THE WORD FROM PARIS

THE WORD FROM PARIS

Essays on Modern French Thinkers and Writers

◆

JOHN STURROCK

VERSO

London • New York

Learning Resources
Centre

First published by Verso 1998
© John Sturrock 1998
All rights reserved

Verso
UK: 6 Meard Street, London W1V 3HR
USA: 180 Varick Street, New York NY 10014–4606

Verso is the imprint of New Left Books

ISBN 1–85984–832–X

British Library Cataloguing in Publication Data
A catalogue record for this book is available from the British Library

Library of Congress Cataloging-in-Publication Data
A catalog record for this book is available from the Library of Congress

Typeset by SetSystems Ltd, Saffron Walden, Essex
Printed by Biddles Ltd, Guildford and King's Lynn

For Mary-Kay

CONTENTS

INTRODUCTION

Asked once why he had not published as much in the course of his life as might have been expected from him, Sir Isaiah Berlin answered that it was because he had preferred the role of 'taxi', by which worldly trope he meant that he had sat down to write only when hailed, or when commissioned to do so by an editor or publisher. The contents of the present volume are likewise the work of a taxi, albeit of a minicab compared with the padded magnificence of a Berlin*. Each one of these essays began life as the review of a book or of an author's oeuvre written in answer to a commission. The commissions came from various editors over the course of thirty years, starting in the mid 1960s; in 1996, they were capped by the invitation of the present publisher to bring the results together in an auto-anthology: an invitation such as a jobbing literary journalist hurries gratefully to fulfil.

It will perhaps sound as though I appear in these pages in the guise of a hireling, whose subjects have had to be chosen for him by somebody else. That, however, is not quite the case. No literary journalist, however vain or hungry, falls in with every proposal that comes his way from an editor. There are occasions when the cruising cab will refuse to pull into the kerb, when the subject on offer is not one he is ready to spend time and thought on. Literary journalists may be for hire but they do well professionally to have a territory that is known to be theirs, and not to lay claim to a diffuse expertise qualifying them to write about anyone or anything.

I am speaking here of literary journalism of a particular kind. The great majority of these pieces were commissioned in the first instance by either the *Times Literary Supplement* or, once it had come into being (in 1979), the *London Review of Books*. These are the two papers I have long worked both for and on,

---

* berlin, n. a closed motor-car with the driver's seat partitioned off. (*Chambers English Dictionary*)

as a contributor and as an editor, having thus been in the unfairly pre-emptive position of being free to commission reviews if need be from myself. They are exceptional papers for allowing their contributors to write at length and to write up, not down, to their readers. You write for them knowing – or maybe fearing – that you are going to be read by people who not only know things, including the things you are supposed to know yourself, but who will not be slow to write in and tell you when you have got those things wrong. This is good for self-discipline: it ensures that you take your time, do your thinking and attend to the quality of your sentences.

Journalism of the sort I am describing is a genre intermediate between two styles of writing that have, over the past thirty-five years, moved irrecoverably far apart: the academic and the journalistic. I have watched this separation happen and seen it become increasingly clearly defined, to the point where there seems little overlap today between the recherché forms of discourse that are favoured by much of academe and the friskier forms thought appropriate to the public prints. There are now large numbers of learned journals in which university teachers can promote their careers by publishing for a peer group: articles of a local interest only, directed at like-minded fractions of the academic community. These scholarly authors have no need to loosen their style or broaden their vision in a bid to attract readers from off the campus.

It's usual to regret that academic writing has over these many years become so inward-looking, when before, when there was much less of it, it seemed little different in either its matter or its manner from the more thoughtful kinds of journalism. Regrettable or not, however, the fault-line that has opened between the discursive styles of the professoriat and the press has given some of us the opportunity to lead a profitably marginal life by occupying a position somewhere between these two contrasting, if not quite opposed, styles, with a view to injecting the gravitas of the one with some of the brio of the other. It could be said that the ideal contribution to papers like the *TLS* or *LRB* should strike academic readers as journalistic and journalistic readers as academic. And having thus set out our stall, we marginals can face in both directions at once and take up our remit as honest brokers. The function of the review-essay, of a roughly chapter-length three or four thousand words, is thus a virtuous one, in restoring a measure of integrity to an intellectual world that is forever looking to fly apart into its various well-defended specialisms.

My own good fortune was to have entered on the broker's life in the mid 1960s, when the days of the literary amateur, of the mere bellelettrist – which has since become a dirty word – were already starting to look as though they were numbered. In universities in both Britain and America, literature was beginning to be taught in new, more complicated and self-consciously professional ways. The first rustlings of Literary Theory were to be heard, and the polarisation among teachers between those who took cordially to theory and those who would have liked to stifle it was under way. With theory of course there also comes difficulty, whether of ideas or of a new vocabulary or both; and at a first encounter with theory, the difficulty itself can be the attraction. It was so for me when I came, more or less accidentally, across the early books of Roland Barthes, was drawn in by their obvious if exotic brilliance, and led on by them to read Saussure and others of the unfamiliar sources on which this very eclectic critic had drawn. After which, French theory seemed to me an excellent idea, and the more of it there was to get to know about the better. Its rapid spread through the academic world was a particular blessing for someone who, though not of that world, had come to specialise in the thought and literature of modern France and could now try to give a wider exposure to the acceptable face of Parisian theory.

The task was the more enjoyable for requiring to be done in a country so gruffly unreceptive to anything even faintly theoretical. And it was the harder for having to try and elucidate for intelligent consumption a body of theory far more sophisticated than anything Paris had sent us previously. Consider, for just one example, the hugely different intellectual demands made on us by the philosophical work of Louis Althusser, the leading Marxist theorist of the 1960s, and that of someone like Henri Barbusse (the unduly neglected subject of an early essay here), whose naive version of Marxism just about allows us to label him as a political theorist of the 1920s and 1930s.

The task of mediation was made easier, on the other hand, by the fact that the new theorists of the sixties had quickly become glamorous, even photogenic figures in their own country: the acceptable faces of French theory, so to speak. The faces were those of Claude Lévi-Strauss, Michel Foucault, Louis Althusser, Roland Barthes, Jacques Lacan and, a little later, Jacques Derrida. Only very loosely could they be said ever to have formed a group, even if they had certain philosophical a prioris in common. They came from a number of academic disciplines, but what was remarkable was the readiness with which their ideas travelled beyond what had once been seen as staunch boundaries between disciplines and were put to use elsewhere. The meta-historian Foucault, for example, whose ideas were often resisted by historians more intellectually timid than himself, acquired many followers throughout the human sciences; Lacan was a hero to the professors of literature who drew on his flamboyantly aired doctrines, if also an ogre to many of his fellow psychoanalysts, to insult and infuriate whom had been a significant part of his professional mission.

The near-coincidence of these various *maîtres à penser* coming to the fore in France meant that they were seen abroad as marking a definite moment in French intellectual history. It was the moment of structuralism, and it gets its full share of coverage in this volume, in which five out of the six thinkers I have just listed appear (the exception is the most personally reticent of them, the anthropologist Lévi-Strauss, who neither invited nor found followers outside his own quite specialised field, so that he is not to be placed in the same transgressive category as the others).

Modern French theory did not begin with structuralism, however. There was first, almost immediately after the Second World War, the moment of existentialism, not in its sombre Heideggerian guise but in the more popular versions put about in France by Jean-Paul Sartre and Albert Camus. Existentialism happened before I did, inasmuch as by the time I encountered the writings of Sartre and Camus, the days of their real influence had passed, even if it was still — *is* still? — easy to find devotees of Camus in particular, who admired to excess the (to me) sanctimonious humanism of a novel like *La Peste*. As the pieces included here on those two pre-eminent figures of the 1950s will show, I am less admiring of both of them than I was brought up to be, first at school and then at university. French existentialism has long since dwindled into an episode of intellectual history and is best understood topically, as an attempt by writers who had lived through the German Occupation to formulate a viable philosophy and a heroic system of values out of a testing wartime experience of rare psychological intensity. Once the war was over, it was as if some substitute needed to be found for the threat represented by a hostile occupying power, so that everyday life could still be lived defiantly and to some purpose. Existentialism, with its invocations of a universe that is cruelly 'indifferent' to human hopes and suffering, was the timely, if now dated, answer.

A second theoretical moment, coming after existentialism and before structuralism, was that of the *nouveau roman*, or New Novel, whose writ ran from the late 1950s to some time in the 1970s. Philosophically speaking, the *nouveau roman* was a reaction against the remote metaphysics of such as Camus and Sartre. Its most vigorous proponent, Alain Robbe-Grillet, argued that the metaphysical age was dead and gone, and that the only philosophy it was now reasonable to adopt was that of scientific naturalism. For him, Sartrian existentialism was a lot of fuss about nothing: if the universe is an alien place in which to exist, so be it; complaining won't make it any less so. Robbe-Grillet's naturalistic alternative was facile but also, coming when it did, refreshing, for sounding a note of iconoclasm and of humour. Literature was thrown onto the defensive, was set to abandon some of the higher ambitions it had formerly had as the barometer by which we weather-watchers liked to measure the vigour or otherwise of a nation's intellectual life.

The point of Robbe-Grillet, however, is not the theories but the novels that he wrote (and the movies that he later made) in obedience to his robust belief that in an age of science we have no business flouting the reality principle and imagining the world differently from the way it provenly is. Whether he ever believed his own insolently dismissive theory of the novel, I doubt; but he prospered greatly from advancing it. His novels are necessarily anti-novels, intricately made in such a form as to demonstrate the deceitful but, as he would say, resistible impulses that daily lead us away from factuality and into fantasy. These novels were taken too solemnly, by those who somehow saw his methods as a real threat to the future of fiction as well as by those who read them, for all the novelist's disclaimers, as exercises in psychological realism. Robbe-Grillet is in fact a very clever and less than serious writer who has over time been handsomely recuperated into French literary history. The essay on him here uncovers in part at least the amusing but clandestine rules governing the composition of one of his narratives; it was written at a time when his methods and intentions were grossly misunderstood.

The second New Novelist included here is a more self-effacing and less programmatic writer than Robbe-Grillet: Nathalie Sarraute, who, for all the novelty of her technique, is admirable above all for having extended, with wonderful if sometimes chilling subtlety, the line of the great French psychological novelists. Sarraute's ambition as a writer, beautifully realised, was to follow far and away the greatest of these, Marcel Proust (who rightly has a section to himself in this collection), down into the furthest reaches of the pre-conscious so as to enlarge, and not for our comfort, our understanding of the quietly vicious ways in which people behave towards one another in company. Sarraute has not outreached Proust in this – no one ever could – but she has found other means than his to stage the invisible small dramas of bourgeois existence. She represents that fine balance between the formally adventurous and the psychologically acute which is for many of us the prime reason for reading French literature.

It is beyond me to say whether my own liking for formalism stemmed originally from a desire to enjoy the status of an alien without leaving home, for in the pre-theoretical times when I got my literary education formalism was looked down on, all very well for the Cartesians of France perhaps but sadly limiting for the spontaneous and inventive British. The strongly formal element in much later twentieth-century French writing I found profoundly attractive, and its enduring attractiveness explains the presence in this collection of one of France's most engaging *fous littéraires*, Raymond Roussel, who took formalism in writing to fantastic new lengths, along with that of two later writers, Raymond Queneau and Georges Perec, who were much influenced in their exploration of literary possibilities by what they had learnt from reading Roussel.

Rather than the formalistic, this strand in modern French writing could better be called the ludic, or playful. For a long time it went pretty much unrecognised abroad, either despite its charms or else because of them: a writer like Queneau, for example, is so seemingly throwaway and jokey (though only seemingly, there is invariably a dark edge to the farce in his novels) that he has had to fight hard to make his way onto university syllabuses, which are not as welcoming as they should be of writing that is easy to enjoy. We have our own ludic tradition in this country, of Edward Lear, Lewis Carroll and other sportive souls, and it is surprising that we were not more immediately receptive to the antic prose of such writers as Queneau or Boris Vian (another inclusion here). That has now changed, up to a point, especially in the case of the peculiarly likeable Georges Perec, who in a short time has become the most exhaustively translated French author of the past thirty years. French literature has splendid comic traditions, and it is right to salute them.

Few of the earlier pieces collected here reappear word for word in their original form. Most have been partially rethought and rephrased, and one or two that had aged without maturing have been rejuvenated. I could see no good reason for essays that were by now thirty years old to be reproduced unedited; and every reason for their author to go over them critically, as the work of some earlier self with whom he is no longer intimate. The ideas and opinions expressed in these pages are thus all of 1997, either because they are ones that I reached when preparing this volume or because I am happy to endorse those that I reached earlier by now re-asserting them. Anyone who has cause to go slowly over his old writings must hope to find evidence of immaturity in them, as he will then be able to tell himself he is a wiser and more perceptive fellow now than he was then. But alas, what we usually find in these re-encounters with our intellectual past is how little our minds have changed, not how much. The gloomy view to take would be that this is evidence of an immaturity we shall never outgrow; I here take the more encouraging view that it is evidence of an intellectual consistency we are not always sure we possess but which can serve in part to justify the appearance of a volume such as this.

Certainly, it is a pleasure to find writings of one's own that had previously been scattered through time and space coming together in a coherent, even if it is not a permanent, format. Laid end to end like this, they can provide a serial record of one commentator's admiring and persistent engagement with modern French thought and writing. No one commentator can engage with the whole of that extensive subject or write about it from more than a single perspective. Here, however, the advantage of being a literary journalist comes into play, and of having your topics determined for you in part by the editors that employ you. For those editors want the coverage they give to a foreign country to reflect a certain consensus as to what is going on there of the greatest intellectual interest and significance. They don't want coverage that, by its very nature, must be extremely limited in terms of space, to be merely idiosyncratic. This isn't, therefore, the entirely personal volume that at first sight it may appear: it engages with many of those modern French writers and thinkers who already stood out, and in doing so, it shares the perspective of a whole community of those who look to France as a source like no other of intellectual stimulus.

ACKNOWLEDGEMENTS

As I have explained, every essay in this book began life as a contribution to a journal or review. Since all of them have been revised for their reappearance here, some to the point where they would be scarcely recognisable if set alongside the originals, there seemed no sense in indicating the dates and places of first publication for each separate essay. Instead, I express my thanks once and for all here, for permission to re-use previously published material, to the editors of the London Review of Books, whence a majority of these pieces derive, of the Times Literary Supplement and of Salmagundi, where the essay on Paul de Man originally appeared; and to Penguin UK, since I have also drawn in part on the introductions to my Penguin translations of Marcel Proust and Georges Perec.

John Sturrock
September 1997

PART I

THINKERS

1

INTELLECTUALS SINCE 1945

The idea has taken hold, since the death of Jean-Paul Sartre in 1980, that France no longer has intellectuals, and that French public life is a lot less distinctive for their eclipse. It is as if the hushed act of street theatre that was mounted around the Cimetière Montparnasse on the day of Sartre's 'private' funeral marked the end of a defining cycle in French cultural history, and not simply the end of a single, if outsize, intellectual career. The two questions that now impose themselves are: *is* France suddenly without intellectuals, and, if so, is this a pity?

Intellectuals are made, not born, and French intellectuals were first made as a distinctive grouping within society by the Dreyfus affair, that inspirational episode of injustice at the end of the nineteenth century. Treason, the crime for which Dreyfus had been wrongly convicted, is a crime regarded as peculiarly grave by a nation's political class and by the *bien pensants*. It calls in question both public and private values, and was thus well calculated to divide the country and inspire high feelings among those who were eventually to be proclaimed (by the neo-intellectual of the 1980s, Bernard-Henri Lévy) 'intermediaries between the world and the universal'. Dreyfus was the victim of certain malign passions of the day – anti-Semitism, nationalism, militarism – and in speaking up for him, intellectuals would represent the undying principle that sets justice above all considerations of convenience or policy, and so intervene as the voice of the ethical and the universal in a political world otherwise given over to low pragmatism. The role is that which Julien Benda allots in his *La Trahison des clercs* (The treason of the intellectuals, 1927) to a spiritual elite who must resist incorporation into the nation's partisan feuds.

Few French intellectuals in this century have wanted to live up to this role. Far from rising above party, they became the happy theoreticians of party – whence the deeply pessimistic tone of Benda's little book, in which the term 'intellectual' appears only in an appendix and is applied far from flatteringly

3

even then. For the role of intellectual was taken up in a partisan spirit at the time of Dreyfus and was seldom played in any other spirit in the years that followed. High ideals may be easily used to serve low, opportunistic ends. The ends of the intellectuals who came to the defence of Dreyfus were not low, but they were opportunistic, given that this gross miscarriage of justice was a historic chance for intellectuals on the political left to get back at those whom they saw as the traditionally oppressive classes and institutions in France: the *haute bourgeoisie*, the Church and the army.

The Left had the best tunes at the time of Dreyfus, if only because Dreyfus himself was innocent, and it was a leftist, Radical journalist (as he then was), Georges Clemenceau, who first brought the term 'intellectual' into common usage, in one or other of the 666 [sic] articles he wrote about the affair in the space of four years. But no sooner had the word been introduced honorifically on one side of the political divide than it was being used pejoratively on the other. Simultaneously with an intellectual tradition, an anti-intellectual tradition was born in France, subscribers to which were fully as 'intellectual', in terms of the social stratum they came from, the education they had received and the professions or careers they followed, as those to whom they were opposed – the stridently nationalistic writer Maurice Barrès, for example, or the long-serving editor of the *Revue des deux mondes*, Ferdinand Brunetière. And if numbers count, we should remember that the reactionary Ligue de la Patrie Française, which was founded soon after the Dreyfusard Ligue des Droits de l'Homme in the winter of 1898, signed up ten times as many members as its reformist rival, including many members of the intelligentsia. Left-wing intellectuals have always counted for more than their right-wing counterparts, but the French intellectual tradition has always been capacious enough to support the full range of contemporary opinion. That indeed is its greatest virtue.

After Dreyfus, involvement by intellectuals in public debate came to be expected; it was a political sideshow, but important for enriching by its talent for abstraction what would otherwise have been the impoverished, short-term thought-processes of parliamentarians. Between the two world wars, French intellectuals played their role to the hilt as *animateurs* both locally and internationally, responding to the establishment of a Communist regime in Russia and later to the rise of Fascism in first Italy and then Germany (see the essay on Henri Barbusse later in this volume). After 1944 that tradition was continued: Paris intellectuals were quick to let it be known what their attitude was towards Stalinism and the Soviet takeover in Eastern Europe (of which more later), towards the United States and the pursuit of the Cold War, towards Algeria and the final liquidation of the French colonial empire, and finally towards the 'events' of May 1968 and what they might or might not portend for the political future.

With their spontaneity and their attractive ludic element, these 'events' upstaged orthodox intellectualism, however: May 1968 was stronger on spectacle and provocation than it was on hard thought. And it is since that date that first the role and then the actual existence of intellectuals in France has been called more and more into doubt.

To the question is France now without intellectuals? an outside observer (this one, anyway) might well answer with a qualified yes. The country is without intellectuals in the fine old sense of the word. It no longer has anyone with the acknowledged standing of a Barbusse, a Malraux, a Camus or a Sartre to tell it what best to think. As intellectuals, they were generalists who made free with their pronouncements on matters of the moment – political, moral, social or aesthetic – and were sure of being heard or read; if they were opportunistic, then the history they were living through was generous in providing them with opportunities. Such generalism no longer holds, intellectuals having come to accept that, rather than give their views on everything, they should, as Michel Foucault advised, be specific, that is, take up only issues to which they already felt a particular commitment (as Foucault did to the reform of the French prison system).

The age that has ended was that of the so-called intellocrats, veterans of abstraction whose acknowledged function was to seek to direct the thoughts of their fellow citizens, to infiltrate as viruses of contestation onto the Internet of conformist opinion. No one performed that function with greater flair or abundance than Sartre, who was ready, also, to prescribe the deontology of the intellectual by generalising from his own activities. The key to it was the *prise de conscience*, a sustained act of reflection on a contentious state of affairs, which the intellectual was asked to undertake on behalf of his society. The intellectual thinks through what others are too short-sighted, too lazy or too trapped in immediacy to think through for themselves; he functions at the serious but preliminary stage of theory, theory in Sartre's rationalist scheme leading smoothly (that is, theoretically) on to the stage of practice.

Sartre flourished in the role he ascribed to himself; he addressed his own nation and was invited regularly to address others. Indeed, the 'Plaidoyer pour les intellectuels' (Plea for intellectuals) that was his personal manifesto was originally delivered as a series of three lectures in Japan in 1965 (it appears in his *Situations VIII*). He was a constant *presence* in the world at large. That presence had been mediated, in the first instance, by books: Sartre was known as a writer before he was ever known as an intellectual. Indeed, before the Second World War he had been apolitical, taking no part in the anti-Fascist agitation of the 1930s; his Resistance activities during the Occupation were prudent, let us say, rather than explicit. He came late, in his early forties, to the fierce, and erratic, career of *engagement* or 'commitment' that gave him such prominence after 1945. This, however, was in accordance with his further definition of the intellectual as someone who brings the competence-cum-notoriety earned in a specific context to bear on a wider public issue. The intellectual, that is, qualifies as such by stepping outside the sphere of his or her professional activity. The nuclear physicist who only ever pronounces on nuclear physics is not an intellectual; the physicist who argues for nuclear disarmament is. And the same with writers: the writer who only writes or writes about writing is not an intellectual; the writer like Jean-Paul Sartre, who chooses to lecture his society, is. (Given which, the inclusion of 'pure' writers, like Samuel Beckett and Nathalie Sarraute, in a *Dictionnaire des intellectuels français* published in 1996 is both a shock and a depressing sign of how, with the times, the definition of an intellectual has become ruinously stretched.)

It was as an author of fiction, of *La Nausée* (Nausea) and the novel sequence *Les Chemins de la liberté* (The roads to freedom), and of philosophy, of the vast Heideggerian treatise *L'Etre et le néant* (Being and nothingness), that Sartre was able first to appear as an intellectual, just as his great adversary of the postwar years, Albert Camus, was best known as the author of two novels, *L'Etranger* (The outsider or The stranger) and *La Peste* (The plague). And even once they had become rival paragons of the intellectual life, Camus and Sartre sustained their presence before the public as much by writing books as by journalism or appearances on public platforms.

The intellocracy could not expect to survive if its members showed themselves to be intellectuals and nothing else; they needed the backing of their other publications, even when, as in Sartre's own case, these seemed to undercut his more *engagé* activities. It is here, above all, that things have changed in France, and for the worse, certainly since 1980. The book, or the published oeuvre, is no longer the only, or even the accepted, measure by which to judge whether or not someone is an intellectual. Books indeed may now seem to stand in the way of certain authors being thought of as such. Is Jacques Derrida, for example, an intellectual, or is he something else? He has written many books and has taken a moral or political stand on a good many issues over the years. But he is, as Sartre never was, a university teacher, and it is usual to find him being described on the strength of his publications rather than his political or moral interventions, as a philosopher.

In the 1940s or 1950s, Derrida would surely have been classified differently, as an intellectual *pur sang*. However, he has not played the intellectual game by the new rules; he is personally discreet, a notoriously subtle thinker opposed on principle to simplicity – 'let's complicate things' is his slogan – and a man seemingly more embarrassed than flattered by the following he has acquired (mainly in the United States) as the theorist of literary deconstruction. He is not, one can safely say, at all well suited to the age of the media intellectual into which we have moved.

For where once there were intellocrats, there are now 'mediocrats', that being the neologism found for them by Régis Debray, who long ago appointed himself as the obituarist of the old-style intellectual. He declares himself to be one of these, an intellectual 'à part entière', or fully paid-up. Debray's case, which he was making even before Sartre died, is that French intellectuals have sold out. Rather than the lords of the library shelves, they prefer now to be lords of the airwaves, to be heard or seen on radio or television, never just read. This is the transition, or declension, that Debray summarises in a fine phrase (and with a crude juxtaposition), as being one from 'the priesthood to the hit-parade'. The old austerity is dead and buried, the new populism is all.

Debray exaggerates and is no fit spokesman for austerity, with his jazzy prose and talent for self-promotion. Contemporary intellectuals are not as corrupt, nor is their situation so final, as he would have us think. The intellectual role in France has been mediatised but not abolished. It does not follow that an appearance on, let us say, Bernard Pivot's celebrated television chat-show, *Apostrophes* (now discontinued), spelt intellectual death, nor that an intellectual automatically degrades him or herself by addressing an audience very much larger than intellectuals could ever have hoped to address in the past. Would the great purists, the Julien Bendas of this world, have forgone making their case before Pivot had they been invited to do so?

Intellectuals in the 1990s may still lay just claim to the moral high ground, as the universalist heirs of Benda. The most impressive of them, Alain Finkielkraut, does so in his *La Défaite de la pensée* (The defeat of the mind,

1987), a book that renews the argument made in *La Trahison des clercs* against what Benda called 'the glorification of national particularisms'. But where Benda took to task an intellectual clerisy seen as having betrayed the disinterested, timeless ideals for which it ought to stand by forever allying itself to this local interest or that, Finkielkraut indicts French culture – and by extension other modern cultures – for having succumbed so completely and so willingly to the Herderian idea that cultural and ethnic difference is what we should value most highly. The unhappy result, for the Kantian Finkielkraut, is that today 'mankind is declined in the plural'. And events in Europe early in the 1990s gave him a chance to make that case very forcefully, when war broke out in what had previously been the one nation of Yugoslavia, and a rabid ethnocentrism led to the deaths of thousands of Croats, Bosnians and Serbs. The Balkan war, and above all the question of whether the West should intervene in it, was an event asking to be argued in full and at a higher, less self-serving level than that which is endemic in the world of national or international politics.

Finkielkraut was not alone among intellectuals in France in making his (pro-Croat and then pro-Bosnian) views known during the crisis; and he was *médiocrate* enough to use the radio and television to help him do so. His very explicit commitment to what he was convinced was a just cause is in itself an answer to the subsidiary question that I posed earlier, as to whether, if intellectuals have vanished from French public life, we should regret it. We should indeed, just as we should regret that their standing has declined to the degree that it has. And this is not exclusively because intellectuals alone may articulate on our behalf what we believe to be the most morally or politically acceptable positions, but for the wider reason that they are free to articulate any position at all, acceptable or not. It is easy to admire a Finkielkraut, who is both liberal and peaceable; but if we believe in intellectuals we should also be able to admire rampaging, on occasions bilious, ideologues like Jean-Paul Sartre.

This is not the universal view, and one specialist on France who is opposed to it is Tony Judt, of New York University. He, on the contrary, thinks it an excellent thing that Sartre and his kind should have gone, the moral of his 1992 book, *Past Imperfect: French Intellectuals, 1944–1956*, being that, in the years immediately after the Second World War, they were not an asset to their country, but a national embarrassment.

Judt's book is an uncommonly damning study of those intellectually exciting years, the years when the divisions among intellectuals in respect first of Soviet Communism and second of a moribund French colonialism in Southeast Asia and Algeria were productive of much writing and polemic. Judt himself approaches his subject – or rather, his subjects – as a sharp, even a vindictive, moralist. He is, that is to say, a belated participant in the intellectual politics of the time, not a mere observer returning detachedly to them from the future.

His main indictment of the intellectuals he discusses is that they failed, for entirely dishonourable reasons, to test the political thought in which they publicly traded against the political reality as it existed around them. The guilty ones, in his view, are those who made up the *marxisant* Left in France during the years following the liberation of 1944, who continued to argue the need for 'revolutionary' change in their own society and to give their unflinching approval to the regimes of the Soviet Union and its satellites in Eastern Europe – even as more and more of them were being exposed in the West for the sinister methods by which they had won and then maintained control of their societies. Judt evidences the retarded, sometimes murderous, politics practised in Moscow, Budapest and Prague in order to castigate what he calls the 'moral bifocalism' of left-wing sympathisers in France, who either could not or would not apply the same ethical standards to Communist regimes in the East as they applied to their own government.

He has plenty of evidence with which to support his argument, and no one doubts that some French intellectuals on the Left practised 'moral bifocalism'. What we need not concede is that this is so very terrible a sin. Intellectuals are as fully members of their own society as anyone else, and whatever views they hold are a function of their perceived place in that society. In the sly definition once given by the sociologist – and some might say, intellectual – Pierre Bourdieu, they represent, as relatively powerless members of the power-holding bourgeoisie, 'a dominated fraction within the dominant class', an ambiguous position that Bourdieu uses to explain the extreme views they are led to adopt politically, and which might certainly be used to explain any 'moral bifocalism'. Dislike of the political and social arrangements under which we find ourselves living goes hand in hand with expressions of admiration for alternatives to them that we can be sure will provoke the defenders and beneficiaries of our own polity. The admiration expressed by Sartre for the Soviet regime, or later by the firebrands of the review *Tel Quel* for Maoism, is meant for internal consumption; it is in that sense parochial. Its 'moral bifocalism' is of the essence.

The postwar years with which Judt is concerned were years of high intellectual adventurism in France, as the mental shutters were raised following the blackout of the German Occupation. The rugged new philosophy of existentialism, whose bible was Sartre's *L'Etre et le néant*, boosted among its adepts the belief that now was the time to put themselves about because of its – wildly unrealistic – teaching whereby autonomous individuals should create their own lives and values by their actions. This was 'commitment' in the broadest sense, with political commitment as a large part of it, the need for that being then so apparent. New political gestures and programmes were stirring for generations who had had to endure first the grubby machinations of the 1930s, when thinkers to both Right and Left in France were contemptuous of what they saw as the terminally decadent institutions of the Third Republic, and then the military fiasco of 1940 and the four servile years of the Occupation. These dire experiences had proved the decrepitude of the old regime; intellectuals, by reflecting on the reasons for that decrepitude could now set the agenda of a Fourth Republic that would be more genuinely and more positively democratic.

Not that everything in wartime had been negative: the Resistance had done well, if not as well as, or with anything like the mass backing that, a postwar mythology claimed for it. But to the new activists it was an inspiring example and to the Communists in particular, because they had been tough, principled and disciplined as resisters. As a result, after 1944 the Communists acquired a political influence greater than any they had known before 1939.

Nineteen forty-four also brought the chance of revenge: the *épuration*, or purge, of those who were known or were rumoured to have been collaborators. This unpleasant, bloody episode, in which thousands died, set a new political tone. There had been bitter divisions between Right and Left even in the Resistance, and as these became institutionalised, French intellectual life slid into what Judt describes as an 'angry Manichaeism'. The Left had the advantage of a radical political philosophy that was well suited to the hopeful hour, and the Soviet Union, to which it looked for inspiration, enjoyed the prestige that came with having fought a brave and ultimately decisive war against Fascism.

Leftist intellectuals were not, however, straightforwardly pro-Communist; rather, they were anti-anti-Communist: internationalist on the surface but parochial underneath, so enclosed within their partisan enmities in Paris that they could never bring themselves to see or to admit that life in the Eastern bloc was anything but pleasant. The supple casuistry with which clever fellow-travellers like Sartre, Maurice Merleau-Ponty or Simone de Beauvoir were able at one time to argue away the brutalities of Stalinism has long been a matter for wonder and dismay. But Judt also incriminates other, less-known intellectuals, notably those on the Catholic Left, associated with Emmanuel Mounier and the review *Esprit*, who managed to combine a religious with a secular theology and to see in Marxist atheism the contemporary form of a Christian commitment to the welfare of the underclass. And all this despite having been given to read incontrovertible accounts of the existence of Soviet labour camps and first-hand reports of the rigged trials in Hungary and in Czechoslovakia that led to the executions of Laszlo Rajk in Budapest in 1949 and of Rudolf Slansky and thirteen others in Prague three years later.

Some on the French Left found these reminders of the 1930s Moscow show trials too much and broke ranks. But many did not and sought for further sophistries with which to justify the nakedly outrageous. Judt makes especially telling use of the Czechoslovak case, the liberal political traditions of that country after 1918 ensuring that its fate after 1945 will always seem the saddest of all.

Left-wing intellectuals by this reading were either deluded or perverse; they thought too much and saw and felt too little, heedless of those who suffered in Eastern Europe, who, according to Judt, were themselves constantly looking to Paris for support. He finds common ground between the internecine manoeuvrings of party bosses in Prague and the philosophical contortions of a Sartre in Paris, inasmuch as both turned on the notion that 'justice' was what those in power decided that it ought to be.

But Sartre's endorsement of Communist malpractice was not collusion with that malpractice. He knew, as intellectuals always do know, that it was never going to fall to him to decide what justice was in France, that he was enjoying what the wild man of the pre-war French Right, Louis-Ferdinand Céline, had once, frustratedly but correctly, termed 'the sonorities of impotence'. Another word for sonorities here might be 'irresponsibility'. To be impotent, as a member of Bourdieu's 'dominated' sub-class, is to be set free from the responsibilities of power and to be as extreme as you like.

This is a perfectly defensible line to adopt, even if, to a moralistic historian such as Tony Judt, intellectuals are to be admired only if they show themselves to be 'responsible'. The responsible intellectuals were those like Raymond Aron, himself so judicious, disenchanted and sensible that the journalist Jean

Daniel once wondered openly whether it wasn't 'easier to be wrong with Sartre than right with Aron', which shows if nothing else does on which side the attractions of being an intellectual are thought to lie.

The notion of intellectual responsibility can be framed in different terms from those that Judt uses: his responsible intellectuals are simply those who advanced the views he finds sympathetic. But who in fact must intellectuals be responsible to, and for what? They are by definition outside the political process: in their introduction to the *Dictionnaire des intellectuels français*, the editors, Jacques Julliard and Michel Winock, give as their reason for excluding figures such as Clemenceau and de Gaulle from their (all too hospitable) pages that they only ever wrote or spoke from within the political world, so disqualifying themselves. And being outsiders, intellectuals are entitled to the privileges that go with their marginal status, including the privilege of irresponsibility, of answering only to themselves.

No one knows, because no one has a way of adequately measuring, the effect that intellectuals may indirectly have on the political process, and if this is so with respect to their own country, their effect on the political process of other countries would be even harder to evaluate. Judt's idea that Sartre and co. were letting down the dissidents inside Russia or Czechoslovakia with their Parisian sophistry is not true in any practical sense, since nothing that Sartre or any other intellectual – not even Raymond Aron – could have said or written would have had the slightest mitigating impact on the then leaders of the Soviet Union or its satellite states. (When Sartre died, in 1980, the event rated just five lines in the Communist Party newspaper in Moscow.)

When de Gaulle ordered Sartre's release from custody in 1968, after he had been arrested for selling copies of the inflammatory paper *La Cause du peuple*, he managed to praise and to marginalise Sartre in a single breath: 'He is our Voltaire,' was the president's reason for letting him go free, thereby recognising both Sartre's high place in the history of French culture and his practical insignificance. Sartre had been patronisingly but effectively returned from the political to the philosophical world. But the philosophical world is that in which moral issues should be debated, and although politically Sartre was ineffective, he was not so morally. By arguing for thirty years in his tireless, perverse, irresponsible way he was demonstrating to the full the value to a society of someone who takes it as his vocation to be forever thinking against the grain.

2

JEAN-PAUL SARTRE

History took its time in demanding that Jean-Paul Sartre give it his full attention. A sequence of grossly disorienting experiences was required: war, captivity, Occupation, liberation. The Sartre who entered on this sequence was someone with as yet only a modest public presence; the Sartre who emerged from it five years later was primed to become the most brazen and prolific of all postwar European intellectuals. The war had changed him; or, if that makes this expert Hegelian sound too much like the slave rather than the master of his circumstances, in wartime Sartre elected to change.

In 1939, when the war started, he was thirty-four and known to some in France as an author of fiction (*La Nausée*, *Le Mur*) and to a few academic readers as a published philosopher. Remarkably, given what he was later to become, he was known to no one as a public intellectual: he had shown little or no interest in either domestic or international politics. He had gone on teaching, writing and amusing himself through the years when French intellectuals had been agitating against Fascism, against militarism and ultimately against the futile appeasement of Hitler by the French and British governments. But there was no word from Sartre on all this. Asked in 1941 why he had had nothing to say at the time about the iniquity of the Spanish Civil War, he answered that he had not felt it was *his* war. He didn't even feel that 1939–45 was his war right away.

By the time of the liberation, however, he was more than ready to start educating and mobilising French opinion, so that the existing political hiatus might be turned to the advantage of the revolutionary Left. The previously indifferent Sartre had been radicalised in no uncertain manner and was to remain so, obsessively if erratically, right up until his death in 1980. He was the foremost promoter of the new political ethic of *engagement*, or commitment, this being an extension into the public domain of the existentialist notions he

13

had evolved in respect of individual freedom and responsibility. Under existentialism, each individual is condemned to be free in the choice of his or her values and to 'assume', that is, take ultimate responsibility for, his or her actions. As individuals playing a public role, intellectuals must be always *engagé*, that is, seen to take sides whenever there was sides to be taken, as Sartre himself was seen to do, on the Cold War, on decolonisation, on Vietnam, on Maoism, on the 'events' of May 1968, on whatever major issue presented itself. For thirty years, his was the intellectual programme that dominated all others in France.

Because it came about in wartime, and under the more or less secretive conditions of the German Occupation, this remarkable outward turn in Sartre can seem mysterious: a *coup de théâtre* that had had to be enacted offstage. But it was not so mysterious and not so theatrical; the two halves of Sartre's life can be brought to fit together smoothly enough. The war re-oriented him just as it gave him his chance. Before it, he was by every account the loosest of intellectual cannons, holding forth to the *lycée* classes he was employed to teach and to his friends in Paris cafés; after it, he was as loose as ever, though ingenious at disguising his free-lance thoughts as ideological imperatives and addressing audiences that extended around the world.

It could be said, then, that the war did well by Sartre. It did not for one thing much threaten him physically: he had a war well suited to his profoundly civilian temper, with no heroics and a great deal of free time in which to philosophise and to write. He was called up in September 1939, served in the army in the east of France and was taken prisoner during the collapse of May–June 1940. He then spent nine months as a prisoner of war (in Trêves, or Trier, Marx's birthplace by a nice coincidence), before sitting out the Occupation, almost entirely in Paris. No matter where he was, Sartre wrote, with a crushing facility: he wrote in barrack rooms, he wrote in the prison camp and he wrote, at length, as a civilian.

He gave a part of his mind but not his person to the Resistance. After returning to Paris from his stalag in 1941, he organised a groupuscule of intellectual resisters, under the name 'Socialism and Freedom'. It did not last long; it was amateurish, quarrelsome and unclear on how to go about things. It gave rise, on the other hand, to one unexpectedly athletic episode when, in the summer of 1941, the famously unfit Sartre, together with his life's companion, Simone de Beauvoir, set off on a marathon bicycle trip round the unoccupied zone in the South, to recruit supporters. They called hopefully on both André Gide and André Malraux, and succeeded with neither.

Sartre in fact had nothing of the war hero about him, and nothing of the patriot either. Even in wartime his vision of the future far exceeded France's immediate needs. To look ahead, as the vast majority of his suffering compatriots did, simply to their country's liberation was not enough for him, because it promised simply a tame return to a despised bourgeois regime. When he produced his own manifesto, on the other hand, laying out the aims of the 'Socialism and Freedom' group, it ran to a hundred closely handwritten pages and was later described by one of his fellow members as a parody of its genre. It might equally well have been described as a paradox, since even at this desperate historical moment Sartre was set on formulating a political programme that would be recognisably his and no one else's. 'Socialism and Freedom' failed ideologically because, at a time when a certain esprit de corps was called for, Sartre proved that teamwork was not his thing. In 1941 there were two alternatives open to serious resisters: they could join the Gaullists on the Right of the Resistance or the Communists on the Left. Sartre would not contemplate submerging his independence of thought in either; already he was practising the politics that made him at once so militant and so prominent a figure after the war – a plague on both your parties.

Within a few months of his return to Paris, Sartre was thus thinking ahead, against the day when France would be free and in need of a new political direction. Applied philosophy was now to be his forte. But how and where did he come to see that this was the appropriate future for him? Without doubt, the best place to start looking for an answer to that question is in his *Carnets de guerre* (War diaries). These were once thought to have been lost and they were never published during his lifetime. A majority of them were indeed lost, since we have only five *carnets* out of the fifteen that he filled during the long, cold months of the 'Phoney War', between September 1939 and June 1940. In their spontaneity, they are formidable as evidence of the variety and drivenness of Sartre's thinking.

The title, *Carnets de guerre*, is something of a joke, given that Sartre never quite went to war. Indeed, he wastes no time as a diarist in welcoming the absolute decline into which, by 1939, the military ideal had fallen in France, even though that decline was hardly good news for a serving soldier faced by armies from a country where the military ideal was emphatically not in decline.

However, Sartre's own avowed ideal at the time when he was called up was the mutinous one he had brought with him from Paris, of cynical insubordination. As nothing higher than a private soldier, second class, he was at the bottom of the military heap, a bourgeois suddenly placed in a position where he might envisage himself as an honorary member of the underclass.

The nine months of the 'Phoney War' were phonier for Sartre than for most. He spent them behind the lines in Alsace doing what he had been trained to do years earlier, by his contemporary and rival at the Ecole Normale Supérieure, Raymond Aron, when they were on national service together: releasing weather balloons and taking sightings on them. (Curiously, Albert Camus once earned money as a meteorological assistant in Algeria at a time when he was hard up: is there some logical kinship between the role of French intellectual and that of weather forecaster?) This quaint, undemanding routine was all that the army seems to have asked of Sartre; there is no mention in his diaries of parades, drills, weapon training, fatigues. In his small unit the military ideal was not in decline, it was irrelevant.

Sartre the war diarist is taken up instead with himself and with his ideas. The war as a political event does not concern him, nor does what might be happening elsewhere in Europe. The 'historicity' that later came to govern his political thought may be present conceptually but not yet concretely, to the point where he might want to analyse the sources and prospects of the present situation. The act of diarising, or of writing, is in itself a pleasure, as well as an incentive to think in a discontinuous form that is new to him. 'I have never felt such freedom of thought,' he told Simone de Beauvoir in a letter from Alsace. 'And it is not just because of the war and all it has thrown into question, but because of this little notebook: its free, fragmentary style liberates me from the slavery of previous ideas.'

If military life for this as yet unrepentant individualist lacks both the servitude and the grandeur it once held for Alfred de Vigny, it does offer him the rare opportunity of exile: from his familiars in Paris, from having to teach philosophy to schoolboys, from the compulsive pursuit of women. The sudden impoverishment of his external life – the bohemian grace of Paris exchanged for an icy, under-furnished barrack room – prompts him as never before to look within, to enjoy a rich, voluble season of introspection which he claims is a novelty for him.

To think as much and as freely as Sartre did during his active service is in itself an act of defiance; the soldier's mind is intended to be dulled into grumbling obedience. But Sartre's meteorology was soon done and the rest of his time was spent reading and writing: ten or eleven hours a day of it, during which he read a great many books, covered a great many pages of his notebooks, wrote long letters to Simone de Beauvoir in Paris and finished what turned out to be only a first draft of *L'Age de raison* (The age of reason), the first, and by far the best, of the three volumes of his trilogy, *Les Chemins de la liberté*. He read critically: Flaubert, the writer who was to preoccupy him later on, derided at this stage for, of all things, 'the awkwardness of his style'; Gide, admired but also found wanting as a diarist because he remains irredeemably religious; Jules Renard, another diarist, dismissed for his short-windedness, his brevity being taken by Sartre as evidence that he was incapable of thought altogether. Sartre the reader of other diarists loves to score points against them; he is competitive to the core.

He got some hard philosophy done too, to be worked up a year or two later into his seminal treatise, *L'Etre et le néant*. The fundamental polarity in his ontology was by now in place, with the 'in-itself' (*en-soi*) set in stark opposition to the 'for-itself' (*pour-soi*) – the distinction from which so much of the later Sartre was to flow, once he had come forward as the libertarian champion of the *pour-soi*. Where the *en-soi* is inert, alien, objective, the *pour-soi* is reflexive, hence free, voluntaristic, even heroic: a creative Nothingness mysteriously supervenient on the non-conscious order of Being. The associated, highly Romantic notion of individual freedom, with the need for each of us to 'assume' all our actions, was only waiting to be anchored politically. Once it was so, a fundamental contradiction became apparent, between the quite unreal weight placed on subjectivism in Sartre's philosophy and the need for that subjectivism to be suspended in obedience to the collective discipline of any rational politics.

By this stage also he had set Heidegger above his earlier philosophical mentor, Husserl, whose idealism Sartre now condemned. The bleakness of Heidegger's existentialism, however, strikes one as more overdone than ever when set before us by a pleasure-seeker such as Sartre, who shared nothing of the asceticism and unsociability characteristic of Heidegger himself. In the *Carnets* he reveals, perhaps unwittingly, how macho Heidegger's philosophy is: a stoical response to the regrettable indifference of the cosmos to human wishes; a philosophy designed for brave and lucid minds like Sartre's.

The contingencies of war having, as Heideggerians would say, 'thrown' Sartre into his present situation, philosophy eventually became less of a professional and more of a human matter for him. He no longer had a class of

Paris *lycéens* to teach, but there was still something rather likeably boyish about him, a levity that was later to disappear from view, once the great postwar success of *L'Etre et le néant* had given him new prestige and a cumbrous vocabulary to go with it. 'I'm sufficient unto myself, in the nihilating solitude of the for-itself . . . I'm not at ease except in freedom, escaping objects, escaping myself; I'm not at ease except in nothingness – I'm a true nothingness, drunk with pride and translucid.' Lyrical flights of self-analysis like this from the *Carnets*, where the psychological converges with the metaphysical in a typically Sartrian fusion, are the last flourishes of the pre-war Sartre, here defending himself and his friends from the accusation of degeneracy with an assertion of their 'intellectual power and gaiety'. In its larval form, Sartre's philosophy had been the language game of an exuberant metropolitan clique, the conspiratorial expression of a milieu. As monstrously expanded in *L'Etre et le néant*, its power became diffused and its gaiety was stifled.

On one crucial matter the *Carnets de guerre* are silent: the obscure process by which Sartre came so quickly to place his political hopes in the revolutionary potential of the proletariat. In the army he had for the first time actually to mix with men from the working class; it was not a contact he enjoyed. In the period covered by the *Carnets*, he was keener on avoiding than on communing with his fellow soldiers. In captivity, however, it was different. In the anonymity of the camp, as one of thousands of French soldiers all reduced to equality before their captors, Sartre found his place and a certain solidarity, not least because there was a camp intelligentsia with whom he could mix and argue about philosophy. The experience both carried him back and projected him forward: 'In the stalag, I rediscovered a form of collective life I had not experienced since the Ecole Normale – in other words I was happy.'

He was also more serious; he had a proper audience again. In the *Carnets*, he presents himself as a 'moral clown' putting on an act for others, and though we are left mostly to guess what those others thought of this superior person they found slumming in the ranks, he gives hints of their complicity in the role he assumed on their behalf. 'Hey Sartre, you're a philosopher, do you think I should . . .?' a soldier asks, as if Sartre had finally been allotted a pastoral responsibility in the barrack room.

The form of this interpellation is like a pastiche of that by which France as a whole would one day be addressing him: 'Hey Sartre, you're a philosopher, what do you think about . . .?' At this first, preparatory stage, the audience was nowhere near smart enough to permit him to be his furiously speculative self. He clowns before it because only by clowning can he preserve what had by now become the sovereign virtue of 'authenticity'; were he to have taken himself seriously he would have been committing the corresponding sin of acting 'inauthentically', or in bad faith.

It was during his fallow winter of army service that he seems indeed to have come into full possession of this thoroughly dubious moral polarity, by which a favoured class of authentic agents and actions could be segregated from the far larger class of the inauthentic. Within the space of a single week, or so he wrote to Simone de Beauvoir, he had 'completed [his] morality'. 'Everything seems to revolve quite naturally around the ideas of freedom, life and authenticity.' To live authentically is to live and act without wearing a disguise, to be 'transparent' both to oneself and to others, a hyper-Cartesian ideal that was to stay with Sartre for the rest of his life, reappearing for the last time in the 1970s when he was advocating what he called 'libertarian socialism', or a fantasmal regime under which we would all of us be able to live useful, absolutely candid or 'transparent' lives and authenticity would thus be universal.

Sartre was none too generous, alas, in allowing authenticity to those who thought differently from himself. He wrote that wartime had made it easier for people to be 'decent and authentic' because under its attendant duress the great mass of previously self-deceiving individuals found it harder to conceal the dark truth of the human condition from themselves. Yet to imply as Sartre does that decency and authenticity go hand in hand is to give his own judgemental game away, since we mark behaviour down as 'decent' according to objective criteria determined by a consensus, but as 'authentic' by some Sartrian intuition shared by initiates alone. Strangely, in the *Carnets* Simone de Beauvoir is said to be 'naturally' authentic, which seems to rob her of the credit she could have earned if she had had to learn to become so.

Another of Sartre's women friends, however, is less favoured:

> I see, for example, how L . . .'s desire for authenticity is poisoned by inauthenticity. She'd like to be authentic, from affection for us, from trust in us, in order to join us and also from an idea of merit. She suffers at seeing a supreme value posited that is alien to her.

This is ugly: malice dressed up as insight. L . . . had already been dropped by Sartre as a lover and is now triumphantly ostracised. She is an example of how savagely and quickly he was able to fictionalise those around him and, leading on from that, of the extent to which sentimental concerns could help to shape his public or philosophical attitudes. There was no violence in Sartre's life, but much violence in his feelings, and the instance of the wretched L . . . is all too premonitory of the virulent way in which, for example, he turned against Camus during their celebrated quarrel following the publication in 1951 of Camus' *L'Homme révolté* (The rebel). Unsurprisingly, Sartre was then the one who condoned violence in what he argued was a good political cause; Camus rejected it no matter what the cause might be.

Sartre found nothing to like in his unfortunate fellow soldiers. Paul, the NCO, says to him, 'Me, a soldier? I consider myself a civilian in military disguise.' That, however, is the role Sartre had taken for himself and Paul comes under the lash:

> That would be all very fine if he weren't making himself a soldier whatever he may say to the contrary – through his volitions, his perceptions, his emotions . . . He thus stubbornly continues to *flee* what he's *making of himself* – which plunges him into a state of wretched, diffuse anguish. (Sartre's italics)

Sartre is not observing his fellow soldier, he is appropriating him, showing him off as a man incapable of lucidity in respect of himself. The inauthentic Paul is an illustration, shrink-wrapped and stored, to be used if need be in the pages of *L'Etre et le néant*.

The other 'character' whom Sartre introduces, Pieter, is more sympathetic because he is urban and faintly criminal, the emanation of a working-class quarter of Paris. But Pieter's fate is to be exultantly turned into an exhibit from *La Naus*ée, an unlovely paragon of viscosity:

> While he masturbates his lip, he utters a thousand slurping smacks – reminiscent of the greedy suckings and lappings and 'yumyums' of a nursing infant, or the pantings of a male on the job, or the consenting groans of a woman satisfied and then the lip re-emerges, obscene and slack, glistening with saliva, and hangs down a bit, enormous and female, spent with bliss.

As a psychophysiological caricature this is brilliantly unpleasant, but it was written in a diary, in the communality of army life, possibly in the presence of the uncouth Pieter himself. The distance that other writers achieve by seclusion and over a period of time, Sartre could achieve instantaneously.

His 'project', or that deep impulsion which, in his philosophical schema, determines the unity of a consciousness, was writing.

> Even in war I fall on my feet, because I think at once of writing what I feel and see. If I question myself, it's in order to write down the results of my examination; and it's clear to me I only dream of questioning my desire to write, because if I really tried even for an hour to hold it in abeyance, place it in parenthesis, all reasons for questioning anything whatsoever would collapse.

Which makes it less extraordinary that in early June 1940, when the French army was in chaos and the nation was foundering, Private Sartre continued calmly working on the revision of *L'Age de raison*.

Writing was the one way he knew of being-in-the-world. But, in order to persuade himself, once he had entered on the path of *engagement*, that writing could in itself be an effective form of political action, Sartre was forced to draw a suspiciously impermeable distinction between the pragmatic and the literary modes of writing. Pragmatic writing was urgent, unequivocal, hortative; literary writing was deliberate, ambiguous, introverted. Literature was what a writer worked on, for his own satisfaction. Having once posed this distinction, Sartre had to try and live with it, had to keep convincing himself that writing could be a sufficient form of commitment to the political struggle. Literature, inescapably, was a practice exclusive to the bourgeoisie, so that to write it was to emasculate oneself politically and to seek shelter in aesthetics.

The dilemma was first posed for Sartre during the years of the Occupation, when he had to decide how far the will to 'insubordination' should take him. In the event, it took him no further than an intellectual resistance; he thought and he wrote, he did not pick up a gun or plant a bomb. He had nevertheless shared in some of the abruptly levelling experiences of wartime, when the hierarchical structures of civil society are provisionally suspended and the hopes of radical thinkers for their eventual permanent dissolution are correspondingly enhanced. At the time of the Liberation in 1944, however, Sartre was happy to mark a caesura between the collective state of mind that had been appropriate during the Occupation and the state of mind appropriate to the new conditions of peace. 'The end of a war leaves man naked, without illusions, abandoned to his own forces, realising, at last, that he can count only on himself.' It was as if the existentialist philosopher had only been waiting to get the war out of the way so that he might rejoin the high road of Romantic individualism.

Despite all the years of agit-prop that followed, during which Sartre became

the energumen of the far, never-quite-Communist Left, he could not live down
the fear that he belonged in truth to literature, not to politics, that he would
continue to be acting in bad faith unless he could somehow disinvest himself of
his bourgeois status as a writer. His disinvestment was to take the typically
contradictory form of a book, and a literary book at that: *Les Mots* (Words), his
essay in autobiography, published in 1964, when he was almost sixty. *Les Mots*
was to be the bourgeois writer's suicide note, in which he takes his guilty leave
of the class that bore him and the privileges that go with his membership of it.
In late middle age, he would prove himself capable of an act intended as at once
a recantation and a renewal, so that the remainder of his life might be dedicated
more purely to the cause of the proletariat, with whom he had never ceased to
express his solidarity.

Les Mots traces the process by which Sartre believes he has come – or been
induced by others – to look on himself, quite falsely, as an elite subject; and it
closes with the extraordinary, Rousseauesque declaration that he is now cured
of all that, that he feels himself to be '[a] whole man, made out of all men, as
good as any man, better than no man.' But this declaration is addressed, alas,
to his bourgeois readers, or to that class from which he has just seceded; it is
not addressed, because it never could be, to the working class to which he is
demanding admission.

Work of literature that it was, *Les Mots* had the inescapable effect of
reinforcing Sartre's bourgeois status; instead of being solved at a stroke, his
dilemma was if anything made more acute. Nothing brings this out better than
his reaction to the stirring 'events' in the streets of Paris in May 1968. Sartre
had not expected them (who had?) but he could not ignore them, they were an
opportunity. He became an activist, taking on, briefly, the running of an
inflammatory news-sheet, *La Cause du peuple*, and helping at the foundation of
the, at that time, extreme leftist newspaper, *Libération*. But there was no
question of him giving his all to what might, just, have been the revolutionary
movement that overthrew the bourgeois order.

By 1968 he had already been working for many years at his enormous,
obsessive study of Flaubert, eventually to be published as *L'Idiot de la famille*
(The family idiot). He refused to give up writing it, elitist in the extreme
though he knew it to be, a barely accessible work of literary criticism that
would never be read by more than a few people. It wasn't reasonable, he
complained to interviewers, to expect him simply to abandon this huge piece of
work, and he set to wondering, a little pathetically, whether one day, by some

unspecified process of 'mediation', 'this sort of book might serve the masses'. Which, for those who have attempted, and been worsted by, the outrageous size and frequent obscurity of the unmediated *Idiot*, has to rank as the most utopian of all Sartre's speculations.

Flaubert, whom Sartre had long before, in the *Carnets de guerre*, accused of being 'awkward', was the writer who represented for him, in an extreme form, the temptation of the *bel écrit*, or 'fine writing'. Flaubert was notorious not so much for writing as for re-writing; he accepted nothing that simply came to him. He sought, and achieved, a style. But for Sartre style was sinful because its effect, so he oddly thought, was invariably to ambiguate, and the writer who has political designs on the minds of his readers wants nothing to do with ambiguity. It was by the act of revision that the intellectual reverted to being a writer.

In his last years, Sartre was of the opinion that some at least of the books he had written would continue to be read. He was surely right to think that. By the nature of things, however, the books that will continue to be read are those over which he took the most trouble, the ones that he *wrote*, or even revised, as opposed to those that he simply set down on paper and then left. The final, posthumous irony of Sartre's career is that his literary books – *La Nausée*, *L'Age de raison*, *Les Mots* – will always find readers because the prose in which they are written is democratic, it is there to be understood by all, whereas the non-literary books – *L'Etre et le néant*, say, or *La Critique de la raison dialectique* (The critique of dialectical reason) – are cast in a language that is intellectually beyond all but a handful of resolute academic readers.

3

ALBERT CAMUS

When Albert Camus was killed in January 1960, after the Facel Vega sports car in which he was a passenger had swerved off the road between Sens and Paris, the manuscript of *Le Premier Homme* (The first man) was found among his things. He had been working on it for nearly a year at the time of the accident and still had some way to go. Yet only in 1994 were we given it to read. It is extraordinary that it should have been thirty-four years before it was published, disappointing that there should then have been no word from the publisher or the manuscript's editor, Camus's daughter, to explain why. It's not as if the book is so underweight that anyone can have thought his reputation likely to shrink as a result of publishing it, nor does it show Camus in any unfortunate new light personally or philosophically. On the contrary, it shows him in an unwontedly sociable light, because here for once we have a first, animated draft of Camus, whose finished prose often reads as if it were set in stone.

The author of *Le Premier Homme* is certainly not the Camus familiar to us these many years from *L'Etranger* and *La Peste*, those lapidary best-sellers whose earnest didacticism has not worn well. *Le Premier Homme*, too, is earnest but at a personal, not a collective or metaphysical, level; the moralising Camus has here come pleasingly down to earth. This is not 'a work of order', which is what the disorderly Sartre accused Camus of having written when he reviewed *L'Etranger* at the time of its first publication in 1942. *Le Premier Homme* has its stilted, preachy moments but they are more than offset by the uncharacteristically mundane account that it gives of his childhood in his native Algiers. According to the publisher's description on the cover, it is a 'novel' and, as one would expect, a 'great novel'. Great it isn't; nor is there much to be gained by thinking of *Le Premier Homme* as a novel. Few will read it as that; rather, they will take it to be the great writer's honest, confirmatory look back, in his mid forties, at the straitened colonial boyhood from which he had long ago emerged.

It is a success story; except that this great writer would like us to believe that his literary success has been as nothing, because it has involved him in a deep betrayal of his origins.

Like all autobiography, *Le Premier Homme* has a case to put: it is a skewed look back at the past. Camus has chosen to afford himself some light protection (Camusflage?) by changing most of the names: the family is no longer called Camus but Cormery, and Albert has given way to Jacques. These aliases don't quite hold throughout, however: on one page, Jacques's widowed mother, who is sometimes Lucie and sometimes Catherine – Camus's mother's real name – becomes the Veuve (or widow) Camus; and on another page, the primary schoolmaster who was the principal agent of Camus' eventual escape from poverty into literature reverts from Bernard to his real name, Germain.

With revision these trivial backslidings from fiction into fact would have been corrected, and, no doubt, much of *Le Premier Homme* rewritten by Camus. He would have sat down to refine it into a 'work of order' because he was too self-conscious a writer to let people read what he had written until he was satisfied it would do him credit. Ever since the time of *L'Etranger*, and despite the romanticism of the 'absurdist' philosophy that then attracted him, he had been labelled a 'classical' writer. For Camus that had to be a good label, an accolade: his way of writing was being assimilated to that which he had been taught to admire above all others. For he was a scholarship boy from a backward province whose literary education had been formal and hard-won. He had reason to make a cult of the classical. And when he himself came to write, it could never be with the insouciant prolixity of such as the *normalien* Sartre, but rather with the dour work-ethic that was endemic among his struggling Algerian relatives and which made him suspicious of the words that came too easily.

We are fortunate that *Le Premier Homme* was never able to be put through his habitual grooming process, a process intended to increase its specific gravity and raise it onto the same plane of extreme seriousness as *L'Etranger* or *La Peste*. Those were parables – cryptic in the one case, blatant in the other – well attuned to the serious times in which they were written and published, during or just after the war, when a heroic humanism, transcendent of politics, such as Camus seemed to stand for could find many grateful takers. Camus himself, however, felt that something was missing from books like these. Even before *La Peste* had appeared, he commented in one of his notebooks, 'What makes for the success of my books makes for their mendacity for me.' And this same 'mendacity' was just what the people in his books lacked, with the depressing result that 'they are not in the world.' Camus presumably meant by this that his people were too diagrammatic, too thought out, too much at the service of his conscious requirements to seem real. His hope was that he would one day be able to let more of himself show when he wrote, to strike a balance 'between what I am and what I say, and perhaps when that day comes, I hardly dare to write it, I shall be able to build the work of which I dream.' *Le Premier Homme* surely comes closer to that ideal balance than anything else that he published.

We have his daughter's word for it that the manuscript was drafted in obvious haste, and the welcome freedom of its manner testifies to the urgency with which Camus undertook this barely fictionalised return to his youth, to the sparse, unfailingly authentic setting of his Algerian family. Just before he started on *Le Premier Homme*, he had written a new preface for the reissue of his first book of essays, *L'Envers et l'endroit*, which he had published in Algeria when he was twenty-four. In it he talks of trying to rediscover his lost 'centre': 'If, in spite of all my efforts to construct a language and to make myths live, I do not succeed one day in re-writing *L'Envers et l'endroit*, I shall not have succeeded in anything, that is my obscure conviction.' *L'Envers et l'endroit* contains a short piece called 'Entre oui et non' (Between yes and no) in which the already estranged Camus thinks and feels his way back into his childhood home, in an act of what he calls 'repatriation', even though at that time he had yet to leave North Africa for metropolitan France. To that extent, *Le Premier Homme* is a re-writing of the earlier book; or, better, a de-writing of it, a much fuller 'repatriation', by which Camus hoped to write his way back across the Mediterranean Sea and so close the divide that had opened between the fêted, speechifying intellectual in Paris and the obscure, almost wordless household in which he had been raised.

That could have been a theme, guilt-laden as it is, to bring out the pompous worst in Camus, but *Le Premier Homme* is a plainly conceived book. It aspires to the lyrical only once, in a revealing connection (of which more in a moment). You might say that this prolonged home visit was to have been Camus's version of *Les Mots*, the book that Sartre disingenuously claimed was his 'farewell to fine writing': the book by which the guilty elitist would purge himself of his elitism and throw in his lot with the anonymous masses. Camus had a deeper reason to throw in his lot with those masses than ever Sartre did. Sartre was a bourgeois, root and branch; Camus was not, he was an oddity, an intellectual on the liberal Left in Paris who had actually been born into the proletariat. So where Sartre was required by his ideology to disown his origins, Camus could lay claim to virtue in espousing his. *Les Mots* is a cruel and witty book, without a good word to say about the institution of the family. *Le Premier Homme* is the reverse: it has only good words to say about the family, words too good, in the end, to be quite believed.

It is in fact a fulsome act of restitution performed by Camus to the mother from whom he had long before become radically separated, in both physical and mental space. The dedication of the book is to the 'Widow Camus. To you who will never be able to read this book', a wording that commemorates, as if to preserve rather than to abolish, the conclusive intellectual distance that had long ago opened up between son and mother.

The narrative such as it is begins with an account of Jacques Cormery's birth in rural Algeria in 1913, a mixture, let's suppose, of how Camus imagined that inaugural event of his own life and what he had been told about it by others. That much is fiction; what follows is memory. Jacques is making one of his regular visits from Paris to his mother in Algiers, having just, for the first time and at her request, been to Brittany to visit the grave of his father. Exactly like Camus's real father, Henri Cormery had been mobilised in the opening weeks of the First World War and fatally wounded on the Marne, when his son was only a few months old. At the graveside, Jacques realises, first, that he is now ten years older than his father was when he was killed, that the 'natural order' has been overturned when a son can be older than his father; and then, that 'he can't invent a piety he doesn't feel' towards a father whom he never knew. This reflection is bound to carry the mind instantly back to Meursault, the affectless young man who, in *L'Etranger*, instead of putting on a show of grief after his mother's funeral, has sex with his girl and goes with her to the cinema to see a Fernandel farce. This refusal to invent a piety he can't feel does Meursault no good: once he is on trial for murder, it is brought up as evidence of his callous nature and plays as great a part as the crime itself in getting him sentenced to death.

I imagine that most readers of *L'Etranger* have always seen the fatally impious Meursault as being in the right – as acting bravely indeed, if one can concede virtue to someone so devoid of an inner life – in not feigning the piety towards his parent that society demanded of him. *Le Premier Homme* clouds the issue, however, for here Cormery is precisely what the indifferent Meursault wasn't: he displays nothing but piety towards his mother, with an insistence that comes to grate. By Jacques Cormery's lights, Meursault *is* the asocial monster that the judge and jury of the novel decided he was. The puzzle is to know how Camus

himself conceived of Meursault, morally speaking, at the time when he wrote
L'Etranger: was he genuine culprit or authentic victim? In moral terms, the
reverential view taken of the mother figure in *Le Premier Homme* has the effect of
banishing poor Meursault into the outer darkness, and in doing so poses the
intriguing question whether its author is not here attempting to exorcise the
Meursault element within himself. In short, is the filial piety in this book truly
autobiographical or is it invented?

The mother in it, Catherine Cormery, is now seventy years old, able for the
first time in forty years to live without working, thanks to the money she gets
from her sons. As a war-widow on an insufficient pension she had been obliged
to go out and clean in order to bring up her children. She has worked,
something that for Camus was of the utmost importance; one remembers the
motto of the self-effacingly heroic Doctor Rieux in *La Peste**: 'We must do
our job.' (Rieux also had been born into the working class and could only ever
in consequence take the side, as he said, of life's 'victims'.) Catherine has
worked selflessly, but it doesn't show. Jacques finds her 'beautiful' and
remembers the 'desperate' love he had felt for her as a boy.

Ominously, however, as Camus describes her, this altogether estimable
woman is practically without a mind. She has no inner life of any kind, and her
stoicism seems more vacuous than admirable. She is deaf, hardly speaks, is
barely literate (hence the dedication, 'To you who will not be able to read this
book'), and is apparently quite uninterested in what is going on around her. It
is as if she has been emptied of her identity so that she can act the part in *Le
Premier Homme* of an ideal of resignation and of anonymity, and as such stand
pathetically opposed to the 'folie de vivre', to the energy and the will to break
out that have marked the life of her anything but anonymous son. Then, having
reduced her to a nonentity, he declares that, whatever he may have achieved in
the world, compared with his mother he is 'nothing'. Some 'nothing' is all one
can say. That the aggrandisement of the mother should at the same time require
this belittlement of the son suggests even more strongly that, in *Le Premier
Homme*, the writer is now pronouncing a phantasmal death sentence on himself,
rather than on the innocent Meursault, for his secret betrayal of Catherine
Camus.

There are pleasures in Jacques's boyhood, but they are found always out of

---

* Self-effacing yet also self-regarding, inasmuch as he turns out near the end of the book to be
the narrator of his own heroic story: an ambiguous position highly revealing of the admixture
within Camus himself of moral high-mindedness and authorial vanity.

doors – in the streets, at school, on the beaches – scenes which are described with an admirable vigour and concreteness. Home is impossibly hard, ruled over by a tough old Spanish grandmother who is quite ready to beat the children and who makes all the decisions, not least the life-changing one that, despite what it is going to cost, the clever young Jacques be allowed to go on to the *lycée* rather than leaving school to earn a wage. For this pinched, unsmiling way of life, Cormery yet expresses an absolute regard. This is the 'kingdom of poverty', a condition that has 'something royal' about it. For him to go back now to Africa from Paris is to 'return to the childhood from which he had never been cured, to the secret of the light, of warm-hearted poverty that had helped him to live and to overcome'.

This was Algeria as the Parisian Camus required it to be, located, as he put it, 'midway between want (*misère*) and the sun. The want stops me from believing that all is well under the sun and in history, the sun taught me that history isn't everything.' By coded statements such as this, he made clear how alien a presence he felt himself to be in the intellectual life of Paris. Few if any of those he associated with, as a journalist, in the theatre, or on public platforms, had had his first-hand experience of want; and none could set against that real deprivation the profound, solar sensuality that went with being born beside the Mediterranean. 'Our climates are incompatible,' he once remarked of Sartre, as the explanation of how it was that the latter's books and ideas had failed to influence him. The same Sartre was of course the implied target of the remark about history not being everything, Sartre having become the postwar devotee of a 'historicity' that he blithely used to justify forms of political violence that Camus found abhorrent.

There is plenty of 'light' in *Le Premier Homme*, of the North African sun, the sea and the bodily pleasures that go with them. What is much less apparent is the 'warm-heartedness'. The Cormery family are tenaciously supportive of one another, but more out of obedience to the ethos of their milieu than out of any explicit warmth of feeling. Camus is determined that poverty should be acknowledged, if not as a moral good, then as a moral alibi, inasmuch as the poor are to be excused from condemnation by their condition, a peculiar, sentimental view to find coming from someone who was otherwise so obdurate in his moralism.

But then at the time when he was writing *Le Premier Homme*, Camus had unusually good reason to exalt his mother and her ill-favoured kind. He had been living through the difficult, frequently murderous terminal years of French rule in Algeria, years that had seen terrorism by the nationalist FLN in support of the movement for full independence and brutality by the French army and by extremists among the *pieds-noirs* or colonists against an Arab population that they despised. Camus, who, in *L'Homme révolté*, had come out against the (Sartrian) view that it was acceptable to kill those who obstructed you in the furtherance of a political end perceived as good, found himself both isolated and appalled, as an Algerian expatriate having to argue with uncompromising colonialists on the one side and with reckless left-wing intellectuals on the other, with those like Sartre who maintained their support of the FLN undeterred by its acts of violence against French civilians. This bore out what Camus had complained of ever since he arrived in Paris from Algiers: that the metropolitan French were dangerously ignorant of the realities of Algerian life, whether Arab or European. Had it been written a few years earlier, *Le Premier Homme* could have been taken as an attempt to educate its French readers in the sociology of the colony.

The ignorance that Camus deplored centred on the lives of those Algerians like his own mother, the poor Europeans who had been settled there for generations but had never prospered. 'There aren't only rich ones there', was his despairing counter to the prevailing anti-colonialist mythology, which had it that all settlers were by definition members of the capitalist class. As he saw it, from the first-hand experience that he intended should be seen as undermining the abstractions of political science, his own proletarian family had never oppressed anybody; they were in class terms as much victims as the Arabs (not all of whom were poor). Camus had long asked, in line with the moderate elements among the Muslim population, for full democratic rights to be granted in the colony, but he wanted also to preserve its links with France. In the fifties he argued for a form of federalism, a compromise that was by then hopelessly out of phase with the prevailing extremism on either side. Above all, he asked that there should be a formal truce, to stop civilians from being attacked and killed, in both Algeria and mainland France: 'If a terrorist throws a grenade in the Belcourt market where my mother shops, and if he kills her, I would be responsible if, to defend justice, I defended terrorism. I love justice but I also love my mother.'

This much quoted, and much derided, remark (made in 1956 to a Swedish journalist when Camus was in Stockholm to receive the Nobel Prize for Literature) helps to explain why his mother should be cast in the role she has in *Le Premier Homme*: her living presence in Algiers had determined Camus to an unpopular and troubled independence of mind over the future of the colony. There is terrorist activity in the city during Jacques's visit, an explosion outside the apartment, French parachutists driving about in jeeps. The terrorists are referred to as 'bandits', a description that establishes a sinister continuity between them and an earlier generation of Arab troublemakers, the more traditional and less obviously political 'bandits' who are loose in the countryside at the time of Cormery's birth and whose 'atrocities' are part of settler folklore.

Catherine Cormery herself is as oblivious of what is happening politically as she is of everything else; she knows only that she won't do what her son suggests and remove at this late stage in her life to France. There isn't much by way of explicit politics, in fact, in what we have of *Le Premier Homme*, nothing to show quite how Camus's views might be evolving, if they were, during the time when he was writing it. The book includes, however, numerous notes and fragments that he jotted down for possible future use. One of them is, in its strange, utopian way, political, and worth giving in full:

> And he exclaimed, looking at his mother, and then the others: 'Give the land back. Give all the land to the poor, to those who have nothing and who are so poor that they have never even wanted to have and to possess, to those who are like her in this country, the vast army of the poor, most of them Arabs and some of them French and who live or survive here out of obstinacy or endurance, in the one honour that is worth anything in this world, that of the poor . . . and I then, poor once again and at last, cast away in the worst of exiles at the far end of the world, I shall smile and die happy, knowing that the land that I so loved and those and she whom I revered are finally reunited beneath the sun of my birth.

How seriously might we take this, as Camus's last, visionary answer when it came to the Algerian problem? By the time he presumably wrote it, in 1959, de Gaulle had agreed that the country should have its independence, which was not at all the outcome that Camus had wanted. In *Le Premier Homme* he was going much further than he had felt able to go before in reasserting his own Algerian-ness and the extent to which it had formed him. Jacques Cormery's despairingly unreal solution for the country's future is one that does away with the racial difference fatally bedevilling French Algeria, by subsuming it within a class difference, allowing the disinherited of both races to merge and, tellingly, to become the definitive embodiment of that quintessential Mediterranean value, honour. By this bold dispensation, the 'kingdom of poverty' takes on a new, geographical resonance and the revered Catherine Cormery is freed to live at peace with the Arab majority, in the anonymity that Camus has chosen to be the ennobling characteristic of the poor. He too, for all the distance that he has travelled up and away from his origins, can seemingly become a part of this same glorious ecumenical order by divesting himself of his name.

This is a 'repatriation' too far. The one place in *Le Premier Homme* where Camus sets out very obviously to raise the tone, to lift his language to meet the grandeur of his theme, comes when he turns, quite briefly, to evoking the arrival of the first French settlers in Algeria, in the middle of the nineteenth century. The tone then is one of epic, as he exalts the hard lives and often unpleasant deaths these people suffered, whether from disease or from the hostility of the Arab population whose country they were settling. Nineteen fifty-nine was a tactless moment to be writing in terms like these, but Camus thought that the ordinary colonisers like his own family had been falsely incriminated, that they deserved better for the stubborn way in which they had survived. Whether they deserved the better he was set on doing them is another matter. The Algeria to which, as Cormery, Camus returns in *Le Premier Homme* is an allegorical, no longer a physical, territory: it is 'the land of oblivion where each one was the first man'.

A psychoanalyst who had known him once assured me that Camus's accidental death wasn't the impeccable contingency that it appeared to be: that the driver of the car, his close friend Michel Gallimard, had drunk freely with his lunch (a 'light meal' only, according to Olivier Todd in his fine new life of the writer, published in 1996), that, as Camus well knew, Facel Vegas were fast and reportedly unstable, that Camus hated speed but still got into the car, that he was in one of his suicidal phases. If this is right, then the portentously named 'land of oblivion' might be a less sunlit destination than French Algeria: it might be the state of death in which the incurably, guiltily famous Albert Camus would become nothing at all.

4

ROLAND BARTHES

What should a man famous in his lifetime for having wished the Author dead wish for himself once he becomes a dead author? To leave no trace behind him would seem the obligatory answer. But if Roland Barthes was hostile to the neighbourly image of the Author as an extra-textual being, he took pleasure in the thought of himself returning posthumously as a biographical subject (which is to say, a biographical object). In the preface to his tripartite study, *Sade, Fourier, Loyola*, he laid down the quite meetable conditions under which he would agree to pass into the hands of futurity: 'Were I a writer, and dead, how I would like my life to be reduced, by the attentions of a friendly, nonchalant biographer, to a few details, a few tastes, a few inflections, let's say "biographemes".' At the end of the same book, by way of illustrating the kind of casual memorial he had in mind, he included perfunctory 'lives' of two of its three subjects, Sade and Fourier: a few numbered biographemes, strewn through space 'like the atoms of Epicurus'. Epicurus's atoms are famous of course for having been hooked, and Barthes's typically sensuous fancy was that these errant particles might link up with hospitable fellow atoms among the living, so ensuring for him a small measure of – fragmentary – survival.

Certainly, there was to be no coming back after death as an entity; the posthumous condition that Barthes imagined for himself was a sociable version of the one he had sought to inflict most unsociably on the humanist notion of the integral Author. In *S/Z*, his scandalous taking apart of Balzac's little-read novella *Sarrasine*, the virtual entity 'Balzac', as the hypothetical source of that text, is separated ruthlessly out by Barthes without detectable remainder into constituent sources, or into the five generic 'codes' to be found interwoven in the text. The Author is thus meticulously degraded from the role of essential soloist in the literary performance to that of visiting choirmaster. This was Barthes at his most insolent, a feral literary thinker going too far for the sheer pleasure of it. The 'codes' — never, to my knowledge, to be systematically exploited again, by any of Barthes's followers or admirers — were a brilliant contrivance with which to shatter the dogmatic slumbers of literary academics and devout Balzacians. Barthes had already published to the same stirring effect a few years before: a short book on Racine, in which that supreme icon of French classicism was re-interpreted in the light of ideas drawn partly from anthropology and partly from psychoanalysis. *Sur Racine* (On Racine) is an eccentric study, in the precise meaning of the term, and it was resented in those places where Barthes wanted it to be resented: in the dusty, unimaginative haunts of the then professoriat. The book was a blow, powerfully struck, for critical pluralism and against the authoritarianism of those who were still teaching that there was a canonical way to read and understand the canonical oeuvre of Racine. And as with Racine, so now with Balzac, traditionally presented as the very specification of a creative genius, as autogenic, owing nothing to anyone but himself, but shown by Barthes as owing just about everything to the formal imperatives and stock of commonplaces prevalent in Balzac's own day. The demonstration is the more valuable for being excessive, because it brings to light, as something more cautious could not, the degree to which all literary creation, however apparently singular, must depend finally on collaboration. For some of us, the concept of authorship has not been the same since.

There was, however, another, milder, almost sentimental side to Barthes, which came more into view in the last years of his life, when he admitted among other things that he cringed at a lot of what was said and written by adepts of his own work and that he got a deep, pre-theoretical satisfaction from reading 'bourgeois' fiction, not least from reading Balzac. The most engaging of the 'biographemes' from which a suitably splintered Life of Barthes might be constructed is an occasion in the late seventies when he agreed to play (badly, by all accounts, and on location in Leeds) the role of William Makepeace Thackeray in a French film about the Brontës; at that late stage of his life (he died in 1980), this wasn't the sardonic piece of cinematic miscasting it would earlier have seemed.

Even in his laboratory phase, when he was jubilantly dissolving Balzac in an acid bath, Barthes didn't in fact insist that the Author figure be banished altogether from the discourse of criticism. The Author might be denied existence in the familiar guise of a phantasmal unity, or of Sole Originator of what we read, but he could remain as a vaguely cordial presence in the form of

— this in *Sade, Fourier, Loyola* again, a book published nine years before Barthes's death — a 'simple plurality of "charms", the site of a few tenuous details, the source still of quick novel-like gleams, a discontinuous song of amiabilities'. That is exquisitely worded but a shade suspect ideologically. For whoever or whatever is permitted to be both 'site' and 'source' looks to be on the way to reconstitution as an ontological item, and Barthes seems to be straying into contradictoriness. His remarkable animus against anything that is normally conceived of as being undivided or continuous sometimes sounds puritanical, as if unity were a state so desirable it was his duty to assure us it was an illusion.

We can be fairly sure that no biography, of Barthes or of anyone else, will ever be written in the elementary, discontinuous form of biographemes, however charming, for even if there are biographers austere enough to attempt it, there will never be publishers suicidal enough to indulge them. The point of biography is to gather its subjects together into the semblance of unity, not to collude in the posthumous distribution of their ashes. When Barthes himself drew — as no one doubts that he did — on his own experience as a lover in order to write his *Fragments d'un discours amoureux* (Fragments of a lover's discourse), he did so both discreetly and discretely, the first-person *je* of that book left teasingly intermediate between self-reference and a merely grammatical subjectivity, so that we have only intuition to go on in deciding how many autobiographemes it might contain. Given how extraordinarily well it sold — 80,000 copies in the first year is a figure quoted — the consensus has clearly been, right from the start, that it contains a great many autobiographemes, that the mainly unhappy amorous tropisms of which it consists were experienced before they were written, by Roland Barthes.

This was the book by which he effected his own elevation from being read as a critic to being read as a writer. The distinction between these upper and lower classes of literary society was one that he had long believed was false and had worked hard to undo. *Fragments* is a book indeterminate in genre, elegant in expression and acute in its understanding of the emotion with which it is concerned: it is enough on its own to ensure that Roland Barthes belongs to the history of French literature and not to the lesser, merely ancillary history of criticism.

The preface to *Fragments* is a masterly example of its author's rare gift for textual coquetry, for appearing in person, then disappearing within a few short sentences. In it Barthes says that *Fragments* is emphatically not a psychological portrait, but a 'structural' one, and that the 'voice' we hear in the book is not that of the – or even of an – author, but that of the Lover. As it registers the ups and downs – mostly the downs – of the amorous condition, *Fragments* functions theatrically, as though the discoursing Lover were marooned, alone and provisionally partner-less, on a stage and made to give a public performance. Barthes imposes no false continuity on him: there is no narrative element, no full, circumstantial setting. The 'fragments' themselves take the form of eighty 'figures', or independent excerpts from a soliloquy, likened by Barthes to the exercises a ballet dancer does when limbering up. Each figure is epitomised in a headword, and the headwords are arranged, dictionary-wise, alphabetically, so as to deny any personal or narrative significance to their ordering.

Fragments is thus both a dissection of the lover's state, conducted by someone who has evidently had experience of it, and a staging of an especially rich field of discourse or, as a Foucauldian would say, of a 'discursive formation'. Barthes has constructed a model of the discursive resources available to the contemporary Lover at different moments in the cycle of a love affair. The components for the model are drawn from literature as well as from life. The discourse of love is one unusually well provided for, and more easily reiterable than most, given the urgency with which it is called on. Barthes is open in acknowledging his borrowings from stock, giving the margins of the text over to identifying the books he has been reading and thanking the friends to whom he has been talking. He claims, with some justice, that what he has written is 'an encyclopedia of the affective culture'. He is instructing us in, as well as expanding on, the spoken or written 'codes' of love, especially those framed in the nineteenth century by Romanticism and in the twentieth by psychoanalysis. The result is entirely Barthesian: a seductive cross between a textbook in what may one day sink to being institutionalised under the heading of Amorous Studies, and a personal confession.

Barthes had flirted before this with the procedures of autobiography, in a book with a title that is either solipsistic or else pre-emptive, *Roland Barthes par Roland Barthes*. This opens in a surprisingly homely way, with a series of family snapshots, though whatever hint of poignancy these might convey is neutralised by the elaborately generalising captions they are given. The text that follows reveals rather little about its author as the word reveal is normally understood: he writes on the very first page (using the third person) that 'he finds any image of himself hard to endure' and thereafter skirts systematically round the stable characterisations which might have risked turning him into a fixture on the page. This writing subject is wonderfully good at refusing to forestall his own objectification.

Halfway through a now-you-see-me-now-you-don't book, however, there is a small clutch of autobiographemes in a section marked 'Pause: anamneses' (an unusual plural, no doubt meant to indicate that each of the entries under this heading has been the product of a separate act of remembering). The anamneses in question are a dozen or more suitably tenuous memories, nearly all of them going back to his childhood in Bayonne in south-west France. They end in an ironic 'etc.', and, in the possibilities they contain for expansion, they are Proustian: indeed, the second of them is a memory of coming home to have broth and toast by the fireside, as if Barthes might be led at any moment to dunk his toast and find Bayonne-Combray coming flooding back in all its lost vividness. He wants us to know perhaps that when he was writing *RB par RB* he was tempted by an ordinary nostalgia, but that he was man enough to resist it. For the rest, the book concentrates on defining his *imaginaire*, in the Lacanian sense of that term. (Pause for anamnesis: Barthes across the lunch table at the Terrazza in Soho, wryly complaining that though he read everything '*le père*' Lacan wrote, Lacan would never read anything of his.)

Lacan's Imaginary is not where any straightforward autobiographer would choose to remain when writing. It is the region of that sustained but delusory effort that Lacan supposes we all make at affirming an identity for ourselves out of our exchanges with the world and with our unconscious. It is Barthes's little joke in *RB par RB* to take up residence there: reasonable for him no doubt, but frustrating for the rest of us, as we watch him trying and failing to establish an identity for himself.

Like Camus, and like Sartre, Barthes grew up fatherless – 'Oedipally frustrated', as he mockingly put it. He was one year old when his naval-officer father was killed in the North Sea in October 1916, a death which meant that from then on the boy and his mother would be financially hard up. His mother's was much the grander of the two families, her father having risen to be a colonial governor in French West Africa. On that side there was money, but it didn't come to her, or not until too late. Barthes went on living with his mother throughout his life, until her death in 1977, three years before his own. They stayed effortlessly close, though to begin with their life was pinched, visibly so; and the embarrassment that this could lead to Barthes marked down as one source of the 'marginality' he said that he had felt throughout his life.

He at no time quite fitted in: even in the sixties, by which time he was teaching charismatically in Paris, his reputation was that of an academic misfit whose students too were misfits. (Let it be said that the sidelines are just where the practising semiologist, as a detached student of the signifying practices endemic in his society, should feel most at home.)

The feeling, or the fact, of Barthes's marginality was seriously over-determined, however; it had other, more formative sources than the pro-fessional one. The family's Protestantism counted for something, in a strongly Catholic part of France; on top of which there was a family scandal that led to a certain ostracism: when Barthes was twelve, his widowed mother had another child by a local painter. Then there was his homosexuality, of which he seems to have become finally certain only in his late twenties. Barthes thereafter was promiscuous, but without ever wanting it to be known, even in the late seventies when, thanks largely to Michel Foucault, 'outing' was in in France. Finally, there was his tuberculosis, which forced him to spend eight years on and off in sanatoria, including during the Second World War, and effectively ended his hopes of having an orthodox academic career. Not until 1947, when he was thirty-one and more or less free from the disease, did Barthes get his first regular job: as a librarian at the French Institute in Bucharest, a few months before the regime there closed it down.

That was also the year that he began publishing, when part of *Le Degré zéro de l'écriture* (Writing degree zero), a quite difficult essay on what might be called the politics of style in literature, was serialised by Maurice Nadeau in the left-wing newspaper, *Combat*. A few years later, Nadeau started commissioning the epochal pieces of journalism that were collected into a book in 1957 as *Mythologies*. Barthes was forty-one and, once *Mythologies* had appeared, famous, launched on his tortuous way through various research and teaching jobs to his final promotion to a chair of literary semiology at the Collège de France.

For many it is the semiological Barthes, the inspired decoder of contemporary culture and its masked ideologies, who continues to count for most. He was 'intuitive', certainly, in the way he went about things, but all the more influential for that reason in conveying the pleasure and the usefulness to be had from interpreting the social world around us – in which Barthes was being true to the missionary tradition in semiotics of Charles Morris in Chicago, who had valued the study of signs as having the power to form more alert and less easily manipulated citizens.

Mythologies remains a delight to read, endlessly ingenious and acerbic in its repeated demystifications of bourgeois culture, notably as mediated in the press: a holy book, I trust, in our burgeoning departments of cultural studies. There was more to Barthes than culture-reading, however. There is also his contribution to literary theory, whatever in the long run that turns out to have been.

Barthes had a hugely liberating effect on the language and method of criticism, and not only in France. He it was who showed that criticism, too, could be *written*, could offer verbal and conceptual excitements of its own while still engaging with the chores of interpretation. Barthes was the academic outsider who made very good. In the sixties, he took on, for the good of us all, the backwoodsmen of the French university system, embodied by Professor Raymond Picard, who expressed himself disgusted by the arrogance and waywardness of Barthes's 'anthropological' reading of Racine. That was a skirmish between modes of criticism – the one stale and pedantic, the other erratic but alive – a skirmish won definitively by Barthes, with the result that French universities today are far more open-minded places in which to read literature than they were thirty years ago.

That Barthes should have been so robust and sardonic as a polemicist – see his *Critique et vérité* (Criticism and truth), in which he answered the plaintive Picard witheringly back – is interesting, in the light of what we know about the sort of man he was. He was by temperament a keeper out of trouble, a sensualist who looked to gratify the body that had given him so much grief when he was young, not to expose it. He was assertive only when he wrote, and political only in print. In the days of *Mythologies* people took him for some kind of Marxist, given the venom he expressed in it against the bourgeoisie and all its hegemonic works. He was using the techniques of semiology to unmask that alienating 'conspiracy' of capitalism whereby the oppression of one class by another is made to appear a fact of nature rather than a changeable fact of history. Challenged in those days by Albert Camus to declare where, politically, he was coming from, Barthes claimed to be a 'historical materialist'. For the sake of argument, he might have added. He was no militant, looking on militancy as one more form of 'hysteria', of the theatrical, over-emphatic behaviour to which he had a horror of himself succumbing. In 1968, when he might have been expected, given what he had written against the academic establishment, to come out in support of the students, he wrote their movement nervously off as 'petty-bourgeois narcissism', which may not look so out of order thirty years later but does Barthes little honour as a conclusion reached in the heat of an exciting moment to which he had surely contributed something at least by his unorthodox teaching and writing. Heat, however, wasn't to Barthes's liking. He was fearful of crowds and of demonstrations: 'Structures don't take to the streets' was the sarcastic slogan that he coined to excuse his passivity.

He was a private, indoors man, where he could be safe with his cigars, his piano and his oil paints. He never hid his domesticity, nor the passion for order that was a part of it. He worked to exactly the same timetable every day and the rooms that he worked in, whether in Paris or in his holiday home outside Bayonne, were identically – let's say, isomorphically – arranged, a décor planned by and for a *structuralisant* to do his thinking in. To go with that there was the extreme orderliness with which he made notes when he was reading, filing them away on index-cards for use later, which prompts the question whether we shouldn't take his cult of the fragmentary to be an unusually honest reflection of the way in which those who write criticism reduce what they read to a card-pack of disjointed responses, only to deal them out later fused deceptively together as continuous prose.

The only physical risks that he took were when he was sexually driven and went out looking for young men, at successive stages of his working life, in Bucharest, Alexandria, Paris or Morocco. That was exceptional behaviour, a product of the 'desire' that he meant should be satisfied only covertly in his daily life but which, in compensation, was displayed flamboyantly enough as a concept in his writing. Right at the outset, in *Le Degré zéro de l'écriture* and his essay on the great nineteenth-century historian Michelet (the book of his that Barthes said he liked the best, maybe because no one else ever much admired it), he asked that the writer's 'body' and its 'history' be given their due, as being the one possible source of his 'style'. Michelet's obsessive industry, for example, Barthes locates first in the migraines from which the historian suffered very acutely and which led him, by some never quite spelt out Barthesian logic, to 'eat' history as the one form of nutrition that would keep him alive. And having once found ways of locating a writer's 'body' in his texts, Barthes was well on the way to constructing a 'materialist' theory of writing. Whatever is distinctive in a text is corporeal, it is where the writer's desire shows through; whatever is style-less is so because it is in some literal sense disembodied. The doxa or received opinion, that *noir*-est of *bêtes noires* for Barthes, is contemptible because it has no desire behind it – though why he should have supposed we are incapable of investing our desire in the doxa is unclear; it frequently appears as the only outlet available to us, even if recourse to it may succeed in concealing the evidence of our investment. The Barthes who wrote was a creature of paradox because that is what he very much desired to be, and a peculiarly mobile thinker because he was ultra-sensitive to the need to move beyond his own paradoxes once they were taken up and in danger of becoming in their turn an orthodoxy.

All through his writing life, Barthes was engaged in a private dialectic, between formalism on the one hand and subjectivity on the other, or between the gregarious and the idiosyncratic. The alternation is one movingly invoked in the essay on photography that appeared in the year of his death, *La Chambre claire* (Camera lucida). For this, Barthes found a final doublet of opposed, mutually defining terms, by which to differentiate the two possible responses to photographs. He opposes the *studium* to the *punctum* (neglected Latin terms that are themselves a reminder that Barthes began as a student of classics, and was fond as a neologiser of drawing on ancient Greek). The *studium* is a term reserved for those photographs that interest Barthes simply as a member of a collective, as one more student of culture. *Studium* photographs may inform but they do not move him; his response to them is a shared, formalisable one. With the *punctum* it is different: that is perfectly individual and affects him deeply, as the photographs included at the start of *Roland Barthes par Roland Barthes* will have affected him deeply, though he was not at that stage prepared to let it be known. No one else can respond to the *punctum* with the peculiar intensity that he does. So the *studium* is what brings together, the *punctum* what isolates.

By the end of *La Chambre claire*, Barthes has confessed the impossibility for him of treating photography purely as a cultural or semiological phenomenon, as he might have treated it twenty years before. It matters ineradicably to him as a suffering human being: 'The choice is up to me, to submit its spectacle to the civilised code of perfect illusions, or confront in it the reawakening of an intractable reality.' His choice, bravely admitted to, is to remain with the 'intractable reality', the phrase itself a coded reference to the recent death of his beloved mother, under the impact of which *La Chambre claire* was written. Detachment, and the old playfulness, are now out of the question; the best he can do is to try and universalise his own feelings and construct a theory of photography that is heavily dependent on his grief and sense of mortality.

We should be grateful that in the later part of his life, Barthes was impelled to offer far more of himself for view in his writing than we had any right to know. The tough-minded among his followers regretted this or found it an embarrassment, undermining as it may seem to do his credentials as a theorist of literature. In fact, the intimate revelations that he allowed us lend a new conviction and pathos to his thought by embodying it, true to his own teaching. As biographemes they prove that expounding literature was for Barthes more a passion than a profession.

5

LOUIS ALTHUSSER

In 1974, Michel Foucault found and published a nineteenth-century French murderer's first-person account of his crime: 'Moi Pierre Rivière ayant égorgé ma mère, ma soeur et mon frère . . .' (I, Pierre Rivière, having slaughtered my mother, my sister and my brother), a statement precious, in Foucauldian terms, as a rare public instance of the normally suppressed discourse of madness. Some twenty years later we were given to read, by someone who had coached Foucault in philosophy when he was a student at the Ecole Normale Supérieure, another bold and engrossing first-person work that could have borne the title 'I, Louis Althusser, having strangled my wife . . .' but was in fact entitled *L'Avenir dure longtemps* (The future lasts forever). This was the garlanded Marxist philosopher's long essay explaining how he came to strangle his wife late in 1980. If Pierre Rivière's was the extrovert testimony of a deranged Norman farmboy and literary simpleton, Althusser's account is infinitely more adroit, the manipulative product of a theoretical intelligence turned narcissistically in on itself, and a pre-emptive exercise in the discourse *on*, not of, madness.

Pierre Rivière wrote his apologia on the orders of the judge at his trial, though he boasted that he had meant to write one *before* carrying out his murders, so as to secure for himself a double glory, as author first of a spectacular crime and then of a memorable piece of literature. With the publication of *L'Avenir dure longtemps* in 1992, two years after its author's death, this double glory became Althusser's. There are signs in the book itself, however, that he was uneasy about the ambiguity of his intentions, when to confess in style and at length to a murder could but add to his celebrity, as a uniquely perceptive and articulate felon. But Althusser is at pains to reassure us also that what he is making is no more than the statement in his own defence that he wasn't allowed to make at the time, because no charge was laid against him. Instead, he was discreetly diagnosed as being in too chaotic a mental state

43

to answer for his act, and consigned to what he calls the 'tombstone of silence', of psychiatric restraint. Coming from a man who, unlike his irrevocably muted victim, had been left free to break his silence, that metaphorical 'tombstone' is all too indicative of his desire to usurp the role of victim and attract to himself the public sympathy presumed to go with it.

For Althusser, the legal and medical rules in France that stop an accused person from speaking out in the event of a non-suit are cause for prolonged complaint. He believes that he has suffered from having others speak out in his place, and so trespass on the autonomy he takes to be his right. *L'Avenir dure longtemps* was written in 1985, five years after the 'drama' of his wife's death, and that he should have been made to wait so long before breaking his silence is his founding grievance in an impenitently complaining book.

Althusser expresses no simple guilt or regret for what he did, he comes to no unequivocal conclusion about why he did it. Rather, he ushers the murdered Hélène Rytmann away towards the margin of his own very troubled life. 'La vedette, c'est le coupable' (the culprit is the star) was the response of one journalist in Paris who had been disgusted by the manner in which the affair was reported at the time when it happened. That was the fault not of Althusser but of his fame, as the most prominent and innovative Marxist thinker of the postwar period in France. And in Althusser's defence now it could be said that the guilty man who turns autobiographer can't help but function textually as the star of his own story and compel everyone else who appears in it to serve his own rhetorical and apologetic ends.

Althusser's most blatant end is the exculpation of himself. As an autobiographical event, the strangling of Hélène Rytmann is a pure contingency, for which motives may be and are found but no one sovereign motive that might resolve and classify the crime as the understandable dénouement of a long and tortured relationship. We might accord it the status in his narrative of an 'irruption', that term of which he makes such striking and regular use in his theoretical writings in order to de-originate, or perhaps better 'disaffiliate', particular structures – the capitalist mode of production, the Freudian unconscious – that we are not to believe are simply derivative from the structures which preceded them. Contingency is a vital concept for the theoretician, as when, for example, 'the concrete individual that is the young Marx appears suddenly [*surgit*] in the *thought-world* of his time, to *think there* in his turn . . .' (Althusser's italics). Contingency is a vital concept for the apologist also, in effecting a break between the emotional situation in which his crime became possible or even likely and the act itself.

The great revelation for most of us reading *L'Avenir dure longtemps* (and the first volume of Yann Moulier Boutang's biography of Althusser, which appeared at much the same time) must be the depth and frequency of the mental crises from which Althusser suffered throughout his adult life. In 1980, this was hardly if at all known, so that his rapid disappearance into psychiatric care instead of into prison made it look as though a special, and objectionable, leniency had been shown him because of the high intellectual prestige he had previously enjoyed.

In fact, Althusser had endured before 1980 a bleak thirty-year history of manic depression, to an extent which makes it remarkable that he should have had a public or a teaching life at all. Boutang calculates that he had to be taken into a hospital on average once every three years and that he was 'immobilised' by depression for perhaps half his working time. He was treated with electroconvulsive therapy and with drugs, and was later permanently in psychoanalysis. At one time, according to Althusser, early in their life together, it was only Hélène's hatred of institutions that saved him from being hospitalised for good.

He offers a partly Freudian, partly Althusserian explanation for his incurably fragile condition, rooted in his petty bourgeois family. The family, along with schools and the church, was for Althusser what he called an 'ideological state apparatus', an exploitative – 'violent' is the word he uses in his autobiography – social 'formation' that embodies the ideology of the state and is the more insidious for being experienced by its victims as a necessary fact of life. The task of Althusser the political theorist was to unmask that fact of life by theorising it, and so turn it from an ideological imposition into a 'scientific' datum. Thus the 'unmasking' of his own mother and father as the two people bearing ultimate responsibility for his problems of affect is simply a domestic version of the larger theory, with Althusser now cast as 'the concrete individual' and his own circumstances representing what, in writing about the young Karl Marx, he describes as 'the irruption of real history into ideology'.

Althusser introduces a self-serving dialectical element into his family situation, however, in contrasting the life led by his parents with that led by his maternal grandparents. They were country people, able to induct their grandson into what he looks back on as a savingly physical, simplified way of life quite contrary to the one he knew in the dystopia of his urban home. 'I experienced an intense happiness, free and full, in the company of my grandfather and grandmother, even when my parents came with me, in the paradise of their house in the forest. . . .' The polarisation of the two environments, and the sentimentalising of one at the expense of the other, sheds an interestingly personal light on the millennial elements in Althusser's political thought, when he turns (in his essay 'Marxism and Humanism') to envisage a future, post-capitalist society, 'a world that may be without shadows, without dramas'. In this redemptive projection of a golden past into an impossible future, one might say that Althusser was robbing Freud to pay Marx.

He had indeed a revealingly erratic relationship with psychoanalysis. It culminated in a passionate intervention at the March 1980 meeting of the Ecole Freudienne de Paris, following the ailing Jacques Lacan's imperious decision to dissolve it. Althusser took the analysts who attended it furiously to task on behalf of the analysands, saying that he was appalled by the submissiveness the Lacanians were showing towards the 'magnificent and pitiful Harlequin' Lacan (of whom years before Althusser had been an extreme and fulsome admirer). He was speaking out of his own distress, as a patient known for declaring that analysis had helped him, but also as someone who had written theoretically about both Freud and Lacan (see the *Writings on Psychoanalysis*, published in translation in 1996). Remarkably, however, Althusser claimed, both in *L'Avenir dure longtemps* and elsewhere, never himself to have read Freud and, more generally, to have acquired his philosophical knowledge more by 'hearsay' than by his own reading. The claim is ambivalent: he suggests that his fellow teachers admired him the more for getting by on so little first-hand knowledge; he offers it contrarily as evidence that he was in truth an 'impostor' who had no right to the position he held.

Althusser's Freudianism shows in the determination with which, in his autobiography, he recreates his childhood to his own best advantage, by casting himself in the pathetic role of a vicarious or unnecessary being. At his birth (in 1919) he was given the name of an 'uncle' Louis, to whom his mother had been engaged but who had been killed at Verdun before they could marry. The mother had instead married Louis's older brother, Georges. Little Louis, literally nominated to take the place of the dead uncle, is launched on a profound mission of oblation: he will be the one to 'save' his mother from his boorish father, as later he was to 'save' the martyred Hélène. And to save his mother he must 'seduce' her, to be for her what the other Louis Althusser was to have been. He has been 'reduced, in order to exist, to *making myself loved*, and, in order to love (because loving governs being loved) reduced . . . to artifices of seduction and imposture'. Both in private and in his academic profession, Althusser has fulfilled his appointed role of impostor, outwardly plausible and a high achiever, yet secretly void. The Marxist philosopher who knows that he has been listened to by his students and readers, and has followers both in France and internationally, will show in his autobiography that all this attention and influence were based on a misapprehension, that he is not at all the man he has been thought to be.

We can take it that Althusser's family life was by no means the catastrophe he presents it as. Nor do his attempts to make us believe that as a philosopher he was a fraud, having read far too little of Marx to be entitled to have theories about him, carry more conviction. They will be taken at face value only by those keen for whatever reason to see this acclaimed left-wing theorist diminished and who are willing to misread what he writes as a compulsive disclosure of the truth about himself rather than the devious pleading of someone set on courting sympathy by the magnification of his failings. Such ill-wishers would do well to attend to what Althusser has to say about Machiavelli, the strategic genius who, he alleges, made Freud redundant centuries before he was born and from whom Althusser has learnt that artifice and imposture are the standard means by which we handle other people. Machiavelli is the political thinker whom the autobiographical Althusser esteems most, above Marx even, and for strikingly personal reasons. It is because Machiavelli's thought is the most purely abstract, a salutary theory visited on an abject world from outside, from that immaculate vantage point for which Althusser himself had gone in lifelong search.

Althusser displays a certain Machiavellianism by placing the description of the murder at the head of the book. He describes not the act of strangulation, of which he has no memory, but his regaining consciousness early on a November morning with his thumbs massaging the hollows in his wife's neck and with aching muscles in his forearms. There is something of the anatomy lesson in his punctilious setting of the scene, and something as well of the playwright anxious to secure the most telling disposition of his props:

> I am suddenly standing, in a dressing-gown, at the foot of my bed in my apartment in the Ecole Normale. The light of a grey November day – it was Sunday the 16th, around nine in the morning – came from the left, from the very tall window, framed for a very long time past by some very old red Empire curtains tattered with age and scorched by the sun, to light the foot of my bed.

> In front of me: Hélène, lying on her back, also in a dressing-gown.
>
> Her pelvis is resting on the edge of the bed, her legs are splayed on the moquette on the floor.

The clarity of this scene, immediately following on the unconsciousness of the crime, is unnerving, as if Althusser were here enacting the too-familiar swing from depression into mania. But the lurid discovery of the body, once briefly invoked, is left in suspense as he turns back to narrate and comment on the pitiful story of his life.

The Ecole Normale is an anomalous, a crime-writer's setting for a murder, a cerebral and ascetic place unfitted for such morbid spontaneities of the flesh. It was where Althusser worked, where he had long lived and, most important, the one place in the world where he belonged:

> a true maternal 'cocoon', the place where I was in the warm and at home, protected against the outside, which I had no need to leave to meet people, because they came past or called in, especially when I became well-known, in short it, too, was the substitute for a maternal environment, for the *amniotic* fluid.

He became a student there only at the end of the war, at the late age of twenty-seven. He never had to leave it, because after having achieved a brilliant *agrégation* he stayed on as the *caïman* or tutor in philosophy. He taught in the rue d'Ulm, very conscientiously by all accounts, and he lived there, at first alone, eventually with a companion more than somewhat unsuited by her stormy and abrasive nature to share its uterine comforts with him.

Althusser met Hélène Rytmann when he was still a student, at a loss in postwar Paris, shy, friendless and hypochondriacal. He was sexually retarded, and she was the first sexual partner he had had, at twenty-nine. She was ten years older than Althusser and much that he was not: unhappy like him, 'un peu folle', but also brash and experienced. He tells a terrible story of how, as a young girl, she had been raped by the doctor treating her parents and then forced, when they were dying of cancer, to give them lethal injections, one after the other – a story that I think we have to list among the hallucinations, the 'imaginary memories' in his own term, which he admits that he has incorporated into the text of his 'traumabiography'.

Before the war, Hélène had been a militant on the far Left, impatient of all political organisations but seized by 'a true passion, total, demanding' for the working class. During the war she had been with the Resistance in Lyon and had met some of the great names of the literary Left at that time: Camus, the poet Paul Eluard, Louis Aragon and Elsa Triolet. She had in short received what in *Pour Marx* Althusser calls 'the terrible education by facts', even if the facts of her past as he gives them are by no means certain. Althusser's own past had been much less exposed or exciting. He, too, had been political before the war but, after a short-lived flirtation with the Royalists in Lyon where he was then at school, in the genteel youth movements of the Catholic Left; the war years, after the surrender, he had spent as a prisoner in northern Germany, safe, frankly grateful to be so and highly receptive to the regime of manual work he was obliged to follow there and to the monkish fraternity of the camp. Liberation indeed cast him adrift, until Rytmann came to be his belated opening onto the world.

The received wisdom is that she was a disturbed and unpleasant woman who did Althusser nothing but harm. Her reputation was that of a *mégère*, or fury, a reputation borne out by the accounts he gives of her rages and caprices when she was with him. But she raged, he explains, because she was terrified of not being loved; at times, she could be both paranoid and suicidal, so that one reason he floats for his having killed her is that she wanted him to do so, his last oblatory act having been to end her martyrdom for her. When he defends her, Althusser goes instantly too far, presenting her as the most magnanimously loving of women, gifted, though she wrote almost nothing, with a verbal inventiveness greater than that of James Joyce.

Hélène was also accused by those who had known the pre-war Althusser as a decorous *lycéen* and good Catholic of having turned him after 1946 into an adamantine Stalinist. But on the evidence of his autobiography, Althusser was incapable of being adamantine. He denies there that it was Hélène who brought him to Marxism. It is true that he joined the Party in 1948, some two years after taking up with her, but that can be convincingly seen as the logical end point of his leftwards evolution through the late thirties and of his experiences in the POW camp. Nor did he give up being a Catholic when he joined the PCF; he remained in the Church until 1952, even past the time when all Catholics who were also Party members were excommunicated by the Vatican.

Ironically, it is unclear whether Hélène herself was ever a Party member. She claimed to have been one, but the Party denied it and refused after the war to have her. It went further: it told its promising new member, Louis Althusser, that she was not a reliable companion for him and that he should leave her; there were stories that she had worked for British intelligence or even collaborated during the war. Althusser wouldn't give her up because he couldn't; he maintained the liaison, though without publicising it. Such muffled disobedience was typical of the thirty-two years he spent as an internal dissident in the Party. He didn't like its leaders or its cynical policies, and he knew it was corrupt; but he stayed on, through all the thousand shocks that Communism was heir to in those years – the Rajk and Slansky trials, Budapest and Prague – which drove so many other thoughtful members out. Althusser, however, continued to believe in the PCF as the one means of 'acting politically – that is, in actuality – on the course of history'. 'Today,' he adds (writing in 1985), 'things have changed very obviously.'

The Party served Althusser as the POW camp and the Ecole Normale served him. All three sustained him by conferring a soothing measure of anonymity on his activities as an individualist who was forever fearful of the price an individualist may end up paying in terms of social or intellectual isolation. All three were surrogate homes for one of nature's asylum-seekers. To be in, but not fully of, an institution was always Althusser's need. As a wartime prisoner ashamed at his own weakness in finding satisfaction in captivity, he fantasised a mode of 'escape' from the camp which involved not actually leaving it, but hiding for several weeks within the perimeter, until the guards called off the hunt. But that was only to defer the risk of escaping, not to avoid it, and Althusser knew that he didn't have the courage to escape.

The word *courage* leads, by a suggestive Lacanian glissade, to the name of the man whom Althusser extols as the person most responsible for his political conversion, his fellow prisoner, Pierre Courrèges. Courrèges was a pre-war Communist whose impact on the camp when he arrived there was that of a thaumaturge:

> Without a mandate from anyone, simply in his own name and in the name of honesty and fraternity, Courrèges took a hand and the effect was incredible. He was simple, direct, warm, natural, acting and speaking apparently without effort. His mere presence transformed the camp.

In this one grand, alchemical moment there is to be found concentrated all of the nebulous millenarianism of Althusser's political project; it prefigures his own conversion from Catholicism to Marxism. Courrèges is at once lone saviour and collective promise, the omega point where a Christian humanism and the Communist revolution converge.

By the end of *L'Avenir dure longtemps*, Althusser may be outside the Party, but he still has the faith and the perverse hope of a distraught individualist that mass action by those of goodwill – the German Greens, liberation theologians – may yet save the world. The 'one possible definition of Communism' to which he clings 'is the absence of market relations, thus of relations of class exploitation and domination by the state'. As an abstraction, that might just do, a fantastic but honourable vision. But then the eschatological gives way to the scatological, and Althusser offers a crassly figurative version of this same future. 'Socialism' now becomes 'shit' or, to be exact, the 'immense river of shit' that society has to cross, which can only be crossed once the proletariat is running the state. This river is well worth crossing because on the far side 'is the shore, the wind and sunshine of a young spring. Everyone alights, there is no more struggle between men and interest groups since there are no longer any market relations but a profusion of flowers and fruits that all may pick for their delight.'

And just as he has stayed a frantically impractical Communist, so he has also stayed a materialist, though here again Althusser's materialism is not quite as other materialisms. His materialist is someone who 'gets on a moving train without knowing where it has come from or where it is going'. Only by apostasy from what he once wrote of as 'the gods of origins and ends' can we become true materialists, attending wholly to the present and to what is, rather than to what was or will be. As a theorist of Marx, Althusser took issue with the 'analytico-teleogical' method by which the writings of the young Marx have been falsely interpreted as merely a necessary preparation for the writings of the mature Marx, urging on the contrary that Marx be restored to the reality of his life in the body and in historical time, as a creative thinker responsive to the shifts in the *champ idéologique* in which he found himself and not simply realising some inevitable scheme. Marx's heroic evolution was out of the mists of 'ideology' into the daylight of 'science', the same categorical advance that Althusser has wanted to make in *L'Avenir dure longtemps* in coming to understand his own lived experience. He prizes his version of materialism because to adopt it was, he says, to 'stop telling myself stories', to see things as they inescapably were. By writing an autobiography, Althusser hoped finally to find refuge as the aloof theorist of his distressed historical self, as he had been the theorist of the historical Marx; for in the lucidity of the theoretical intelligence there lies, he would say, the one cure for a diseased reality, whether the reality be that of capitalism, the Communist Party or Louis Althusser's own ruinous past.

6

JACQUES LACAN

Sessions with Dr Jacques Lacan were famously short, but none I daresay as short as mine. We met professionally not as doctor and patient, but as author and editor, over the telephone, voice to voice. Newly taken on at the *Times Literary Supplement*, I was the one appointed to give Lacan the bad news, that an article he had been commissioned to write could not be used. He had sent in a sensationally convoluted French text which had been turned by a translator into a blankly unmeaning English one, and it was not thought sensible for the paper to publish something that none of its editors could understand. Lacan was incensed at knowing that he had been spiked, on what to him seemed insultingly practical grounds. He thought it was enough that his name should be on the piece for it to have to be published; I that unintelligibility was a ground for rejection, irrespective of whose unintelligibility it was. Since the disputed article was not echt-Lacan but only Lacan in translation, the argument from authorship was strong but not irresistibly so: the article did not appear.

This two-minute dialogue of the deaf is nothing much as Lacan stories go, for no one was ever more generative of good gossip than that famously rude and quarrelsome man, who could never tolerate being subject to the authority of others, nor to share his own authority with them: he set new standards of fissiparousness in a profession long known for it. My own exchange with Lacan serves, however, to raise the question that is slow to disappear even though he has now been dead for some fifteen years: how far should we feel obliged to go in order to understand what he wrote? I believe strongly that we should go as far as our brains and our patience can take us, that Lacan's was a remarkable intelligence and that the struggle to elucidate its workings as one reads has both its rewards and its pleasures.

At the time when he was asked to write in the *TLS*, Lacan was known outside France – and outside the psychoanalytical profession to which he had long stood in the relation of charismatic Other – only through the *Ecrits*, the large volume of his theoretical papers that had been published in 1966. With the appearance of the *Ecrits*, the claim was made that Freud had finally been brought to France, and that France would have now, as Lacan himself once franglicised it, to *'faire bye-bye'* to a smug and superannuated Cartesianism for which the whole idea of an unconscious mind was a contradiction in terms. The claim was somewhat misleading in suggesting that previously Freud and Freudianism had never got anywhere in France; they had, notably during the 1920s among the Surrealists, whose imperious capo, André Breton, once tried to enrol Freud himself as an honorary member of his unstable coterie. Lacan in his youth had accounted himself a Surrealist; he knew that Freud's ideas were far from a novelty among the Parisian literati, even if, by 1939, there were still only twenty-four psychoanalysts officially practising in the whole of France.

Once he had trained as an analyst, Lacan's ambition was to be Freud and Breton in one: a serious student of the human psyche *and* a literary ringmaster. In the *Ecrits*, this ambition is only too apparent. Nowhere do they read with the benign clarity so characteristic of Freud, but rather as the work of an inordinately subtle concettist, whose mannered syntax and extreme allusiveness seem designed to separate those who read him into the mutually impermeable classes of the devotees and the defaulters. Only later did those of us who defaulted discover that the *Ecrits* were Lacan at his most obstructively difficult, and that we should have paused over the title he gave to that book: writings were what it contained, not speakings, and when he wrote Lacan believed that he should complicate his prose to the point where it stands in actual illustration of the riddling discourse the psychoanalyst hopes to elicit from his patient.

In the consulting room, the Lacanian analyst is given the role of encouraging 'the discourse of the hysteric', that is, of 'hystericising' the patient's discourse under the artificial conditions of a consultation. To a non-Lacanian, this looks like a dramatically reworded version of the old free association, that analytical technique that the Surrealists prized so greatly in the graphic form of automatic writing: 'The analyst says to the person about to begin: "Go on, say anything at all, it will be wonderful."'

Lacan goes much further, however, in claiming that the task of the listening analyst is to act out, from a position of seeming ignorance, the role of the 'one who knows'. All that he is called on to do is to add the 'punctuation' to what he hears from his hystericised patient, to the 'ribbon of excrement' as he calls it, in a typically Lacanian flourish. It is unclear, as so often with Lacan, whether he is being playfully arrogant or arrogantly playful in proposing a model of the analytical situation where the analyst's initial, mock-modest state of ignorance is abandoned apparently only because such is the suffering patient's need. In the *Ecrits* at all events, Lacan seems to have combined the two roles and to have hystericised his own discourse, crossing the method of the analyst with the madness of the patient and giving free rein to the verbal promptings of his own unconscious – so proving on the page his most celebrated dictum, that 'the unconscious is structured like a language'.

There is a counterfeiter at work here, however. Professionally, and by all accounts personally, Lacan was nothing if not magisterial and there is something implausible about his argument that we are wilfully deluding ourselves if we believe we are masters of our own discourse, because as users of language we come, like it or not, under the impersonal empire of the linguistic Signifier, which has the power to make greater or lesser hysterics of us all. Lacan's exuberant promotion of the Signifier, which is to be regarded as always the senior partner in its relations with the Signified in language, was at once the most conspicuous and the most angrily resisted of Lacan's various re-formulations of a familiar Freudianism. His own view was that Freud, for all his concern with the psychopathology of verbal play and verbal error in both dreams and waking life, had drawn culpably back from recognising the real autonomy of the Signifier, or, as we could also say, without resorting to the Saussurian terminology, the real autonomy of language in respect of its users, Freud and Lacan included. Lacan overturns – 'gloatingly', as the author of the single best study of Lacan's thought, Malcolm Bowie, complains – the old hierarchy which sets the 'speaking subject' and the meanings that he or she desires to express above the medium of expression itself. In Lacan's way of thinking, the medium, far from being subservient or responsive to our desires, actually *constitutes* the speaking subject and in the analytical situation needs to be explored so that the patient may come to recognise better the form and significance of his or her desires.

The consequence is that, once we are implicated, every time we open our mouths or set pen to paper, in the Symbolic Order of language, a signifying system that has evolved quite independently of us, we can no longer function as gratifying wholes, because we are subjects divided, the unconscious mind being now invited to have its say in collaboration with the conscious. What Lacan means when asserting that 'the unconscious is structured like a language' is that whatever may be brought to light of the unconscious, in the course of a psychoanalysis, can but be verbal and can but pre-exist its revelation. 'The unconscious is the discourse of the Other' is one of the formulations found by Lacan. Like any act of *parole*, this discourse is determined formally by the objective structure of the *langue*. Lacan, you might say, has used Saussure as the intellectual means by which lastingly to discredit the Ego-psychology imposed by Freud, the predecessor whose nerve failed him when it came to acknowledging the full subversiveness of his own analysis of the psyche.

Nowhere in Lacan, however, have I found any acknowledgment that those who speak and those who write may enjoy a different relationship in respect of language. Psychoanalytic criticism of literature we have had in plenty, practised by Freudians, Jungians, Lacanians and by those who might call themselves eclectics. Such criticism appears to be pursued for the most part on the understanding that the text under analysis is in the situation of a patient, of someone launched, as a Lacanian would say, on a 'hysterical' discourse. But is the Writing Subject really just a Speaking Subject discovered in flagrante? If we allow that the Speaking Subject does indeed go blindly ahead, signifying freely in the more or less guided exploration of his or her 'desire', the Writing Subject is in a different position because he or she – the truly Lacanian pronoun would be 'it' – can go back any number of times over what has been written and at least partly restore the authority there of the (delusory) Ego. The effect of going back over the written text, as Lacan did, in an opposite intention, so as further to hystericise it in obedience to the powers of suggestion latent in its Signifiers, is a willed regression from the written to the spoken, as if there were something reprehensible in the relative lucidity of the first.

Language, however, is the law we have all of us to live and suffer under: 'The psychoanalytical experience has rediscovered in man the imperative of the word as the law that has formed him in its own image. It manipulates the poetic function of language in order to give his desire its symbolic mediation.' As the prose poet of the unconscious, Lacan is a consummate performer, but one only too well aware of the paradox whereby his own authority as a layer-down of the psychoanalytical law was invested in a discourse as much ludic as doctrinaire, and so difficult to follow in many places that the price to be paid by those wishing to contest it all along the line would be self-defeatingly high. He has a decidedly haughty way of vacating the psychoanalyst's seat of authority.

It is a relief for any student of Lacan to turn from the punishing complications of the *Ecrits* and meet with him in the more accessible spoken version, which is transcribed in the numerous volumes of his *Séminaires* (if and when the series is completed, it will contain twenty-six volumes, one for each year of the public lectures he gave in Paris between 1953 and 1979). As a lecturer, Lacan drew the crowds because he entertained them, his caustic digressions, his polemics, his erudite ad-libbing, along with the assurance and energy of his meta-psychological theorising, having made him into a star metropolitan turn. Allusive and acrobatic of mind though he still was on these oral occasions, he used them to exercise his pedagogical cure with a certain responsibility, coming back again and again to the repertoire of key axioms or concepts around which his grand theoretical design should be seen to turn, explicating and expanding on them to the point where they make consistent and often impressive sense. It is usually possible to follow Lacan and surprisingly often to enjoy him in the *Séminaires*, the public performer being more congenial and instructive than the oracular, poeticising author of the *Ecrits*.

Over the years, the Lacan circus had to migrate across town, from its original medical setting in the Sainte-Anne hospital, via the Ecole Normale Supérieure in the rue d'Ulm, to a lecture room lent to him by the law faculty of the Sorbonne. Lacan himself had an amused commentary to offer on the reasons for this enforced peregrination. To have begun his mission to Paris in a hospital was only proper, but at Sainte-Anne, it appears, his seminars – which were never 'seminars' as most of us know them, but uninterruptible solo flights – had contained too much by way of intellectual horseplay – too many 'gags' is Lacan's description (he uses the English word) – and not enough by way of psychiatric instruction for the managers of the hospital to put up with him any longer; the Ecole Normale Supérieure, too, had had its doubts about the value of his presence and he finally had to leave the rue d'Ulm because smoke from the cigarettes of his audience wafted up into the library on the floor above and annoyed the readers there. So 1969 found him lecturing in a third, and this time a legal, setting, telling his hearers that the occasion was now clearly come for him to bestow on psychoanalysis its '*statut juridique*' (juridical status), an apt occasion bearing in mind Lacan's insistence, cited above, that psychoanalysis be seen as the activity that has rediscovered the Law of Laws, which is the inescapable authority of language.

The first of the *séminaires* to be given in this new location was that for 1969–70, and it was eventually published as volume seventeen in the series, under the title of *L'Envers de la psychanalyse* (roughly, The underside of psychoanalysis). It is particularly interesting for belonging to what Lacan describes as the 'structuralist moment' of his teaching. The title refers to one of the four distinct discourses that between them, according to him, structure the psychoanalytical field: the discourses of the Hysteric, the Analyst, the University and, this is for some reason the 'underside', the Master. To these four discourses there correspond four elements or terms in what one might call the primal scene of Lacanianism, in which a Subject desirous of some unknown Object intervenes in the Battery of Signifiers, *né* the Symbolic Order, and in the process undergoes a Splitting. The function of language for Lacan is in fact to disrupt or else to dissolve the Ego, by subjecting it to those alien forces resident in the unconscious over which it has no control. Unlike the Freud of whom he claimed to be the faithful representative, he is the sworn enemy of all so-called Ego-psychology, that reinforcement of the rights of the Ego against the encroachments of the Id that Lacan liked, rightly or not, to identify as a superficial and mainly American perversion of Freudianism.

Each of the elements or terms in Lacan's primal scene is characterised by a 'dominant' discourse: the discourse of the Master is that of the unsplit (that is, deluded) Subject; the discourse of the Hysteric, as we know, that of the split Subject; the discourse of the University (I am quite unclear why) that of the Battery of Signifiers itself; and the discourse of the Analyst that of the surrogate Object of the Subject's desire, the Analyst being called on during the course of an analysis to be also the object of a transference. There are possibilities in this schema for some vigorous games of power politics to be played out between the different discourses, and the timing of Lacan's introduction of this quadripartite diagram was typically knowing. The course of lectures in question was being given little more than a year after the highly disruptive 'events' of May 1968, when the authoritarian discourses of the Master and of the University had come under assault from students demanding, even if they didn't yet know it, their hystericisation. Lacan, man of the world as ever, was cutting his theoretical cloth to suit the time and place, and distancing himself with a suitable acerbity from both the Masters and the University – an attitude supported by the volume's cover picture, which shows Daniel Cohn-Bendit, the most chubbily photogenic of the student ultras of the previous year, grinning insolently up at a helmeted riot-policeman.

Not that Cohn-Bendit's posture is one for which Lacan himself had any sympathy. On the contrary: he assured his audience that he had not had to wait for 1968 to call the discourse of the University into question, and that they would do better to listen to what he had to tell them concerning inter-discursive relations than to imagine that they might escape the Symbolic Order altogether and wreak their will in the order of the Real. (As a concept, the order of the Real is elusive even by Lacan's standards, but it seems to describe everything, of either a psychological or a material nature, that lies outside the process of symbolisation.) Lacan indeed put down the Sorbonne students when they dared to heckle him with the same fluent and scathing disdain with which he had already put down the University, whose discourse he condemned as obsolete in its Cartesian trust in the validity, as the recognised vehicle of Truth, of the first person singular. The discourse of the University is vitiated by being addicted to the 'idealist I, the I that has mastery': it is the meretricious discourse belonging to what Lacan calls the 'Je-cratie' or Ego-cracy. (It is hard not to see a perfect fit between the description of Ego-crat and the role of *maître à penser* as performed with such success by Jacques Lacan.)

The *Séminaire* volume (volume eight, containing the lectures he gave in 1960–61) which appeared simultaneously with the one referred to above makes as good a point of entry as there is to the imbroglio of Lacan's thought. It does so because the topic with which it deals, the Transference, is crucial to any account of what actually happens in psychoanalysis and central to the contribution made by Lacan to psychoanalytical theory. In this volume, his arguments are both reasonably straightforward and made with real wit. The Transference is a subject that Lacan is prepared to gloss without feeling obliged to draw it so completely into the half-light of his own formulations as to make it opaque.

Psychoanalysis as we know it evolved out of an episode of transference, when Freud's early colleague in the study of female hysteria, Josef Breuer, abruptly and embarrassedly broke off from treating by hypnosis a patient who had developed an erotic attachment to him. Breuer – according to Freud – was unable or unwilling to understand this strange turn of events, whereas Freud took thought and concluded that Breuer's patient had transferred onto her doctor emotions originally felt for, but never expressed to, someone else (her father). The aborted exchange between Dr Breuer and the pseudonymous Anna O. was thus the true matrix of psychoanalysis, of the 'talking cure' or 'chimney-sweeping', as Anna O. called it on different occasions, in which repressed emotions would be artificially brought to consciousness and in the process attached provisionally and, all being well, cathartically to a willing but impassive surrogate, the analyst.

Lacan goes to classical literature to find a role model for the analyst caught up in this fraught professional situation. Not, needless to say, to the by now exhausted story of Oedipus, but to the as yet pristine figure of Socrates, as he is presented in the *Symposium*. One by one, Lacan analyses the interventions in that text of all the different symposiasts, showing himself by turns scholarly, ribald and patiently exegetical on his way to an interpretation that he claims – rightly, I can believe – is 'epochal'.

His main business is with the last of these interventions, when the clownish Alcibiades arrives on the scene, late and audibly the worse for wear, to complain to the other banqueters that, although he loves Socrates, Socrates does not love him but has spurned his amorous advances with an offensive indifference. To which Socrates's answer, as re-described by Lacan, is that Alcibiades, his drunkenness no doubt ensuring that his discourse will be 'hysterical', does not know his own mind, or rather his own 'eros'. For the true object of Alcibiades's desire is not Socrates but Agathon, the man in whose house they are feasting. Socrates is thus the object of a transference, and is taken by Lacan as a model proto-analyst, the figure 'who brings back the truth into the discourse'. The striking characteristic of Socrates as he is represented in the Platonic dialogues is his profession of vacancy, of starting out on the discussion from an (assumed) state of ignorance. And like Socrates, the Lacanian analyst is to affect to be nothing in himself and to know nothing beyond what he learns from the hysterical discourse of his misguided patient/lover. Seek not your patient's Good, but his eros, is the advice which Lacan impresses on his followers, meaning I presume that the analyst can have no therapeutic purpose other than to make his patient aware of what he calls 'the margin of incomprehension, which is that of desire'. A successful analysis must make available to the desiring subject the missing sections of the life story that he should, ideally, be free to tell himself: 'The unconscious is that chapter of my story which is marked by a blank or occupied by a lie: it is the censored chapter.'

In his incapacity, as transferee, to respond to the feelings that are being transferred onto him, the analyst must be seen as exemplifying the failure of the Real Order to adjust itself so as to meet the desires of the patient. Lacan himself introduces the concept of a 'pure negativity', one that is 'detached from any particular motive', to describe those moments in an analysis when the analyst simply 'abstains', or remains silent. These are moments when the Real impinges on the Symbolic Order, or the 'rational' on the 'hysterical', though the identification by Lacan of the rational with the mute is ironical to say the least in someone claiming to be carrying through the methods of the supreme rationalist, Freud.

To read Lacan after reading Freud is to be struck by one very conspicuous absence, or Lack: of anything like a developed case-history. Lacan writes as if he had never in fact had any patients, as if his theories had been successfully elaborated without the need for them. His largely admiring expositor Malcolm Bowie concedes that 'such [case] material matters rather little, is adduced rather infrequently, and, when it does appear, finds him already hovering high above the earthbound business of the consulting-room.' At the same time, Bowie argues that, by focusing the attention of the psychoanalyst on what might be called the linguistics or rhetoric of the encounter between analyst and analysand, Lacan is re-directing the daily practice of psychoanalysis to what are potentially beneficial ends.

This is the answer of an admirer to the question that comes to mind again and again in intervals of the struggle to understand the *Ecrits*, or of enjoying the histrionics of the *Séminaires*: what could the application of all this possibly be? What practical purpose could Lacan's own seductively polymathic discourse serve, beyond that of securing to himself a reputation for incomparable brilliance? Well, there are now plenty of practising analysts in France and elsewhere who declare themselves to be Lacanians, and, if Bowie is right, they will be more keenly aware than analysts of other schools, or of none, of their responsibilities as 'practitioners of the word'. There is no reason why Lacanian analysis should not be practised with modesty and self-effacingness, even if its rules were laid down by someone who was laughably far from possessing either.

Freud was a theorist who was anxious to be thought of as an empiricist, setting much store in the *Autobiographical Study* that he wrote when he thought he was dying by the 'laborious findings' of psychoanalysis, lest anyone should think that he had not, before withdrawing to work on his theories, served his time in the trenches, face to face with his patients. His follower Lacan, on the other hand, was a theorist anxious to be remembered as a theorist, as a contributor not to the empirical, nor even the human, but to what he referred to as the 'conjectural' sciences, which are distinctive presumably for lying somewhere outside the prosaic domain of the verifiable. Perhaps we should be grateful that it was so, and that Lacan chose to write in a 'poetic' manner aimed at establishing him as much as a literary as a medical figure. For were we to read him simply as a healer of minds we might well feel outraged that the clinical experiences from which he had started, and which he saw so little cause to invoke, were ones of great individual unhappiness.

7

MICHEL FOUCAULT

An exotic image of Michel Foucault shows him standing, kimono-clad and in sombre outline, against the brilliant emptiness of a doorway, his shaven skull and tinted lenses serving to endorse James Miller's witty description of him (in his *The Passion of Michel Foucault*) as 'a metaphysical Eraserhead'. This was the philosopher as admiringly photographed by a gay friend of his, the young writer Hervé Guibert, who, several years after Foucault's AIDS-related death in 1984, published a short story and a brief *roman à clef* which described what he had himself seen of that death and revealed some of his friend's closest and most troubling obsessions. Guibert justified this ugly indiscretion by saying that Foucault himself had lived his life with a conspicuous 'freedom' and 'audacity', and had never hidden his 'inclinations', however perverse some of these might be.

The justification was disingenuous on Guibert's part, yet it could claim to be loyal to the belief once expressed by Foucault that, in the case of a writer,

> his major work is, in the end, himself in the process of writing his books. The private life of an individual, his sexual preference, and his work are interrelated, not because his work translates his sexual life, but because the work includes the whole life as well as the text.

The belief that the manner in which a life is consciously lived and a published oeuvre can together form an aesthetically satisfying whole is Nietzschean, and Nietzsche was the philosopher to whom Foucault owed the most. His own oeuvre, however, has none of the expressive flamboyance of Nietzsche's, none of the same passionate urge to denounce the servile masses and to lecture them morally.

Foucault's was a thoroughly dissident intelligence, but the style of its expression is notably academic and on occasions – in *Les Mots et les choses* (Words and things) especially – turgid. But then, for all the extracurricular idea that 'the work includes the whole life', he saw no easy connection between the flesh-and-blood being who writes and the texts that eventuate from that writing. Foucault indeed became notorious, after Roland Barthes, for calling into question the traditional conception of authorship, of the Author understood as 'the principle for grouping together discourses, as the unity and origin of their meanings, as the focal point of their coherence'. Against the old view that, for all its semantic capaciousness and variety, a text should be seen as radiating uniquely from the mind of the individual who wrote it, Foucault offered a structuralist view, whereby authors are responsible for the disposition of their discourse and of the meanings it contains but are neither the originators nor the owners of those meanings.

The notion that, behind or beneath an author's oeuvre, we are entitled to search for some extra-textual 'unity' that will serve to recuperate its disturbing miscellaneity is an illusion – an illusion which Foucault did his subtle best to guard against in his own case. He began his inaugural lecture at the Collège de France, for example, by saying that he wished he could find himself already enveloped by his *discours*, without having to launch bodily into it and thus appear to be originating it. And towards the end of his life, he told an interviewer, whose role as a journalist was to impose an identity on him: 'Do not ask who I am and do not ask me to remain the same. More than one person, doubtless like me, writes in order to have no face.' A self-effacing Nietzschean is something of a new, and certainly a contradictory, idea. Yet the description suits Foucault, whose 'audacities' remained mainly a private matter during his lifetime, and whose oeuvre, for all the remarkable influence that it has had, is necessarily discreet, founded as it is on a peculiarly self-denying interpretation of what an Author is.

Foucault followed an orthodox path through French academic life. He began as a student at the Ecole Normale Supérieure, taught abroad for a number of years before becoming a professor in the provinces and was then, in 1970, elected to a chair at the Collège de France. This was not the career path of a reckless outsider. Less orthodox, however, was his refusal to identify himself in his teaching or writing with a particular university discipline. The two books that brought him to public notice in the early 1960s, *Histoire de la folie* (The history of madness) and *La Naissance de la clinique* (The birth of the clinic), both of them works of (Foucauldian) historiography, appeared while he was nominally a professor of psychology in Clermont-Ferrand, and the publication of the second was carefully timed by Foucault to coincide to the day with the publication of a small (and opaque) book on the writer Raymond Roussel, as evidence that this author was no narrow-minded academic specialist. His chair at the Collège de France was in the history of systems of thought, an idiosyncratic title found for the author of Les Mots et les choses, which is very precisely an attempt to systematise three seemingly separate fields of eighteenth-century discourse concerning language, natural history and economics.

Again like Barthes, Foucault was able by his worldliness and the unusual scope of his intellectual concerns to contest the rigidity of the university system within which he spent his life. Should he be thought of as a philosopher or as a historian? Or was he simply a philosopher of history? His admirers can reasonably claim that he was all three of these, as someone who advanced powerful new arguments about how history should properly be practised and the use that might be made of it. His opponents might claim, on the other hand, that his historical agenda was too personal, and predetermined, to validate what he claimed to have found in his institutional studies of madness, or punishment, or medicine.

Foucault's affiliation with Nietzsche shows itself most conspicuously in his fascination with the forms and institutions through which power both has been and is exercised in societies. He accepts the Nietzschean view that the will-to-power is universal, and supports it by arguing that since the seventeenth century in the West societies have continually extended their power over the lives of their members, to the melodramatic point where the only route by which an individual can hope to escape its mechanisms is through death. Foucault glamorises death as 'the most secret, the most "private" point of existence', and death by suicide, very logically, as the ultimate act of protest against the impersonal but pervasive apparatuses of power. 'Bio-power' is Foucault's arresting term for the processes by which a modern society achieves the 'subjection of bodies and the control of populations', as we good citizens submit to all manner of corporate disciplines and rational-seeming imperatives. We submit more often than not without recognising that our actions are in fact submissive: Foucault is playing the traditional, demystifying role of the intellectual in alerting us to the full measure of our daily implication in the 'rapports de force', or power relations, whose pervasiveness he intends to expose. It's as if he were providing the hard historical data with which the Olympian Nietzsche could not be troubled, in revealing to modern, God-less man the stark contrast between the possibility of freedom and his actual servitude. What is missing in Foucault, however, is the aristocratic scorn that Nietzsche heaps on all those craven souls who choose to submit rather than to live by the Dionysian principles advocated by him. There is no explicit call to rebellion in Foucault, nothing in the least inflammatory. The libertarian moral is to be inferred only – hence no doubt the insistence that the writer's life be taken into account also in order for his oeuvre to be complete. The *rapports de force* of which he makes so much may serve as a replacement for the familiar '*rapports de production*' of Marxism, inasmuch as Foucault could claim to be probing more deeply, down to the biological substratum even, into the workings of society and locating a fundamental structure there of which relations of production are merely one, economic manifestation. Foucault remains in his books always the meta-historian, however, writing with an apparent impartiality that helps to mask the grandeur of his ambitions.

Foucault meant to be recognised, and invariably has been recognised, as an anti-humanist, or as a militant in the war on subjectivity that was conducted so brilliantly during the structuralist years in France. Nothing that he wrote was quoted against him so insistently as his prophecy right at the end of *Les Mots et les choses* that Man was 'a recent invention' of Western European thought who, Foucault was ready to wager, would one day be 'erased, like a face drawn in the sand on the edge of the sea'. Quite what these ominous-sounding words are threatening us with, I am unsure. I take them to be saying that we shall one day all of us be Foucauldians, able to recognise that true knowledge is not dependent on the psychology of the knower and does not require to be subtended by a transcendent human subject. In the words of Jules Vuillemin, a philosopher who was one of Foucault's supporters in his election to the Collège de France, his objective was 'to construct a history with no human nature'. This is *echt*-structuralism, a reminder that the systems of thought of which Foucault was on the point of becoming the titular professor exist independently of those who think within them and that without those systems we should as thinking subjects be bereft of thought altogether. The most that Foucault will allow us is the not very creditable freedom to take up 'the subject position' within some particular field of discourse.

The minatory conclusion to *Les Mots et les choses* needs to be borne in mind when reading Foucault, since the conventional way in which he presents his historical findings in his books might otherwise suggest that he is as accepting as any non-structuralist of the influence of individuals on the evolution of human thought and knowledge. He is scrupulous in identifying the sources on which he draws, which are some of them of named, some of them of anonymous and some of them of collective authorship. But he leaves us in no doubt that these sources are no more than illustrative of the attitudes or beliefs he is analysing, and that they are emphatically not to be taken as having themselves originated those attitudes or beliefs. The past as Foucault restores it is a 'field of discourse' consisting of innumerable '*énoncés*', or statements; the identities of those whose *énoncés* have survived, in the extant documentation, is neither here nor there.

For all this, there is, inevitably, a certain humanism in Foucault. Had there not been, he could not have acquired the reputation he now has, which extends well beyond the narrow confines of the human sciences in which it was first established. He has come to be seen as the inspired enemy of a coercive normalisation in society, whether this operates in the sexual field, the psychiatric or the more generally behavioural. By calmly ascribing insidious powers of control to supposedly liberal societies such as our own, Foucault became the patron saint of abnormality and of deviance. And by making relations of power into the specific form underlying all personal or collective relations, he lent high intellectual authority to the political arguments that are now commonly advanced for 'empowerment', the achievement of which for this disadvantaged group or that in society would of course confirm, not disprove, the strength of Foucault's zero-sum case, by demonstrating that a gain in power by one group can only be achieved by power being taken away from another.

His intellectual following is at once more extensive and more politicised than that of any French thinker since Sartre (whom Foucault seems personally to have disliked). It can hardly have been drawn to him by the ease or elegance of his writing. Unlike Sartre, he did not think that to write 'well' was a bourgeois crime, committed against a proletariat that wants action not 'style'. Foucault was no populist. But his books do not set out to attract. Rather, the manner of their composition bears out his description of himself as a 'contented positivist'. They are dense with facts, facts in Foucault's case being references to his discursive sources. This density can become oppressive, but it is an integral part of the grand theory that underlies his whole meta-historical procedure. Foucault approaches the past – and here again he is a structuralist *pur sang* – with the intention of displaying its discontinuities. He is the historian of the gaps, of the problematical and unfillable spaces that separate one item of evidence from another. He rejects the 'alibi' of that historiography which purports to represent some segment of the past as a continuous, seamless story.

To reject the illusion of continuity is to reject also the false belief that the human consciousness can function as the locus of some embracing synthesis:

> To make historical analysis into the discourse of the continuous and human conscious-
> ness into the originating subject of all becoming and all praxis, these are the two faces
> of a single system of thought. In this, Time is conceived in terms of totalisation and
> revolutions are only ever a becoming aware [*prise de conscience*].

The terminology here tells us who, when thus marking his own historical method off from that of others, Foucault had in his sights: those thinkers, with Jean-Paul Sartre chief amongst them, for whom the concept of 'totalisation' stood as the *ne plus ultra* of all attempts at synthesis, and for whom 'revolution' was the huge event that would somehow automatically follow in practice once the theoretical *prise de conscience* was complete. Foucault's method is nothing if not oppositional.

In pursuit of his campaign against the totalisers, he chose a mode of presentation in his canonical books that helps to bring out the discontinuities in which they deal. In *L'Archéologie du savoir* (The archaeology of knowledge), he says that in writing, for example, a study such as *La Naissance de la clinique*, which traces the way in which Western conceptions of disease changed during the eighteenth and early nineteenth centuries, his task was to discover order in 'the space of a dispersion', what was dispersed being all the many *énoncés* he requires if he is to reconstitute the cast of medical thought or underlying 'system' by which these scattered data were informed. And that dispersion is exemplified materially in his prose not only by the weight of citation, but by a prose style marked by parataxis, and by numerous reminders that what we are being given to read is a 'pure description of discursive events', as if those events were being allowed, as we say, to speak for themselves.

The problem for Foucault, however, was that, by the fact of its existence as a solid, independent object, a book is no very congruous receptacle for a 'field of dispersion'. On the contrary: it is a space within which that dispersion has been counteracted, and a synthesis inescapably made. To guard against the danger that this synthesis might appear to us to be the transcendent act of an extra-textual consciousness, Foucault stresses that the physical unity of the book is accessory at best to its 'discursive unity', and that this discursive unity is itself only 'variable and relative': 'The moment one questions it, it is no longer self-evident; it does not point to itself, it is no more than a construct out of a complex field of discourse.' These repeated caveats have, I suspect, no effect at all on those who read Foucault, unless to make them even more aware than they might otherwise have been that it is the arch-dispersionist Foucault and no one else whom they are reading.

Foucault's wish is not the impossible one of abolishing once and for all the concept of the book, or by extension an oeuvre, as an entity; it is to make evident how many discriminations must be made when it comes to defining such an entity. The presumption of oneness is idle, until such time as it has taken into account the play of multiplicity which that oneness conceals. Foucault's is an art of 'unpicking' – a vogue term that his own work will have done much to impose on the discourse of the human sciences (and of literary criticism). He asks that the presumed 'unities' of book or oeuvre be 'suspended', since under close examination they prove decidedly complex. 'The material unity of the book? Is it really the same whether we have to deal with an anthology of poetry, a collection of posthumous fragments, the *Treatise on Conics* or a volume of Michelet's *History of France*?' And similarly with an oeuvre:

> Is it enough to add to the texts published by the author those he had been planning to give to the printer, and which remained unfinished only by the fact of his death? Must we also integrate everything by way of rough outlines, plans, corrections and crossings-out? Must we add abandoned sketches? And what status should we give to letters, notes, reported conversations, remarks transcribed by those who heard them, in short to that immense swarm of verbal traces which an individual leaves around him at the time of his death?

The more of such distinctions there are to be made, amongst material all too easily unified under a single rubric, the more justified Foucault's project appears.

The historical problem par excellence under this dispensation is to determine in just what a unity consists, whether it be a book or an entire field of historical analysis. How far, for example, can we take 'sexuality', the topic of the series of volumes that Foucault was working on at the time of his death, to be a single, coherent concept, applicable equally to the modern age and to the classical age to which Foucault very illuminatingly reverts in the second and third volumes? Few readers of these books will have any difficulty on that score, but will decide that they are all three about 'the same thing', adept, in Foucault's best manner, in drawing fine distinctions between forms of sexual behaviour or sexual teaching that we would certainly otherwise assume were identical or continuous with those of our own society. In the end, it hardly seems to matter whether the concept of 'sexuality' is unitary or not; Foucault has enlightened us in a perfectly familiar way.

What is no longer permissible, however, is to assume that the unity of a field of discourse such as this precedes the analysis of it; rather, it is the product of analysis. For that analysis is itself discursive: it is discourse applied to discourse; and one of the lessons that Foucault teaches is that the role, or power, of discourse is to bring order to what would otherwise lack it. He is very much part of the so-called linguistic turn in modern thought, since his discourse stands towards its subject-matter in the same relation as language stands towards the world to which it is used to refer. Foucauldian discourse, like language, is seen as giving order to the world, rather than taking orders from the world. In the title of Les Mots et les choses, the words come before the things, the grand theme of that (rather difficult) book being that what we normally take to be pure empiricism, or a direct, unmediated cognisance of reality, is always in fact the product of cultural 'codes', but for the existence of which no such cognisance could have been taken. Foucault goes as far as it is possible to go in arguing that discourse maketh the man, not man the discourse.

That he should now be seen as standing squarely on the side of libertarianism and against coercion is in some ways surprising, when he did rather little publicly when he was alive to get himself appointed to any such pragmatic role. Politically, Foucault was for much of his life, and by the standards of the time, reticent. He was a member of the French Communist Party for three years, in the early fifties, but broke with it over its refusal to recognise the sordid truth of the 'doctors' plot' in the Soviet Union, and for ever after despised it. In 1968, when the student 'events' erupted in Paris, he happened to be teaching in Tunisia where, as he later sardonically observed, dissident students took far more serious risks in making their case against the authorities than ever students in Paris had. Only a year or so later, however, in the early 1970s, he emerged as an activist, most notably in the setting up of the Groupe d'Information sur les Prisons (GIP), a body whose purpose was to bring about improvements in the conditions under which prisoners were kept in French gaols.

The inspiration for the GIP had come from the political Left, which was outraged by the treatment some of its members had received when arrested in the aftermath of the 'events'. Foucault's own involvement was humanitarian, however, not an expression of any partisan allegiance. He campaigned in the first instance as a historian of punishment and of prisons who had taken the opportunity to intervene in person in the very processes that were to be the subject of his remarkable book *Surveiller et punir* (Discipline and punish), which appeared in 1975. At a press conference early in 1971, he began with a startling, if somewhat forced, assertion of his solidarity with the prison population: 'None of us can be sure of avoiding prison', and followed with the claim that 'We are living under the sign of *la garde à vue*.' This was to read life in terms of (his own) literature, in the best Nietzschean spirit. For what Foucault was referring to was the practice whereby suspects may be held in custody by the French police without charge for up to twenty-four hours: a reasonable procedure that I imagine is standard throughout the Western world. The phrase *garde à vue* has an ideally Foucauldian ring to it, however, since in *Surveiller et punir* his argument is that, over the course of the last two centuries, there has been a profound shift in the ideology and practice of punishment in Western societies, away from the infliction of pain on the body of those deemed to be guilty, to a regime of surveillance involving not only the detention of criminals but attempts at their moral rehabilitation. Foucault's exhibit A, for an example of the sinister new utilitarianism that has come to dominate modern penology, is Jeremy Bentham's famous Panopticon, an architectural fancy which embodies both the will of authority to absolute control over the lives of those imprisoned, and the will to economise on manpower in so doing, since in the Panopticon a single supervisor is able to keep watch over a large number of inmates. Bentham's projected building is the perfect expression of a regime of *garde à vue*, casting its portentous shadow over Foucault's rhetoric as a newly recruited prison reformer.

In *Surveiller et punir* he comes out as so extreme a progressive in penological terms as to be uniquely reactionary. In that book, he sees our modern, post-Enlightenment, supposedly more civilised ways of dealing with criminality as crueller than the more violent methods that they displaced. It begins, notoriously, by quoting a sickening description of the bungled torture and slow execution of an eighteenth-century French regicide, as an example of the extreme penalties once judicially inflicted on the body of the criminal. Whatever *frisson* we may get from reading the details of such an elaborate and ritualised putting-to-death, most of us would say that it was an abomination, and that a regime founded on incarceration marks a moral advance on one founded on a sanctioned and at times spectacular brutality. Foucault argues, and powerfully, to the contrary: to the effect that there may be cathartic social benefits to be had from the spectacle of cruel physical punishment, and that in any calculus of cruelty the gentler rigours of the penitentiary might count as a regression, since to be kept perpetually under surveillance for a long period may be more harmful than being tortured. Either way, the prison stands for Foucault as the exemplary institution of a coldly rational, ordered society, whose authority extends to the invigilation of all forms of what it labels as 'delinquency' or 'deviance'.

Since our kind of society is never going to legislate a return to judicial torture, we have to assume that, in arguing as he does in *Surveiller et punir*, Foucault was out to provoke, not to persuade. He was thinking, more obviously than he ever had previously, against the grain, or 'dangerously', as a Nietzschean might say. And thinking dangerously, moreover, on a matter that was intimately bound up with his own private life. For by the time he died, Foucault had learnt how to live, as well as how to write, dangerously, and so to subscribe to his own posthumous unification. During the 1970s, he had supported various movements for gay liberation in France, but quietly, without any resonant public declarations of his own homosexuality. That was an identity that this faceless man could do without. At the same time, he was being taken up as an academic superstar by universities in the United States, especially at Berkeley, a campus noted for its explosive and ambitious radicalism. In breaks from his teaching at Berkeley, it seems that he made voluptuous excursions into the homosexual counterculture of San Francisco, and in his fine biographical study James Miller has some uncomfortable pages itemising the kind of thing Foucault may have got up to there with his fellow s/m adepts. Here, if anywhere, the 'relations of power' dear to the historian could be realised with the fullest imaginable intensity, in s/m's punitive rigmaroles of domination and submission. And here, if anywhere, the life and the oeuvre of Michel Foucault achieved the rare convergence that he had so desired.

8

JACQUES DERRIDA

'If, in fact, equivocity is always irreducible, that is because words and language in general are not and can never be absolute *objects*. They do not possess any resistant and permanent identity that is absolutely their own.' This was Jacques Derrida setting up residence philosophically in 1962, in the first work that he published: a translation of, and more important a commentary on, Edmund Husserl's *Origin of Geometry*. This was the first example of how life-threatening Derrida's close embrace could be in his deceptively modest role of scholiast. His commentary is in the event an act of sabotage against its host-text as it works to uncover the presuppositions that, so Derrida argues, both underlie and undermine Husserl's thesis of the ideal objectivity of mathematical entities. It also marks the first public appearance of Derrida's own elusive but remarkably influential philosophy of language that over the years to come was to make his fortune, not, interestingly, among Anglo-American philosophers, where his converts have been few, but among philosophically minded professors of literature.

As the few lines that I have quoted hint, Derrida was prepared from the outset to draw radical and provocative conclusions from the view of language that he had inherited from Saussure and from structuralism. The Saussurian doctrine of the linguistic sign involves analysing it into two aspects, a material aspect and a semantic: into a Signifier, which may be either acoustic or graphic, and a Signified. What structuralism had also done, however, unnoticed by almost all, was to reinforce the idealist belief that the semantic plane of language is independent of the material plane and as such determining of it. Understood thus, the semantic plane consists of infinitely many, pre-established meanings-in-waiting, attending on their realisation in one natural language or another. Derrida came to the philosophy of language as a materialist, and he was set on exposing the falsity of this common metaphysical understanding of the way in which language works. It is only a pity that the campaign against it that he launched back in the 1960s should have been conducted in so alembicated a prose style and, in its later stages, so self-indulgently; that made it easy for his genuine insights to be written off as the vapourings of a philosophical mystagogue.

Derrida has published far too much over the years and too little of it in prose recognisable as being that of a methodical thinker concerned that his arguments should become widely known and understood outside the circles of his adepts. His logorrhoea, which has done him harm, is the more regrettable for coming from someone who has also campaigned as a pedagogue to defend and if possible extend the teaching of philosophy in French schools and universities. Even in 1962, however, when he was analysing the phenomenology of Husserl, he was already prepared to invoke the name of James Joyce, the master of equivocation, as a corrective to any Husserlian view that words might function as ideal, self-contained objects. The semantic abundance of *Finnegans Wake*, a 'materialist' text in which the Signifiers so very patently call the tune, proves otherwise, and Derrida was looking ahead in his own practice as a writer to play the Joycean game and thus deny his fellow philosophers the comfort of supposing that what they were professionally engaged on was the establishment of unequivocal, language-transcending truths.

In the fifteen years or so following the little-remarked appearance of his Husserlian commentary, Derrida became an object of reverence with some and a corresponding scorn with others. The reverence came mainly from within academic faculties of literature, and mainly from the United States. It stemmed from a belief that, as someone very sophisticatedly – in the full sense of the word – concerned with the textual construction of meaning, he had new and precious lessons to teach as to how works of literature might be re-interpreted. The scorn came mainly from Anglo-American philosophers raised in the analytical tradition, who dismissed Derrida's enterprise as irrelevant or mistaken, since it appeared nowhere to connect usefully with the Philosophy of Meaning as they understood it. His prose style also they found alien, both wordy and opaque, deriving as it does from a continental tradition steeped in Hegel and Heidegger rather than the limpidities of a Russell or a Quine.

One can sympathise with both the devotional and the dismissive points of view towards Derrida. Over these early years, he achieved enough to justify both the high regard in which some people held him and the intemperance with which others met each new publication. There were a daunting number of these: three separate books published in the calendar year of 1967, four more in 1972, a reckless and overwhelming rate of production. He had passed very quickly from being a philosophical thinker of substance to being an academic celebrity who wrote too much, and to increasingly counterproductive effect so far as some of us who had earlier admired him were concerned.

The moment when Derrida's first career began to suffer from the fallout of his second can be dated to the publication in 1974 of *Glas*, a huge text that combines, in two divided columns of print, what he calls a 'violent decipherment' of Hegel's philosophy of Absolute Knowledge with, as its companion, a commentary on the seditious, homoerotic fantasies of the gaolbird turned writer, Jean Genet. Anyone who wants Hegel but not Genet might read exclusively down one side of the page, anyone wanting Genet but not Hegel exclusively down the other. But the twin columns are supposed to resonate off one another, like two bells with a single clapper, this last being the role allotted to the poor ricocheting reader. Hegel and Genet have been brought together on the say-so of Jacques Derrida, and only committed Derridians will feel they have to submit themselves to the wearisome convolutions of *Glas*.

The avant-garde format of *Glas* is a far cry from that of the Husserl book. That was orthodox, with Derrida's commentary preceding (and far exceeding in length) the translation. *Glas*, however, represents in its layout Derrida's fundamental assault on the concept of the book as the locus of an implied semantic convergence. We are given not only two slender columns of prose, set in different type sizes, but interpolations at the side of the page, some short, some quite long, some set in bold, others in plain type. This, we can tell by looking, is a Derridian Text, a prosework that has been denied the appearance of unity which goes with regular, continuous pages of print. The format embodies the principle of 'dissemination', or that ungovernable scattering of meanings which, whether we like it or not, is language's vocation, as a medium of communication which, by virtue of its structural, transpersonal nature, deprives us of anything more than a partial control of what it communicates. Derrida may have taken issue with the Lacanian division of the analysand's 'speech' into the categories of 'full' and 'empty' (for Derrida, all speech is 'empty' in the Lacanian sense), but he is at one with Lacan in arguing that, once implicated in the Symbolic Order of language, we surrender our autonomy as speaking subjects and must yield to the influences of its objectifying 'play'.

Glas thus has a ludic point to prove, though it is worth observing that, illustrative as it is of a particular model of language, it serves to re-instate its 'author' in a position of power. It is an ostentatious mix of commentary on his paired authors and antic verbalism, in which Derrida has set a good example and apparently allowed the surface accidents of the French language to determine his own textual progress in the best Joycean manner. Punning had become an important part of his schema, instituting a love of wordplay whose depressing effects are still visibly with us in the publications of those who seek to write prose as exuberantly given over to verbal ingenuity as that of the Master.

Two years before *Glas*, in a volume called *Positions*, where he replies helpfully to questions put to him by interviewers, Derrida had tried, disingenuously, to underline the ancillary status of his writings, which are to be read it seems as parasitical on those with which they interlock: those 'in whose tracks [*traces*] I write, the "books" in the margins and between the lines of which I delineate and decipher a text that is at once both closely alike and quite other. . . .' This was a just about legitimate description of the kind of 'decipherment' he had been engaged on up to that point, in the Husserl translation, and in *La Voix et le phénomène* (Speech and phenomena), a further commentary on Husserl's ideas, *De la Grammatologie* (Of grammatology) and *L'Ecriture et la différence* (Writing and difference), the three volumes, published all in the same year (1967), that together form the canon of the serious, philosophical Derrida. By the time he came to write *Glas*, however, his own 'text' was so 'other' in respect of those he was commenting on that the effect on the labouring, often mystified reader is one of the wilful misappropriation of both Hegel and Genet. 'Ancillary' was no longer a description to which Derrida could lay honest claim.

This swerve away from philosophy and into word-spinning was unfortunate in that it cast a retrospective blight over his earlier work. It made the substantive, analytical books he had published seem that much less fundamental and mind-enlarging than they were – and still are. The earlier Derrida had gravitated consistently and for the general good to the bounds of thinkability, or at any rate to the tacit preconceptions conditioning the thought of those thinkers with whom he took issue: apart from Husserl, these included Rousseau, Lévi-Strauss, Foucault, Freud, Plato, Saussure and others besides. Wherever he looked, Derrida believed he could point in their thought to 'the metaphysics of presence', or a covert idealism from which Western philosophy has never been able, or wanted, to break away in more than two thousand years. To undo the philosophy of language and meaning on which that pervasive idealism rested was the far from modest ambition of this purportedly 'ancillary' figure.

The attack on the metaphysics of presence had in fact begun with the analysis of Husserl's phenomenology, though the term itself was introduced only a little later into Derrida's considerable and seductive armoury of new concepts – his fertility in this regard is no small part of his attraction for his followers. In *La Voix et le phénomène* he finds fault with Husserl for his separation of the linguistic sign into an indicative and an 'expressive' function. The 'indicative' function depends on the sign's objective status as a constituent of the language system: it pertains to the sign as such, irrespective of the circumstances in which it may be used. The expressive function by contrast pertains to the axis of *parole*, or of language in action: it is animated by the 'intentionality' of the language-user at the moment of use. The twin functions, separable in theory in just the same way as the Signifier and the Signified are separable in theory for Saussure, stand to one another, according to Derrida, in the relation of body and soul; indeed, he goes so far as to argue that our traditional, and comforting, notions of metaphysical dualism in respect of bodies and souls derive from a misunderstanding of the true nature of the linguistic sign, which can never be expressive in the intimate sense in which Husserl argues that it is.

La Voix et le phénomène makes Derrida's case against Husserlian idealism patiently and without show. The title in itself points to his fundamental objection, which is to the normally implicit 'phonocentrism' of most, if not all, thought about language – including that of Saussure, who failed to recognise the true subversiveness of his own structuralist doctrine. A phonocentric view of language holds, roughly, that the expressive function counts for more than the indicative, that when we use language to 'express' we are somehow 'present' in it in a way that we can't be when language is reduced (as phonocentrists would want to put it) to its indicative function. The 'voice' gives life to language, just as the soul animates the otherwise inert body. Against this view Derrida develops the strategy by which he is best known, of taking *écriture*, or writing, rather than speaking, as the exemplary form of language-use, that being the form in which the presumed immediacy of 'expression' is certainly disrupted if not actually suppressed. In writing there is no voice and the indicative function of language resumes its priority at the expense of the expressive. Derrida had set out to remove the age-old prejudice in favour of speaking and against writing. Writing is language cast adrift: it exists in the absence of the writer and may be read by millions or by no one at all. Speaking is different: it is language granted the benefit of a living human presence, individualised, 'felt'. Or so, pre-Derrida, we used comfortably to suppose. His far less comfortable view is that *all* language is cast adrift by virtue of its being language. Language is structural, a system of relations not of hard-and-fast entities, and hence never unconditionally 'present'. This is structuralism carried to its logical limit, and Derrida has made the case for it, over and over again, with great virtuosity.

I find it hard to believe that those persuaded of its truth react any differently as a result when it comes to interpreting speech; our social lives require that we connive daily in the illusion of phonocentrism and assume a certain 'presence' of our interlocutors in what they say. Not so, however, when it comes to interpreting writing. Literature has commonly been understood in a phonocentric light, as if the texts we read were in effect being spoken to us by their authors, whose 'voice' we come to recognise and to like. Derrida's fortune was to be made, understandably, among those teachers and critics of literature who craved a more austere, less sociable model of textual appreciation.

Derrida has nothing to say about literature as such in *La Voix et le phénomène*, but he had plenty to say about it subsequently, and all of it going in the one direction: against the presupposition that literature is, before anything else, expressive of the most private attitudes and feelings of those who write it. Language does not work like that is Derrida's cautionary message, and one richly worth our heeding. He may not convince us that the notion of expressiveness is no longer worth anything, but he has done enough to expose its problematical nature. His arguments came as a relief to those professors of literature who had long found themselves at odds with the prevailing, sub-Romantic ethos of subjectivism. That those arguments should have arrived couched in a new conceptual patois was a bonus: the battery of quite difficult, alien-seeming concepts introduced by Derrida – the metaphysics of presence, phonocentrism and the rest – meant that initiates preserved a ready advantage over those who either could not or would not learn the new vocabulary of criticism.

La Voix et le phénomène is a brilliant exercise in what was soon thereafter to become known as deconstruction, or that adversarial mode of reading which aims to expose a particular text's implicit (that is, unwritten) premisses and, in so doing, demonstrate that these are actually contradictory of some of its explicit premisses. This is a worthy and productive mode of reading, but only in the right hands. Derrida's own hands were right; those of many of his followers were not. The danger in deconstruction is obvious: it invites the textual commentator to erect him or herself as the person who is alone astute enough to have noticed where the logic of the text under analysis has failed, where its 'blind spots' are to be found. The blind spot exemplifies the failure of an author to 'master' language, which has generated meanings beyond those he or she has authorised. It is noticeable, however, that the textual exegete bent on expelling the hypothetical presence of an authorial voice soon becomes a presence in turn, and guilty of betraying the structural purity of the whole critical enterprise. In the hands of a critic as powerful as Paul de Man, for instance, a text's blind spots become its most significant moments, as if it were only those places where the author's mastery lapses that are now of concern to us. And we may well gaze in admiration at the subtlety with which a de Man teases them out. The deconstructor is invited to play the role of dishonest broker, or of a usurping presence.

The target of Derrida's own first essays in deconstruction was pointedly chosen. The specific claim of Husserlian phenomenology is that it describes the act of perception or cognition free from any of the a prioris that may otherwise distort our view of it: it offers itself as epistemology of a back-to-basics kind. Derrida believed he could show differently, that for all its scruples phenomenology had failed to notice the 'metaphysical presupposition' (of presence) on which it rested, with the unintended, indeed disastrous, consequence that 'the phenomenological critique of metaphysics' reveals itself to be simply one more 'moment within metaphysical self-assurance'. This was in effect a proof that no language-user, not even one as meticulous and self-analytical as Husserl, could rely on the coherence of his own arguments. Even a Husserl could be shown up as the victim of linguistic signs richly capable in their combinations of containing meanings he would have taken steps to exclude had he been aware of them – and in the process, needless to say, generating new inconsistencies.

Had it remained in the hands of philosophers, deconstruction would have seemed neither path-breaking nor so very presumptuous, since the history of philosophy has consisted in large part in the reinterpretation or dismissal by new generations of thinkers of what had once seemed secure philosophical theses put forward by their predecessors. This is true up to a point of the interpretation of literature also, even if literary reinterpretation is normally more tentative because more impressionistic, and readier therefore to admit to its own provisional nature. Deconstruction, however, introduced a new element, by appearing, like structuralism before it, to invite the text to analyse itself. The deconstructor was merely the agent through whom its contradictions or incoherences would be revealed. Except of course that deconstruction is a demanding and unusually abstruse mode of analysis, and whoever executes it successfully is more, rather than less, eager to claim the credit for doing so. It is paradoxical, but revealing, that deconstruction should have flourished in a university system, that of the United States, whose teachers are encouraged to make themselves a name by the ancillary articles and books they publish.

The premiss for the extension of deconstruction's remit from philosophy into literature is that both are textual, even if philosophy normally makes truth claims and literature does not. Philosophers recognise the equivocity of the language they philosophise in, but they also do their professional best to disambiguate whatever they publish. Writers of literature may not actually seek ambiguity but are far less likely to want always to suppress it, since they have traditionally taken a more relaxed or even grateful attitude towards the disseminatory powers of their medium. The will that deconstructionists display to tar all texts with the same brush, as if philosophy were literature by any other name and literature philosophy, is thus misleading. They can alas point, in their own justification, to the example set by a text such as *Glas*, where the literary and the philosophical are inextricably plaited together. It is an irony, on the other hand, that when, unusually late in his academic career in France, Derrida had to make the statutory public defence of his doctoral thesis, he took care to dissociate himself from much if not all that had been done in his name. Deconstruction, he declared, is 'a word whose fortunes have disagreeably surprised me'. One sympathises; but then one might also point out that Derrida above all had no right to be surprised by the fortunes of a word over whose semantic potential he presumably expected not to keep control in the first place.

Derrida's prime purpose when he started out was, as I earlier suggested, to deconstruct Saussurian structuralism, which had failed to recognise the full implications of its own principles: what he referred to on an especially significant occasion as 'the structurality of structure'. The occasion was a conference held at the Johns Hopkins University in Baltimore in 1966, when Derrida spoke on the topic of 'Structure, Sign and Play in the Discourse of the Human Sciences'. The reading of that paper has been held ever since to constitute that problematical thing for structuralists, an event: the event that launched deconstruction as an academic fashion in the United States.

The paper itself (it appears as the penultimate item in *L'Ecriture et la différence*) was austere enough, but its main theme will have struck quickly home to an audience already familiar with, and perhaps friendly to, the doctrines of structuralism. Derrida's argument against structuralism as currently understood was that the notion of 'structurality' had been 'neutralised, reduced: by a gesture that consisted of giving it a centre, relating it to a point of presence, to a fixed origin'. This neutralisation was most suspicious, because 'the concept of a centred structure . . . is contradictorily coherent. And as always, coherence in contradiction expresses the force of a desire.' The guilty desire that so expressed itself was that of avoiding the realisation that in fact structures can have no centre, no transcendent 'point of presence', no origin, no telos. This realisation could but be a source of *angoisse*, or extreme anxiety.

By suggesting to his audience that the harsh truth of structuralism's centrelessness had been suppressed because we were not man (or woman) enough to withstand it, Derrida had contrived to dramatise his argument and lend it a psychoanalytical glamour. An element of repression was now involved, so that to be a Derridian deconstructionist was to show a certain courage and face up to the unwelcome truth that a structure such as language consists in practice of the literally interminable 'play' of its elements as they are endlessly combined and recombined. This was to repeat the argument made many years before by the American Pragmatist philosopher C.S. Peirce that there need be no end to the process of 'semiosis', inasmuch as one combination of linguistic signs must always be interpreted or responded to by a further such combination: a process of which we become uncomfortably aware when struggling to make our own thoughts more perspicuous.

In order to bring out the full implications of structurality Derrida introduced a whole series of 'infra-structures', or concepts – *différance*, the 'trace', 'temporalisation', 'spacing-out', the 'supplement' – whose common feature is that they all refer to a relationship between terms and thus exemplify the Saussurian principle that language is differential, whether acoustically, graphically or semantically. The consequence is that, in Derrida's words,

[I]n the absence of a centre or origin, everything becomes discourse . . . that is to say, a system in which the central signified, originary or transcendental, is never absolutely

present outside a system of differences. The absence of a transcendental signified
extends the field and play of signification into infinity.

This is portentously put, but it embodies a fact of the language-system that we
have all of us to acknowledge, that, as Henry James wrote in quite another
context, 'relations end nowhere'.

Derrida-ism would not have been taken up with such fervour in universities
had it not also had a 'political' dimension, 'political' in scare quotes to show
that the 'politics' in question are of the academic, not of the more public,
variety. This politicisation follows from the attempts he has made to dismantle
intellectual hierarchies such as that which I have already cited between speaking
and writing. Derrida thought not to reverse this value system but to abolish it,
by replacing it with his notion of a pure structurality underlying speaking and
writing alike. This was an egalitarian quest he later extended in a number of
other profitable directions: into, to take one example, the hierarchical division
by which we value the 'inside' of something more highly than the 'outside'.

Derrida has pursued this distinction into the field of aesthetics. In a book
called La Vérité en peinture (Truth in painting), he meditates on what he terms
the 'parergonal', or marginal aspects of a work of art. (The parergon is one of
the numerous Greek terms that Derrida has tried to bring back into use; a
striking facet of French thought in the age of Derrida, Barthes, Foucault and
Lacan is the extent to which all of them were drawn at different times to the
classical languages and literatures.) In the case of a painting, the parergon is the
frame, a necessary but normally unconsidered 'supplement' to the picture itself.
The painting normally has need of a frame in order to be displayed in public,
but the frame is not part of the picture, or so the protocols of art dictate.*
The parergon has been marginalised, but Derrida will restore its significance as
an easily grasped example of his favourite category of the 'undecidable': is it a
part of the aesthetic whole or is it not? La Vérité en peinture argues for a more
open-minded interpretation of the word art, and in that sense it is 'political',
for quarrelling with the hallowed criteria of delimitation which tell us that a
picture's frame doesn't count for much, even though we perceive picture and
frame as one.

* Just before I wrote these words, I went to an exhibition in London of the work of the British
painter, Howard Hodgkin. Hodgkin is well known for painting the frames of his pictures, so as
to include them very obviously 'in' the work. In one or two cases, he even extends the picture
beyond the frame, as if aspiring to paint the gallery wall as well. This is a well-judged Derridian
challenge to hierarchical notions of inside and outside.

Derrida's philosophy is what Rodolphe Gasché well calls a 'heterology', a philosophy of 'otherness', founded, if it can be said to be founded at all, on the 'equi-primordiality' of alternatives, which is as far as our minds can reach towards a pure, unconditional differentiality. This differentiality is 'pre-ontological', since existence, along with its Other, non-existence, forms a typical pair of disjunctive predicates, itself to be accounted for by heterology alone. Philosophy in the West has striven to suppress the awareness of this fundamental differential principle because it desires (but whence such a strong, universal and guilty desire? I don't think Derrida has explained this) a total, unflawed 'self-presence' in which there is no place for the morbid and intrusive presence of the Other. 'Self-presence' is a fantasy, however, because in order to be present to ourselves we have to be divided into an I and a Me, the circuit between which passes through the objectivity of language and of meaning.

There is a furtive ethic at work in deconstruction then, whose lesson is that any presumed integrity of the self is delusive, since we can relate to ourselves only as mediate beings. I am I only by virtue of the not-I. All communication, even that conducted in a soliloquy, is in Derridian terms tele-communication, or communication at a distance, since there is in principle no less a distance between I and Me when we commune privately than between two separate beings at opposite sides of the world. We are alienated even in our solitude. Or so Derrida would have us accept. The Derridian thesis is by its nature an austere one, but it has been argued for over many years with so blatant a sense on Derrida's part of intellectual spectacle that it has long seemed more an expressive than an indicative phenomenon.

9

PAUL DE MAN

This chapter is an interloper. Paul de Man was not French but a Belgian who emigrated to the United States soon after the Second World War. There he taught for many years at Yale and was far and away the most influential proponent of the deconstructionist methods in criticism that derive in large part from the work of Jacques Derrida. The occasion for writing about de Man, however, was the discovery, following his death in 1983, that he had, as a young journalist in wartime Belgium, published articles favourable to the Nazis, and at least one that was anti-Semitic. Taken together, his collaborationism and his later Derrida-ism are reason enough for de Man to be intruded here.

On the day that I began writing this essay, Parliament was voting to change the law so that suspected war criminals from 1939 to 1945 known to have come to Britain and to be still living there might be charged with assisting in the wartime murder of Jews in Eastern Europe. In France, coincidentally, a case was being prepared against Paul Touvier, a member of the collaborationist *milice* who was accused (and subsequently found guilty) of responsibility for the killing of French Jews during the Nazi Occupation. The harrowing crimes thus revived were acts against Jews, but they were acts of murder, not of anti-Semitism, and I use them for a reminder that anti-Semitism should not be criminalised, least of all with hindsight, as if it were itself physically injurious: there is no continuum of delinquency running from racial slander to homicide.

Paul de Man was anti-Semitic in public only once, as a young journalist in occupied Brussels, but then not again. As wartime misdemeanours go, his was a small one, but its ultimate discovery gave rise locally, in the United States, to a weight and a passion of commentary quite out of proportion to its gravity. It inspired, finally, in 1989, six years after de Man's death, the close on five hundred, double-column pages of *Responses: On Paul de Man's Wartime Journalism,* in which thirty-eight authors, American academics for the most part, come at the incriminating fact of the one genuinely anti-Semitic article he wrote in 1941 from many angles, in an orgy of perspectivism, from commentators who prove by turns acrobatic, portentous, polemical, eirenic, abstract, evidential. To adopt the terms that the philosophically very sophisticated de Man himself might have used, commentaries such as these draw attention more to the virtualities of reference than to the nature of the referent itself.

The very bulk of *Responses* indicates to what extent that referent has been expropriated from its historical moment and incorporated into another time, another continent and another intellectual setting. De Man's fall from grace occurred in 1941, in Brussels and in the columns of a newspaper; these 'responses' to it were written in 1988, in the United States, and in the setting of the university. It is puzzling to an outsider to know why this many North American professors should wish to have their say about something that happened forty-seven years ago in occupied Belgium. Why should the belated revelation of de Man's moment of anti-Semitism have been found so frankly inspirational? After reading *Responses*, a first answer might be, because of the great dexterity of mind that it has called out in those invited here to come to terms with it. Dexterity of mind is required because of the immaculate purism which de Man had long stood for as a literary critic, he having argued that 'historical' and 'aesthetic' readings of literature denatured it by according priority to the world supposedly represented there instead of to the act of representation itself, and that a right reading must take the rhetoric of literature to be what matters, not its ontology. Many find this post-Mallarméan reversal of priorities dismayingly negative, as if the world must at all times be recognised as preceding the word, lest language come to seem exclusively mythopoeic. It is not negative, however, but interrogative, and it frees us from the naive and philistine belief that verbal constructs are unintentional or determined unequivo- cally by the way things are in reality: that literature is given not made.

But what when it turned out that the unforgivingly ascetic Paul de Man had once implicated himself, very grubbily, in print, in the real world beyond the text? Could the severe verbalism or 'philology' which he had advocated as a critic not now be read as a sign of guilt, of his wish to exculpate himself by sabotaging the direct relationship we all know exists between language and reality?

Certainly, the discovery of his wartime journalism threw into question his own declared hermeticism in respect of what he called 'the ethics of the profession'. In an interview given to Italian radio in 1983 (it is printed at the end of the essay-collection *The Resistance to Theory*), he concluded from the experiences he had had of teaching in Europe and in the United States that 'in Europe one is of course much closer to ideological and political questions, while, on the contrary, in the States one is much closer to professional questions.' This comparison, as drawn by de Man, is intended to be structural, not historical or autobiographical: in Europe (in Zürich to be exact) he had been teaching future secondary-school teachers; in America, future university teachers – potential colleagues, that is. In Zürich he had felt 'alienated' (de Man's word) because his students, once they had graduated and started work, would make no further use of what he was teaching them; he was therefore happier in America where, the implication is, his students might be formed in his own image and teach other university students accordingly when the time came.

De Man's complaint about Zürich is redolent of the privileges that he came to enjoy in America, as a teacher comfortably enclosed within a system of higher education large enough to enclose, when their turn came, those whom he was teaching. Swiss schoolteachers might come face to face with 'ideological and political questions' following their release into society; de Man himself and his American students would be spared them, they would find only 'professional' ones. His whole comparison between the two experiences of teaching is suspect for being so sharply contrasted and so gratifying to himself; it appears autobiographical rather than structural, and defensive, as if Europe were for him a more exposed place, which he was glad to be out of, than the United States, where university teachers as well-placed and intelligent as himself can sublimate the vulgar questions thrown up by real-life politics by emphasising the irreducible ambiguity of the terms in which they are framed.

De Man's own career as teacher and writer in the United States was founded on a philosophy of natural language which is such as to make of ideologies a plaything fit only for the philosophically blind or else the dishonourably scheming. In his magisterial essay 'The Resistance to Theory' he wrote: 'What we call ideology is precisely the confusion of linguistic with natural reality, of reference with phenomenalism.' That is a peculiarly broad definition of the term ideology, and it seems to allow that one may be sincerely ideological but never lucidly so, since a proper lucidity as to the mediate status of natural language would reveal to us the confusion we had been in as subscribers to any ideology at all: ideology occupies the mental space more healthily occupied by a proper, self-conscious philosophy of language. De Man's position, arrogant or not, was that of anyone who has made the full 'linguistic turn' in philosophy and accepts that there are no transcendent signifieds, that once we enter language there is no arresting the play of semiosis until we exit again from language. This is the 'negative knowledge' about language of which literature has the virtue of being uniquely aware and which de Man saw it as his task to bring to wider notice: natural language is a medium of human exchange rendered 'unreliable' by the very fact of its being a medium. That is his axiom, and as such a lone, unavoidable concession by him to foundationalism.

I am unclear to what lengths he thought that this negative knowledge should be taken, whether it should be reserved for the study of literature alone or whether we should all of us bear it in mind all of the time, in our living as in our reading. The sensible assumption is that, like Hume ceasing sociably to be a sceptical philosopher when he came downstairs from his study, de Man was able to forget his negative knowledge when he reverted from dealing with texts to conducting his life. But however that may be, his negative belief is not to be exclusively ascribed to his own earlier lapse into a crassly instrumental practice of natural language when he was writing as a journalist and making anti-Semitic propaganda: it would be cheap to suppose that a defensible if extreme philosophical principle was to be explained by the wish to conceal a biographical secret. De Man was far from alone in presuming natural language to be constitutionally unreliable, and also in advocating an approach to literary texts which takes them first and foremost as verbal constructs made ambiguous for us by their 'intentionality' or inherent duplicitousness. The argument that he would not have taught as and what he did had he not sinned ideologically in his youth is foolish.

The posthumous discovery of that ideological sin returned him, however, from the thoughtful milieu of the university campus to the crude and impatient notice of the world 'outside'; and the world outside did not do well by him, unwelcoming as it is of anyone of a style of thinking so uncompromisingly austere and so subtly qualified as his. De Man was extruded from one textual environment into another, infinitely coarser, one: out of the academic discourse of which he was at once a prime instigator and a master and into that of the public prints. The journalists in the United States, and the handful in Europe interested in the affair who took their cue from them, grasped right away that its reverberations were extra-academic, that the element of anti-Semitism meant that real political and not just local professional passions might be stirred up by its means. Their copy appears to have ranged from the facile to the scurrilous. But then it is the need, the responsibility, indeed, of journalism to simplify. In the peculiar case of Paul de Man, however, simplicity itself becomes an ideological issue, because the simple utterance never draws attention to itself *qua* utterance: it is the arch-culprit among utterances for concealing its own mediating status. The *media*, by an irony, would have us suppose that what they give us to read or to hear is unmediated, that we should be fully satisfied by its referentiality without stopping to question its terms of reference. De Man may never have written about the mass media, ultra-fastidious man that he was, but in teaching us to read literary texts so as to grasp their inherent contradictions and the rhetoric which informs them, he was heir to that estimable culture-critical tradition in Europe which has seen it as the task and pleasure of the intellectual to educate the semiotically deficient in the duplicities of the propagators of signs.

No critic could have been more at risk from exposure to the forces of mystification in the media than Paul de Man, nor any style of literary criticism more open to facile mockery or paranoid abuse than the deconstruction of which he, after Jacques Derrida, was held to be the North American godfather. It is ironic no doubt that the journalistic mockery and abuse which he suffered should only have come about because of the discovery that he had himself once worked as a journalist and thus been caught up in the superficiality, haste and intellectual opportunism characteristic even of literary journalism. Had de Man already been a university teacher in 1941, when he wrote anti-Semitically, then worse things might have been said of him, since professors are expected to distinguish themselves from journalists by the deliberation and the care which they take to justify their arguments: their distinctive task when writing as journalists is to bring intellectual discretion to a kind of writing normally adjudged to be the more marketable for its absence.

Deconstruction is of course a soft target, a method of criticism widely distrusted and easily ridiculed for being so proudly abstruse, or else 'foreign' (the French have usually found it too 'American'; so where is its true home?). The deconstructive method itself, however, of an excessively close, 'philosoph-ical' or 'figural' reading of texts, whereby certain contradictions in their argumentation or preconceptions may be exposed, is not strictly at issue, because it is not to be abstracted into any easily digestible formula. But its presumed effects, on the ductile students who are exposed to it, are another story. It is the supposed ethical and political fallout from deconstruction which provides a ready point of juncture between a notably esoteric method of criticism and the relatively elementary world beyond the academy.

The argument of the simplifiers appears to run that as you read literature so will you live your life. Because de Man taught that at once the attraction and the problem of literary language is its conscious rhetoricity, so the finished deconstructionist, once released into the professoriat further to spread the bad, sceptical word, will be someone so doubting of all constituted truths and values as to be a menace to the communal wellbeing. This is one more version of what is by now a long familiar anxiety among cultural conservatives, that students in schools and universities are radicalised for life by the teachings of powerful and secluded intellectuals, themselves disqualified as mentors for being at one remove from life as the rest of us experience it. De Man was a mentor whose fallibility on the practical side, which he had displayed all those years ago in Belgium, was seized on with relish as proof of the civic irresponsibility to which his tuition would lead.

This conflation of deconstruction with a general and irrevocable nihilism seems at best ignorant, at worst hysterical, as if young nihilists were so effortlessly trained up, or as if the questioning attitude towards language actually advocated by de Man, if only in the literary domain, were not by extension a valuable possession for citizens surrounded as we daily are by the evidence of linguistic corruption and mystification. But then those who would vilify de Man for luring generations of admiring students down his own de(con)structive path are those who would also deride him as being no more than an ineffectual professor – a man contradictorily endowed with a power born of his own impotence.

The conflation has been made, however, and it raises an interesting question: how did a teacher and critic as difficult, as Germanic in his own reading and as apparently glacial in temperament as Paul de Man ever come to have a following in the first place? He published no one, continuous book that could serve as a popular manifesto of his critical beliefs, only, in his lifetime, three collections of reprinted essays. The essay was the size of publication best suited to him, so he said, because he was a 'philologist', not a philosopher, and without someone else's text with which to engage he had no ideas of his own. In this he was the archetypal critic-as-parasite, flitting – though does de Man ever quite flit? – from host to host in three literatures, English, French and German. But the parasitic essayists are rare indeed who acquire the authority of de Man.

His self-deprecation was undercut, however, by the range and depth of his reading in philosophy as well as in literature, and by the force of an intelligence which was far from subservient to the texts with which it engaged. De Man took over what he was reading and made it provisionally his own, and such commanding essays as 'The Resistance to Theory' or 'The Rhetoric of Temporality' go far beyond any parasitical reliance on original texts; they will survive as landmarks in the theoretical literature.

Yet such performances, however superior, can not account fully for the admiration which de Man drew to him. That I fancy may have come from a less explicit, pre-theoretical theme in his writing: from the note of high, invulnerable pessimism which he repeatedly strikes in respect of the human condition. In this de Man is reminiscent of the 1950s, of a time when God was only quite recently dead and when a certain tragic humanism was the order of the day, as we faced excitedly up to the news of our cosmic dereliction. 'Existentialist' was a label to which, interestingly and typically, de Man objected: in a book review of 1964 called 'Heidegger Reconsidered', he sets out to rescue that thinker from the over-sensitive readers who have taken his philosophy to be one of pathos instead of a purely philosophical lucidity, claiming that in *Being and Time* 'death . . . is mentioned primarily for epistemological reasons and not, as the much abused term would appear in its popularized version, for "existential" reasons.' This attempt to neutralise the pathetic effects of the death-theme in Heidegger is subtle, and wonderfully unpersuasive. De Man's point is that pathos is only to be felt in the immediacy of life, not in the reflexivity of philosophy, that is, of language. A hard, 'authentic' (a key existentialist category of experience, cunningly turned by de Man against its common, Sartrian usage) knowledge of our finitude as human beings is to be had, it seems, only from a mediate, collective source, to be felt in our brains and not on our nerves. To claim this, as de Man does, as the Heideggerian way in which to read Heidegger, is to play a double, cruel, very de Manian game: he will apply the steel of reason where he knows it will hurt most, at those places in our reading where we feel the most personally and urgently addressed by the text.

In 'Looking Back on Paul de Man', a very eloquent essay, half obituary and half apologia, his former colleague at Yale, Geoffrey Hartman, writes that, in de Man's work, 'the pressure on both text and reader was heightened by a prose that stripped all pathos and uplift from its subject.' I take this as meaning that de Man capitalised in his writing on denying us the consolation of finding pathos in texts which are concerned with a pathetic subject-matter. This is why he gave ever closer attention as he went on to the poetry of Romanticism, not as a phenomenon of literary history but as a corpus of writing seductive for the tension it embodies between the poets' desire to achieve in language the concreteness of actual perception and their more and more conscious resort to imagery, which is the triumphant proof of their frustration. Again, as with Heidegger, de Man contrives very brilliantly to show us Romantic poetry as a crux of epistemology, instead of an exercise in pathos, an illusory mediation in symbols between the human consciousness and an alien, 'ontologically prior' reality. Yet the pathos which he is set on countering by his own allegorical readings, of Keats or Wordsworth or Hölderlin, returns, muted, in his invocations of the anxious state out of which they wrote, of their 'predicament' or 'sorrow of separation' or 'unhappy consciousness', as poets authentically aware of the fragility not only of life but of language too.

Their state of anxiety was one with which de Man thought we could all of us now identify in our predicament (see 'The Inward Generation', an essay of 1955 collected in his *Critical Writings*). Far from reconciling us to our sad sublunary condition, Romantic poetry should, once it is honestly read, remind us again of our final alienation. The stoical bleakness on which de Man presumed is itself a Romantic attitude, however, and lent a necessary, attractive pathos to his rigour as a critic.

It is tempting to look back on de Man as a demystifier, saving us by his hard lucidity from all kinds of mistaken readings of texts, whether or not they are designed for our comfort. But there were really no limits to his scepticism and he refused for himself the comfort of believing that the demystifier replaced error with inviolable truth. Demystification he described as 'the most dangerous myth of all', for seeming to promise us a cure for that negative knowledge about language which is in fact constitutional and not historical. De Man's absolute acceptance of that premiss and the extraordinary intelligence with which he worked at its application to literature make him an exemplary figure in contemporary criticism. And his youthful moment of anti-Semitism has nothing whatever to do with the matter.

PART II

WRITERS

10

MARCEL PROUST

THE CORRESPONDENT

Proust wrote too many letters. He thought so, and so anyone might think, contemplating the twenty-one volumes of Philip Kolb's superlative edition of the *Correspondance complète*, the first of them covering the years 1880 to 1895, the last of them 1922, the year of the writer's death. Sheer numbers would not have mattered had they been stronger letters, but Proust's correspondence is too much of it mechanical or emptily ingratiating, the one remaining exercise of the social virtues by a man who had taken once and for all to his bedroom (with occasional querulous sorties late at night to the Ritz Hotel) in order to be alone with his asthma and the prodigiously radiating manuscript of his novel.

As he declined bodily in his fetid hermitage, Proust came to worry about the hundreds of letters he had written during these years of rapt fictional creation; he was afraid, he told his housekeeper, Céleste Albaret, that once he was dead they would be published, or if not published sold at auction, and he even consulted a lawyer to find out whether he could stop that happening. He was told he could not, and concluded morbidly that his letters would eventually become so many 'arrows returned against him'. This black thought did not slow him down, however, because the more ill and unvisitable he became, the more letters he wrote: the later volumes in Kolb's series are fatter by many pages than the earlier ones. In theory, Proust told Jacques Rivière (in a letter), he was 'un athée de l'amitié', or unbeliever in friendship, but one who yet 'practised it with far greater fervour than so many apostles of friendship'; and the evidence of this confessedly Tartuffian fervour is in the abundance and regularity of his correspondence, as he keeps company with a whole vivarium of big fish and small: with the titled hostesses of whose hollow world he had become the pampered adept when young; with the old literary friends and

young literary protégés whose work he endlessly overpraises; with his publishers; and with the admirers and reviewers of his own work once it had begun
to appear in its full extent after 1918.

Why would Proust have worried that letters as anodyne and mannerly as his
mostly are might one day become 'arrows' and be fired back at him in
retaliation? The acrid, analytical Proust keeps himself after all for the pages of
the novel and is unloosed less often than one might wish in the correspondence,
beyond the occasional complaint in a safely democratic ear about how
depressingly stupid the habitués of the *beaux quartiers* constitutionally are and of
how out of place he always was among them: 'I got into that circle very young.
I said only vacuous things, which were admired. One day I talked intelligently,
and they struck me off their dinner-lists for six months.' Generally, however,
Proust the correspondent shows few brute feelings and bares no disturbing
secrets, he is more M. de Norpois than the baron de Charlus: the urbane
tactician of the drawing rooms, not the serpentine and malicious deviant. But
might this not be just it, might he not have wanted to call his letters back
simply because they *were* so careful, so very much less Proustian than they
should have been, coming as they did from the bitingly candid moralist of *A la
recherche du temps perdu*? If one day they were aggregated and published, they
would betray the double standards of the novelist whose great book had
ultimately exposed the shallowness, cruelty and unforgiving egotism of the very
society that had once attracted and then received the young Proust himself, and
of which as a writer of facile letters to dukes, literary lions and countesses he
appeared still to be an expert member. His letter-writing was a compulsion the
too plentiful evidence of which might much better die with the man who
indulged it.

For Proust, letters were the opposite of literature. They were random social
acts, the graphic equivalent of the slight, disjointed things we say to one another
when we meet. They had none of the depth or continuity of literary art. In his
correspondence a novelist can only fall back into the superficial world of Sainte-
Beuve, that dominant nineteenth-century critic whom Proust despised for
having supposed in his philistinism that the writer's social and creative self were
one and the same, that the person you dined and talked with in the cafés or
salons was the same person who went home and wrote the *Fleurs du mal* or
Madame Bovary. Proust insisted that the true writer must contain two selves, a
surface self for when he was in company and a deep one, a *moi profond*, for
when he was alone, and writing. Letters may be written in solitude, but they

are not written by the *moi profond*, whose arduous excavations of the unconscious and of buried memories are not to be squandered by being put into an envelope and posted to a friend. It was vital that Proust the socialite and Proust the novelist be seen to be two people therefore, not one, and the letter-writer never mistaken for the man who wrote *A la recherche du temps perdu*.

This need for duplicity finds an oblique reflection in a late essay that Proust wrote on Flaubert, which contains in passing the suspiciously gross misjudgement that 'what is alone surprising with such a master is the mediocrity of his correspondence.' Flaubert's letters are in truth far and away the best of their century in French, a wonderfully frank, powerful and animated compendium of his moods, his attitudes and his ideas concerning the practice of his art. Why would Proust go out of his way to condemn them, if not to warn his own posterity that a great writer may (or must?) write second-rate letters because his *moi profond* is nowhere to be found in them?

Even so, and happily for us, the Proust on show in the later volumes of the correspondence is much more the practising author than he had been earlier: a lot of his letters are about the book, about getting it into print, getting it read and getting it rightly understood. The printing of the successive volumes of *A la recherche* was one of the great dramas of French publishing history. When the first of them, *Du côté de chez Swann* (Swann's way), appeared, the misprints in it were a scandal, a good thousand of them, but these were the excusable fault of typesetters who had had to work from galleys that were more palimpsest than proof, the original wording having been overgrown by the author's scrawled and spiralling additions. ('But it's another book,' said Jacques Copeau, catching sight of the 'corrected' galleys on a bedside visit.) So distinctive were this author's proofs indeed that there was a plan later on to bind some of the actual returned sheets into the de luxe editions by way of illustration, if only to show what the publishers had had to endure along the way. *Swann* appeared before the war for the first time, in 1913, published by the reputable house of Grasset but at Proust's own expense. Other publishers had turned it down, including the Nouvelle Revue Française (later to evolve into the firm of Gallimard and to buy Proust out from a resentful but powerless Grasset), on the advice mainly of one of its most influential readers, André Gide. It has sometimes been said that Gide rejected Proust's MS because its overt homosexuality had scared him, but the homosexual theme was as yet more evident in the plan for the novel than in the text; there is no evidence of it in *Swann*.

The reason Gide himself gave for turning it down – in a letter of 1914 to

Proust himself, in which he is already apologising for 'the gravest mistake ever made by the NRF' – is quite different, and it bears out what I have just been saying about Proust's fears of being mistaken for nothing more than an emeritus hanger-on of the Faubourg Saint-Germain set. 'For me,' wrote Gide, 'you had remained the man who frequented the houses of Mmes X, Y or Z, the man who wrote for the *Figaro* [to which newspaper Proust had earlier contributed fawning pen-portraits of celebrated Paris salons]. I thought of you – shall I confess it? – *du côté de chez Verdurin*: a snob, a dilettante socialite – the worst possible thing for our review' (the NRF was at once a publishing house and a literary review). It is an irony that Proust's offer to pay for *Swann*'s publication himself should have confirmed Gide in this idea, to the point where he was able to believe that French literature's supreme modern masterpiece had begun as a piece of vanity publishing – an irony because Proust's real reason for paying for its publication was so that he could keep control of things and not be forced into mercenary compromises over the size of the volume or, in due course, the risqué aspects of his subject matter.

During the four years of the First World War the text of the novel grew exponentially, in private; by 1917, Proust is talking of some three and a half thousand printed pages to go with the one published volume. These began to appear in 1919, when *A l'ombre des jeunes filles en fleur* (Within a budding grove) was published, an event which he first fussed over and then complained about to Gaston Gallimard, in anticipation. When the book came out he had reason to celebrate, on the other hand, for it won the Prix Goncourt for that year, a rare success for literature in the annals of that corrupt award. Proust was suddenly a literary notable, and he liked the idea of honours. The trouble, however, was that the later volumes of the novel were far riskier sexually than the early ones. How would the readers he had now gained – the 'electricians' whom he imagined taking to the novel because it described a world so unlike their own! – bear with the perversions of characters such as Charlus or Mlle de Vinteuil in the increasingly frank pages of *Sodome et Gomorrhe* (Cities of the plain)? Would the gathering explicitness of his text put him beyond the social pale and scotch once and for all his chances of being invested with the Légion d'honneur or a seat perhaps in the Académie française? Proust had hopes of both these solemn accolades and played some jesuitical games with himself so that he might remain convinced of his own respectability, lobbying the poet and, more important, academician Henri de Régnier, for example, in these over-complicated terms:

I should be very sorry to spoil the character of my books out of any aspirations to the academy. But I have in the end to speak the truth, even though it might not favour my candidacy. I finally intended to talk about Sodom and Gomorrah in an objective fashion. But to my great annoyance, the fatality of the characters involved dragged me into a sort of pamphlet, or sermon, very different from the impartial portrait I had intended.

'I'm anti, I'm anti' becomes a minor motif of his letters around this time, in case anyone should suppose him to be soft on homosexuals. He asserts the morality of the later parts of his novel very strongly, even claiming that they are 'religious'. What is curious, however, is his supposing that his 'sort of pamphlet' might do him more harm with the very upright members of the Académie than the 'impartial portrait' to which he had so regrettably failed to restrict himself. He seems to have become entangled in his own homophobic cover-story, and in the irremovable discrepancy between his worldly ambitions and his authorial integrity. As it turned out, the list of those appointed to the rank of *chevalier* in the Légion d'honneur in 1920 included – in a section he thought demeaning, containing as it did various sub-literary figures – the unwontedly full name of 'Proust (Valentin-Georges-Eugène Marcel)'; the Académie, alas, he did not live to enter, though it's obvious from his correspondence what a master he would have proved when it came to drumming up votes among the sitting members for his own admission.

Much the most significant theme in his later correspondence is the novelist's intermittent but forthright commentary on his novel. As the successive volumes came out, he wrote frequently to the journalists and critics who had reviewed them, beginning always with some words of flattery but then passing on to the more serious business of setting them straight by showing where and how they had misread him. He hated above all the idea that *A la recherche* should be taken, as it so readily was, for a *roman à clef*. If it was one, he said, then there were so many keys for each character and episode that to try and correlate them one to one with figures from real life was futile, and worse than futile inasmuch as it denied him his right to imagine a world rather than merely report on one. To those readers like the absurdly tortuous, sulky and by now moribund Robert de Montesquiou, who was quick to pick out as he thought members of his own plush acquaintance among the novel's characters (though he was seemingly blind to any possible resemblance between himself and the increasingly monstrous Charlus, whom he sees rather as a descendant of Balzac's sinister 'invert' Vautrin), Proust asserts the prerogative of the synthesist, for whom no one and nothing can pass untouched from life into literature, the text answering exclusively to the novelist's particular needs. Again, he asks repeatedly that *A la recherche* be judged only once it is complete, that no one should decide on its quality or its overall meaning on the strength of its serial parts. Time is the principal actor in his fiction, and time takes time to work its transformations. The novel is a 'composition', in the same sense as a building or a work of music: its end is predetermined – already written, he emphasises – but to be disclosed only slowly, so that the experience of reading towards it may be brought close to the experience of living. 'It's only at the end of the book, when the lessons of life have been grasped, that my design will become clear,' he had said, writing to the young critic and editor Jacques Rivière, back in 1914. By the same token, the book is not to be understood as a merely subjective memoir or autobiography, because according to Proust it contains not a single 'contingency'; everything in it is there in illustration of those general laws of human behaviour which he has spent his adult life searching out in the society around him. The novel, in fact, is his valediction to that society and to his own unworthy social self, and the comments that he allows himself on it in his letters converge in his desire finally to be free of his past.

Health and money are the other two truly engrossing concerns of Proust's late letters. The first was by this time terrible, by his own account of it. Scarcely a letter but opens with a plaintive bulletin, telling of his 'attacks' and of the difficulties he is having even as he writes with his breathing, or seeing, or sometimes even speaking. Injections of caffeine, adrenaline and *in extremis* morphine keep him working on his proofs, and his room is lucky to get aired once a week from the reek of fumigants – the old woollies he wears in bed are full of holes from where he has burnt himself lighting matches. His correspondents can be in no doubt just how unwell and how beleaguered he has become. By 1920–21, only the novel is alive, its author habitually declares himself to be either 'dying' or 'dead'. Nor is he happy with where he has ended up living, after being forced to move from the old apartment in the boulevard Haussmann where he had lived for many years into what he likes to call a 'slum' in the rue Hamelin (he manages at one point to enrol his old friend the duc de Guiche no less as a go-between in negotiating with landlords). He has had to leave his famous noise-suppressing cork tiles behind, because of the expense of removing them, and to put up as a consequence with the sound of coitus reaching him through the unprotected walls.

And as with his health and his apartment, so it is with his fortune: he is financially done for, so he likes to tell people, a *rentier* brought low by the years of war and then by the postwar depression. In reality he was far from ruined, merely very neurotic and silly over money. All the way through his edition of the correspondence, Kolb has included a helpful and intelligently chosen selection of Proust's incoming mail, and some of the best letters written to him are those of Lionel Hauser, an old family friend and investment adviser, who is almost alone in treating the novelist without any hint of flummery, telling him off plainly more than once for acting the spoilt child. Proust had got through a great deal of money over the years, and made almost none from his writing. He was quite oppressively generous when it came to giving presents: in the one surviving letter written to Alfred Agostinelli, his chauffeur and perhaps his lover, who had left him to go and take flying lessons on the Côte d'Azur, Proust refers to a propitiatory offer he had obviously made to buy the runaway his own aeroplane (the letter arrived in the south on the same day as Agostinelli was killed when his plane dived into the Mediterranean). But he never became poor; the dereliction into which he liked to represent himself to his correspondents as having descended is surely a part of his wish to be seen to have broken utterly with the false values of the arriviste. He is finally the arriviste in reverse.

Agostinelli's aeroplane, had Proust ever bought it, was to have cost 27,000 francs – the precise cost in 1914 in Paris of a Rolls-Royce car (such as the narrator offers unavailingly to buy, along with a yacht, in hopes of luring back the fugitive Albertine in the novel). That we should know of this suggestive equation between the real offer and the fictive is entirely due to Professor Kolb, whose editing of Proust's letters was from the start a fine example of scholarly care and thoroughness. In his footnotes, Kolb explains everything one could want explained and has tracked down every least allusion. When Proust casually writes to someone that 'my age is rising as quickly as the Seine', his editor goes off to consult the files of the *Figaro* and is able to tell us that in late December 1919 the river was abnormally high and that the feet of the stone Zouave on the Pont d'Alma were once again awash. Indeed, it is by the tracing of references like these that Kolb was able to date many of the letters, since Proust himself seems never to have bothered with anything of the kind.

The full correspondence will never, I assume, be translated into English; there would be no point in so vast and expensive an undertaking, given how routine so many of the letters are. The twenty-one volumes of the French have in fact been reduced to four in English, translated – and very well translated too – by the late Terence Kilmartin. These four volumes are enough: the letters have been intelligently chosen and give a fair representation of the correspondence as a whole. But in doing that, they could also do Proust harm. Thanks in no small measure to the unsuitably precious English into which his novel was originally translated by C.K. Scott-Moncrieff (see the final essay in this group), he has continued to impress anglophone readers as the very thing he was desperate in his later life not to be thought: as a writer more remarkable for his worldliness than his intelligence. By putting on show the conversational as opposed to the profound self of Proust, his translated correspondence does more to reinforce that unfortunate impression than to correct it.

THE CRITIC

The collection of Proust's critical essays known to us as *Contre Sainte-Beuve* (Against Sainte-Beuve) are far more than the occasional or subsidiary writings that they might seem to be. They are a robust statement of his overriding aesthetic beliefs and concerns, the same beliefs and concerns that he dramatises to such supreme effect in *A la recherche du temps perdu*. That wonderful novel makes fuller sense therefore for the more explicit knowledge of his ideas that can be got from reading his criticism. Indeed, it is wrong to try to separate Proust's critical from his creative endeavours when, in his case, these were in so unusually close an alliance.

Contre Sainte-Beuve was not published in Proust's lifetime; had it been, his high worth as a critic would have been sooner understood. Nor did he finish writing it, not, as was the case with the huge novel that he had abandoned earlier, *Jean Santeuil*, because he felt disappointed by what he had been able to produce, but rather because what had begun as a peculiarly impassioned work of literary criticism turned in the writing more and more into a novel, into *the* novel in fact. The writing of *Contre Sainte-Beuve* is thus both an odd and a dramatic story, well worth the tracing. No other major work of literary criticism has ever been so intimately bound up with the creation of a work of fiction.

Contre Sainte-Beuve dates from the most crucial period of Proust's writing life, from the years 1908 to 1909, when he finally got down to work seriously on his great novel. This is a well-documented twelve months or so, and it is fascinating to follow the genesis of *Contre Sainte-Beuve* in the various references that are made to it, first as an idea and then as a work in progress, in Proust's correspondence (the relevant volumes are numbers eight and nine in Kolb's edition).

In 1908, when the references begin, the writer was thirty-seven years old and by now acutely anxious that, because of what he saw as a culpable lethargy and a distracting readiness to go into society, he might die before he had had time to produce the great work of literature he felt himself to be capable of writing. This was not mere affectation or a morbidity deriving from his neurasthenia. Proust was severely asthmatic and could not expect to have either a long life or a healthy one in which he would be fit to work whenever he wanted. Thus the opening paragraph of the essay 'The Method of Sainte-Beuve' is genuinely poignant, with the writer urging himself to break out from an unproductive inertia and to write down things he had long carried in his mind but had lacked the energy to make public. He adapts a Gospel injunction, 'Work while ye have the light'; and work he now did, obsessively, for the rest of his quite short life (he died in 1922, at fifty-one).

Proust's fear of his true worth going forever unrecognised was reasonable, and it comes out movingly if obliquely in the complaints he makes about the limitations as a critic of the supposedly all-discerning Sainte-Beuve, who was still regarded in the early part of this century in France as far and away the greatest of nineteenth-century critics. Proust's opposition to Sainte-Beuve was nothing new, it had been brewing for some years and had found occasional expression in various of the essays and articles he had written. But it came to a head in 1908.

From May of that year, there is evidence that he was thinking of writing a full-length study of Sainte-Beuve. In a letter to his friend Louis d'Albufera, he lists the astonishing and impressive variety of literary projects that he currently had in mind:

> For I have on the go:
> an article on the nobility
> a Parisian novel
> an essay on Sainte-Beuve and Flaubert
> an essay on Women
> an essay on pederasty (not easy to publish)
> an article on stained-glass
> an article on tombstones
> an article on the novel . . .

This projected 'essay on Sainte-Beuve and Flaubert' is the first real pointer to the composition of *Contre Sainte-Beuve*. As we have it, this contains a very short essay of four or five pages on Flaubert, relatively sketchy alongside the much longer essays on Sainte-Beuve's method, on Baudelaire, on Balzac and on the poet Gérard de Nerval. The connection of Sainte-Beuve with Flaubert itself refers back, however, to something that Proust had written earlier in 1908, when he had published in the *Figaro* a series of pastiches of French writers, mainly from the nineteenth century, each of whom was imagined as retelling the events recently brought to light in a sensational lawsuit, the 'affaire Lemoine', in which a con man of that name had been sentenced for swindling a million francs out of the head of the diamond firm of De Beers. The series included a pastiche of the critic, Sainte-Beuve, imagined by Proust as reviewing a novel by Flaubert based on the affair. This fictitious Sainte-Beuve is guardedly unfavourable to the novel as such, but unctuously patronising of the novelist, whom he sees as a likeable human being even though lacking in talent as a writer. This combination of literary obtuseness and drawing-room smarm is precisely what Proust takes the critic to task for in *Contre Sainte-Beuve*.

By the end of 1908 the essay on Sainte-Beuve seems to have been still only a project. But Proust had been reading Sainte-Beuve's criticism and making notes on it ('unusually for me', as one of his projected prefaces announces); one of his working notebooks (the *Carnet de 1908*) has survived and some twenty-five pages of it are taken up principally with his sometimes cryptic and frequently barbed observations on Sainte-Beuve's weaknesses. Around the middle of December, Proust wrote to another friend, Georges de Lauris:

> I am going to write something about Sainte-Beuve. . . . I have two articles constructed in my head in a sense (review articles). One is an article traditional in format . . . The other would start as the narrative of an early morning, Mamma would come to my bedside and I would tell her about an article I want to do on Sainte-Beuve. And I would expand on it to her. . . .'

Proust's uncertainty about which format to pursue, the traditional or the quasi-narrative, is a good indication of how inseparable his critical and creative intentions now were.

The second, and shorter, of the two prefaces he wrote contains one of only two instances of his referring to the volume under the title of *Contre Sainte-Beuve*. The other, longer preface, which on the surface is rather little connected with Proust's views on Sainte-Beuve, is a document of high interest and autobiographical drama, referring as it does to a most momentous event in the writer's life: the dipping of a piece of dry toast into a cup of tea, or rather the discovery to which that trivial act gave rise. This is the most celebrated of the various experiences of 'involuntary memory' on which the huge and complicated structure of *A la recherche du temps perdu* was eventually to rest: the key to the novel's composition and to the more or less Bergsonian philosophy of time to which Proust the novelist subscribed. (In the novel the piece of toast becomes a madeleine, in itself a commonplace kind of small cake but chosen by Proust for the religious resonances of its name, *madeleine* being the French for the Magdalene.) The function of the dipped toast, like that of other, comparable experiences of involuntary remembering, also recalled in the preface of *Contre Sainte-Beuve* and invoked in *A la recherche*, is to resurrect, through a sudden identification of the present moment with a particular time and place in the past, huge tracts of the rememberer's experience which had apparently been erased from his memory without trace. The involuntary memory is crucial for Proust because he believed that, unlike the voluntary memory, which is at the beck and call of the conscious mind or intellect, it restores the past in all its lived truth and intensity.

Proust seems to have been unable to keep separate in his mind the study of Sainte-Beuve and the 'roman parisien' he was planning to write. 'Should I make a novel out of it, a philosophical study, am I a novelist?' he writes in one perplexed, pessimistic entry in the *Carnet de 1908*. The first evidence that he had begun writing it comes in June 1909, when he tells de Lauris: 'Georges, I'm so exhausted from having started Sainte-Beuve (I'm hard at work, execrable as it happens) that I don't know what I'm writing to you.' More explicit still is a letter of mid August to a publisher, Alfred Vallette, offering him the chance to publish the book Proust is working on:

> I am finishing a book which despite its provisional title: *Contre Sainte-Beuve, Souvenir d'une matinée* is genuinely a novel and an extremely indecent novel in places. One of the leading characters is a homosexual. . . . The name of Sainte-Beuve is not there by chance. The book ends in fact with a long conversation about Sainte-Beuve and about aesthetics . . . and once people have finished the book they will see (I would like them to see) that the whole novel is merely the putting into practice of the artistic principles emitted in this final part, a sort of preface if you like coming at the end.

Proust asked Vallette not only to publish this oddly hybrid work as a book but also to serialise it ahead of publication in the fortnightly review that he ran. He promised that once 300 pages had been serialised, 'the novel part would have appeared. There would remain the long *causerie* about Sainte-Beuve, criticism, etc., which would appear only in the book-version.' The word *causerie* was well chosen, for that was the term favoured by Sainte-Beuve himself, whose weekly newspaper articles on books from the mid nineteenth century were collected and published – in no fewer than twenty-seven volumes – as the *Causeries du lundi*. Vallette did not take the book on.

By the time *A la recherche* began to appear, in 1913, the *causerie* on Sainte-Beuve was no longer part of it, even if the considerable animus that Proust felt against that critic comes out directly at particular moments, and very amusingly, in the literary pronouncements that he puts into the mouth of the aged and rather fatuous Mme de Villeparisis, whose judgements are, like those of Sainte-Beuve, determined by the social standing and good or ill nature of the author in question.

During the summer months of 1909, the critical study Proust was trying to write, in which he would put forward certain ruling aesthetic principles, finally became swamped by the proliferations of his fiction. Not until 1954, indeed, thirty-two years after his death, did anything resembling such a study appear, and even then it was entangled with chapters of the fiction on which he had been working simultaneously, so hard was it for an editor, working from Proust's disorderly manuscripts, to determine where the one ended and the other began. (A second, much altered edition of *Contre Sainte-Beuve* was published in 1971, with the fictional elements mostly removed.)

Proust's quarrel with Sainte-Beuve was not some austerely academic disagreement as how best to understand the nature of authorship and of literature. More than a quarrel, it was a campaign which Proust pursued for much of his writing life, with a bluntness and scorn which show that uncommonly emotive issues were being raised. Even before he wrote *Contre Sainte-Beuve* he had dropped hints, as I have said, of the charges that he would one day be pressing against the critic. The question to be asked therefore is, why did he feel so strongly about the work of a critic who was in fact decidedly tame in what he wrote and who was anyway long dead; whence the animus?

The answer has more to do with Proust than with the actual or presumed incompetence of Sainte-Beuve. Sainte-Beuve was unlucky in standing so conspicuously for certain ideas from which it was imperative that Proust should detach himself, and be seen to detach himself. His own creative integrity and reputation were at stake. His objections to Sainte-Beuve are peculiarly personal therefore, and the more compelling for being so; in reading *Contre Sainte-Beuve* we can appreciate them doubly, first as an episode in the history of modern literary thought, in which they have an important place, and then as an episode in the autobiography of Marcel Proust. By taking issue with Sainte-Beuve, he can establish his independence of mind. For Sainte-Beuve's values were worse than simply false, they were also tempting: they were values by which Proust had earlier lived himself and by which he had good cause to fear that others would assume he was still living. So *Contre Sainte-Beuve* is an essay in the extrication of Marcel Proust from a value system from which he was profoundly anxious to escape.

He lays two main complaints against Sainte-Beuve. The first is that Sainte-Beuve was a blatantly incompetent judge of his contemporaries, even though he had declared that to rank the writers of one's own time according to their true merits was the highest talent and responsibility of the critic. The second, related, complaint is that Sainte-Beuve failed to allow for the all-important difference which exists between the writer as a social being, who mixes daily with others, and the writer as a writer, who creates his work in solitude.

Proust has some good, sardonic fun with the first of these charges, and not only because Sainte-Beuve failed so glaringly to live up to his own specification of the literary critic's role as being to form, not to follow, taste. In Proust's account of him, Sainte-Beuve appears as an inveterate dunce, forever singing the praises of writers who were tediously mediocre and forever overlooking the literary genius of those few contemporaries who possessed it. Anyone who relied exclusively on Sainte-Beuve for a picture of French writing in the mid nineteenth century, Proust mockingly concludes, would have a wrong and sadly philistine impression of what was then going on. He or she would be made aware that Stendhal had an aptitude for paradox but almost none for the novel; that Balzac's inspired notion, of having the same characters reappear again and again in the novels of the *Comédie humaine*, was inconsequential, a mistake even; that Baudelaire was, contrary to the common idea, a polite and agreeable young person but ungifted for poetry; or that the supposedly unsociable Flaubert was also a good fellow but that a novel like *L'Education sentimentale* was unreadable. For Proust, as for readers today, these writers were the four great names of Sainte-Beuve's time, but Sainte-Beuve somehow couldn't see it.

These are the test cases for Proust, of authors on whom he himself had exact and wonderfully perceptive things to say, things far removed from the biographically minded vapidities of Sainte-Beuve. No critic, however clear-sighted, could in fact have lived up to Sainte-Beuve's self-appointed role as mentor to the age; in evaluating the writers of the day all critics get at least some of them wrong. But, fair or not, Proust's case is instructively made, and the examples he chooses, of Sainte-Beuve's misapprehensions and misjudgements, are damaging.

However, we do not now need to worry whether Sainte-Beuve was really as inept as Proust maintains, since it is Proust himself, among others, who has done much to shape our assessments of the literary past in France, and few of us even read, let alone allow ourselves to have our taste guided by, Sainte-Beuve. What matters is the general point Proust is making, as to the recognition of literary genius in the age in which it is active. Genius itself is not always confident of being recognised, or even, in its Romantic version, desirous of being recognised, when its ultimate éclat will be all the brighter for having gone uncelebrated at the time. It is this century, not their own, that has raised Proust's particular heroes to their, as we see it, rightful and definitive place in French literary history. If that place really is definitive, and safe from future fluctuations of taste, then we might say that once a writer achieves it he is removed from history altogether and has entered the timeless dimension of art.

This is Proust's own belief and one which Sainte-Beuve is faulted for not having risen to. Sainte-Beuve was the prisoner of his own time, like the Guermantes brothers who are introduced into *Contre Sainte-Beuve* as emissaries from Proust's novel and who have preserved, anachronistically, from the time when they had first read Balzac in their father's library, 'the preferences of the readers of those days'. This is to take up a historical standpoint, but the historical standpoint can never be the standpoint of art; only those critics who are able, however incompletely, to escape from it and to judge contemporary works from some prophetic standpoint in the future have true insight into the nature of art. What Proust is asking of a critic, unreasonably, is that he be gifted with double vision, able to look around him at the present with an understanding and a discrimination achievable only in the future. And this double perspective, with one period of time being captured and then evaluated from the standpoint of a later one, stands at the heart of Proust's aesthetic and at the heart of the structure of his novel.

He had excellent, private reasons for being preoccupied by the question of genius and its recognition, because of the disparity between his literary ambitions and his actual literary achievements. At the time when he was writing *Contre Sainte-Beuve*, he had published relatively little: had he died during that (unusually hard) winter, as he may genuinely have feared that he would, his reputation would have been very thin and certainly transient. There could be little to comfort him in the probable historical judgement of his contemporaries. Proust thus had a peculiar and urgent need of the future for his reassurance in the present. He knew, what was more, that the novel on which he was at last started was a work of extreme innovation and that it would surely not be easily assimilated by contemporary critics or readers, who might find it (as some did, when it began to be published) obscure, alembicated, uneventful and shapeless. Here again, the time factor is everything: it takes time for the great innovators to be properly understood; and, in the particular case of *A la recherche*, time for the meaning of the work as a whole to become apparent, inasmuch as not until the end has been reached can the full coherence of the novel's structure be appreciated.

Proust's second principal charge against Sainte-Beuve, that he made no distinction between the writer as a social being and the writer as a writer, is at once more reasonable and critically more substantive – but it, too, has its personal application to Proust himself, as we shall see. This failure in Sainte-Beuve is literally fundamental; what he refused to allow for was what Proust believed to be the vital difference in psychological and ontological individuality between the social and the creative self. The social self, even supposing it is a unity at all, is that which we display to others in our public moments; it is a surface self, conditioned by the company or circumstances in which we find ourselves. Our *moi profond*, on the other hand, which is in eclipse during our daily commerce with other people, is alone capable, once we find ourselves alone again, of genuine creation in art.

The medium in which both selves are materialised is verbal, so the comparison for Proust is between two distinct registers of language, between literature as an upper register and mere conversation as a lower. Sainte-Beuve's gross error was to conflate these registers. The very name of *causerie*, or 'chat', that he gave to his weekly critical essays is degrading because it seems to bring literature down to the level of gossip. Sainte-Beuve was a tirelessly sociable haunter of literary salons for whom solitude would have been more a penance than the condition of true authorship.

> At no time does Sainte-Beuve seem to have grasped what is peculiar to the inspiration or the activity of writing, and what marks it off totally from the occupations of other men and the other occupations of the writer. He drew no dividing-line between the occupation of writing, in which, in solitude, and suppressing those words that belong

as much to others as to ourselves, and with which, even when alone, we judge things
without being ourselves, we come face to face once more with our selves, and seek to
hear and to render the true sound of our hearts – and conversation!

The *moi profond* demands seclusion if we are to become aware of its existence,
and an abstinence from the damagingly intrusive company of other 'words' or
voices. This abstinence extends even to a literary practice that is certainly
solitary and might easily be supposed to be safe: that of reading, about which
Proust had fundamental things to say. He emphasises its charms but its danger
also. In reading, as in conversation, we listen to voices other than our own and,
misled by the solitude in which we do it and the edification which it brings,
may not admit that it is just as great a distraction from that self-communion out
of which art can alone come. Reading can never quite engage the *moi profond*,
can only ever be an incitement to the creative mind. The *moi profond* is the one
source of originality, of the writer's own voice or style, freed at last from
contamination by the styles of others. Here the lesson of pastiche has been fully
learnt, for once a writer has his own style he has transcended, or else expelled,
all those 'melodies' he had been able to hear when reading the words of other
writers.

Proust's is thus a very Romantic aesthetic, in which the creator is a lonely,
privileged figure, a person apart at those times when he is working and never
to be confused with the much shallower person who is to be met with and
spoken to in company. Sainte-Beuve admitted no such vital distinction, hence
his errors of evaluation amongst his contemporaries. Far from it being an
advantage for a critic actually to know the writers about whom he writes, it is
a grave disadvantage, for his judgement of them will be corrupted by
acquaintance: 'How does the fact of having been a friend of Stendhal make us
better able to judge him? On the contrary, it would probably be a serious
hindrance.' The social self even of a literary genius may be 'very inferior to the
outward self of many other men'. Thus Sainte-Beuve was unable to see that
Baudelaire was a genius, and the most profound and original French poet of the
century, in part because he was a friend.

And if first-hand acquaintance was impossible for Sainte-Beuve, if the author
in question were dead, for example, then nothing deterred he set about learning
all he could about him from those who had known him or from reading about
his life. 'Literature for me is not distinct or at least separable from the rest of
the man and his organization' is Sainte-Beuve's declared philosophy. Today we

might say that he was a behaviourist in criticism, who refused to see beyond the facts that he had gathered or to endow writers with the inner and necessarily hidden mental space that they need in order to create. We might say also that he was a simple-minded subscriber to the 'biographical fallacy', or that fashion for interpreting literary works according to the known events of their author's lives or of their 'organisation'. That sort of interpretation leaves out of account the work of transformation that for Proust is the essence of the literary act, whereby lived experience is raised into literature by the shaping power of both thought and feeling.

Sainte-Beuve's method was infected by the positivism of the age in which he lived: it sought to explain everything by facts. Proust's by contrast is the method of a philosophical idealist, who posits an essential self as the source of all genuine creativity. Given that his *moi profond* is a normally suspended function in human beings, it may readily be thought of in proto-Freudian terms as an agency or Muse closer to the subconscious than to the conscious mind. Certainly, it is an infinitely richer, more suggestive and more generous model of the writer's spiritual economy than that with which Sainte-Beuve worked.

Proust had strong reasons of his own for marking off the social from the creative self. In the earlier part of his life, he had been an assiduous caller on the *gratin* of Paris, a diligent socialite, an ostensible dilettante. He had aristocratic friends and a well-mined seam of snobbery. But at this cardinal moment of his life, when he turned aside to work at *A la recherche*, he retired bodily from the glamorous society in which he had earlier participated and became famously reclusive: he became the novelist as anchorite, investing his health, his time and his intellectual resources no longer in fugitive conversations but in the permanence of his novel. He turns from a ready collusion in the ways of that society to a cruel, generally damning analysis of it. His novel is the product of the *moi profond* of which his social acquaintances may have had no inkling, in the days when he still moved and talked amongst them. But until such time as that *moi profond* has been able to manifest itself, in the form of a literary creation, Proust will remain misunderstood and grievously undervalued. Hence his animus against the worldly Sainte-Beuve, who believed that an artist should keep the best of himself for his friends.

The one quality that Proust allowed to Sainte-Beuve was intelligence; he does not attempt to deprive the critic posthumously of that. Intelligence, however, is not necessarily the quality that a critic most needs. The very arresting first words of the preface to *Contre Sainte-Beuve* read: 'Daily, I attach less value to the intellect. Daily, I realise more clearly that only away from it can the writer repossess something of our past impressions, that is, attain to something of himself and to the one subject-matter of art.' In writing, intellect must thus concede the priority to what we would normally call intuition. This remarkable statement, coming from an author of such formidable intellectual powers, must be read as polemic, as only provisionally sincere. It is a part of the case against Sainte-Beuve, and of Proust's urgent desire to distinguish between the two classes, those who are intelligent and those who are creative. He knew – who better? – that without the intelligence to exploit it, 'intuition', or in his case the largesse offered to him by the episodes of involuntary memory, is valueless. The point he is making, however, is that Sainte-Beuve's acknowledged intelligence is in actual fact a limitation on his capacities as a critic, because it could only ever have afforded him a partial understanding of the creative process. Proust is in effect claiming that even the critic must explore his *moi profond* if he is to recognise true literature when he meets it.

PROUST IN ENGLISH

In the spring of 1920, Proust was fretting because the good Gaston (Gaston Gallimard, who had become his publisher during the war) had been, he thought, inexcusably slow in arranging for translations of his now successful novel. In the past twelve months, the first part, *Du côté de chez Swann*, had been published for a second time (the little-noticed earlier edition had appeared from a different publisher before the war, in 1913) and the next part, *A l'ombre des jeunes filles en fleur*, for the first time; and with this, Proust had, remarkably, won the Prix Goncourt, a prize that he had hoped for but which then, as now, generally went to works of an uncomplicated mediocrity. There should by his reckoning have been foreign editions pending of these first instalments of *A la recherche du temps perdu*, and an English edition mattered most of all. English was a language which Proust could read even if he had not learnt to speak it; he had, with the help of Marie Nordlinger, translated Ruskin's *Bible of Amiens* and *Sesame and Lilies* into French. His sense of symmetry, if not of justice, called for his own work, indebted to Ruskin as it was, to be turned into English, and if nothing had so far been done the fault must be Gaston's, because the English themselves were hugely enthusiastic about it: in a letter of May 1920, he promised the young critic Jacques Rivière, who was by now his editor *chez* Gallimard, that there had 'perhaps been eight or nine articles in the *Times* alone'.

The 'perhaps' was disingenuous. There had been at most two notices of his work in the *Times Literary Supplement* and an essay by Albert Thibaudet published in the *London Mercury*. Proust's pained exaggeration was born of the neglect that the novelist was then feeling. He had, however, an advocate on the *Times* who was quite unknown to him: a Scottish infantry officer, lately demobbed, who was well connected but unfortunate enough to have been appointed private secretary to the bizarre Lord Northcliffe, at that time the owner of the newspaper. C.K. Scott-Moncrieff had been keeping up with the books that were being read in Paris and had been led by the award of the Prix Goncourt to the work of Marcel Proust. Indeed, he had already written to J.C. Squire, in these years a hub of the London literary journalistic world, to see if he couldn't now make something of his discovery:

> Do you think that *Land and Water* [a review edited by Squire] would consider for a moment running Marcel Proust's book . . . as a serial in English? I am reading it with great absorption in rare moments of leisure, and I am prepared to make a very palatable translation of it, which is not easy. Publishers here seem very shy of acquiring *droits de traduction* – which costs money – when they can sweat indigenous authors gratis.

Land and Water – or *The Country Gentleman and Land & Water*, to give that weekly its full title – was a wonderfully unsuitable outlet for a serialisation of Proust: the novelist was no countryman and no sportsman, despite the reverence he may have felt for the Anglophile bigwigs who ran the Jockey Club in Paris. *Land and Water* didn't bite; nor did any London publisher. But Scott-Moncrieff was convinced and began his translation just the same, without waiting until he had been given the commission. Quickly, and understandably, he came to find Proust more to his taste than Lord Northcliffe, and Combray a more bracing place in which to spend his time than Printing House Square: he resigned from the *Times* to work at the translation full time. He found a publisher, Messrs Chatto and Windus, who in 1922 brought out the two volumes of *Swann's Way*, thus inaugurating the single largest, most celebrated and most admired work of translation into English of the twentieth century.

Literary translators rarely make a name for themselves, save possibly among their own kind. They are hired dependants of the authors whom they translate.

If Scott-Moncrieff stands alone among the translators of the twentieth century, then that is Proust's doing: their names go together, the extraordinary qualities of the original reflecting glory on its translator. In fact, it was translating that Scott-Moncrieff enjoyed, not Proust as such. He did not start by translating Proust, nor only translate Proust once he had joined forces with him. His first translations were of *Beowulf* and the early French epic poem, the *Chanson de Roland*, whose gory, impetuous verses were a poor preparation for the coiled introspections of *Swann's Way*. For his version of the *Chanson de Roland* Scott-Moncrieff had awarded himself beta double plus, a mark literary translators are apt to favour, as being a fair compromise between their professional vanity and the chronic sense of having let the original down which haunts their working days. (The giving of marks in itself is a reminder that translation is a linguistic exercise first practised in a classroom, and that there will always be a sense of the competitive about it.)

During breaks from *A la recherche*, Scott-Moncrieff took refuge in the shorter and more matter-of-fact sentences of Stendhal (*The Charterhouse of Parma*) and in the plays of Pirandello. If he was drawn to Proust this may have been for technical rather than temperamental reasons, for he was not, judging by such descriptions as one can find of him, a very Proust-like man. But the relentless elaboration of Proust's sentences, the formidable extent of his knowledge and the effortless precision with which he analyses the most intricate states of mind, these offered an ultimate test of the examinee's powers.

We are rightly suspicious when a translator acquires a name, as Scott-Moncrieff did, because translation, to be good, must be self-effacing. If the translator gives the impression that he is blocking our view of the original, he exceeds his brief. The great virtuosos of literary translation of the past did just that, of course: Urquhart (with Rabelais), Florio (with Montaigne), Sir Richard Burton, Edward FitzGerald set themselves up to be conspicuous intermediaries and not mere servile transparencies. The languid but superior FitzGerald, for example, saw no virtue in sticking too closely to what poor old Omar Khayyam had written: 'It is an amusement to me to take what liberties I like with these Persians, who (as I think) are not Poets enough to frighten one from such excursions.'

Scott-Moncrieff was not of this piratical company. He was a genuine translator, unfailingly respectful of the text before him. There is a considerable, and very harmful, difference of tone between his English and Proust's French, as we shall see, but that does not prevent one from saluting an astonishing effort of translation, resourceful in its vocabulary, attentive to the logical development of Proust's sometimes hasty syntax, consistent in its English style over a length of a million words or more. (Scott-Moncrieff did not live to finish it: it was completed, rather clumsily, by Sydney Schiff.) *A la recherche* had found an English translator who was intellectually worthy of it and had found him at once: it did not have to wait, as so commanding a masterpiece might have expected to wait, to be matched with someone who had the understanding, the fluency and the stamina to cope with it.

No translation lasts for ever, however; even though the wording of the original does not change over time, the wording of its successive translations will. Classical works require to be re-translated with some regularity, because translations cannot help but date, they are of their own time, not the time of the original. The originals themselves do not date, they age, and as they do so, the gap widens between the language in which they were written and the 'same' language as it is written and spoken now. Indeed, that gap may widen to the point where a language we think of as our own acquires much of the unfamiliarity of a foreign language. Thus, only a specialist now finds it easy to read the classic works of Middle English and there is nothing philistine about producing a modernised text of Chaucer; in everything but name this is a translation of Chaucer, and each generation of readers may feel entitled to a new one, since a 'modern' Chaucer produced in the 1940s may well seem to be in need of modernisation itself by the 1990s.

Now, where modernisation is concerned, Scott-Moncrieff's Proust is a peculiar case. It was produced in the early twenties, but it was hardly made into the English of the twenties. This translation is a rarity: it was dated from the outset. And, unfortunately but naturally, that datedness was at once read back into the French original, with the harmful consequence that, ever since, those who read Proust in English come away with an anachronistic view of the sort of writer that he is. Scott-Moncrieff's English does not read as if it were contemporary with the prose standardly written after the First World War. If I were to characterise it in historical terms, I would say that it is Edwardian English, pre-1914, and the English moreover of someone who was set on sounding 'literary'. The stylistic register into which Scott-Moncrieff chose to translate is one that would have suited the first Proust, the youthful author of the tiresomely precious *Les Plaisirs et les jours*; it does not suit the infinitely more direct and prosaic author of *A la recherche*, one of whose needs it was to demonstrate how completely he had shed the callow mannerisms of his *fin-de-siècle* self.

Scott-Moncrieff's betrayal of Proust began with the English title he inflicted on the novel. The French title, *A la recherche du temps perdu*, is defiantly functional, it has nothing in the least ornate, let alone lyrical about it.* In one short phrase, it describes both the action of the novel and the purpose of the novelist: there is no excuse for not translating it as 'In search of lost time'. Scott-Moncrieff's preferred title comes instead from a Shakespeare sonnet, two lines from which he chose to quote on the title-page of *Swann's Way*:

> When to the sessions of sweet silent thought
> I summon up remembrance of things past.

These are exquisite lines of Elizabethan poetry on which the translator no doubt seized happily for their seeming aptness. In fact, they are the opposite of apt: their tone is wrong and so is their meaning. The novelist himself protested against the title in a letter he wrote to his English translator only weeks before he died. Scott-Moncrieff had missed, he complained, the 'deliberate amphibology' in the French. Once the 'Stalactites of the Past' and similar extravagances had been rejected, Proust had wanted to call the novel simply 'Le Temps perdu'. This is slightly ambiguous in French: it may mean 'lost time' (as in the English phrase, 'making up for lost time') or else 'wasted time' – either of which alternative readings is entirely suitable to the novel, given that *A la recherche* has to do not only with the restoration of a past believed to have been lost through being forgotten, but also with a past and present felt by the narrator to be wasted until such future time as he can overcome his culpable inertia and begin writing. The 'lost time' of the beginning would eventually be balanced out by the title of the novel's redemptive final section, *Le Temps retrouvé*, or 'Time recovered', and the 'A la recherche de' for which Proust eventually settled is a phrase serving to link the originary state of loss to the final state where that loss has been redeemed, so bringing out the all-important architectonics of the whole.

Scott-Moncrieff's 'things past' will not do, therefore, since those words

---

* Cf. some of the very fancy titles contemplated by Proust in a letter (undated) he wrote to his friend Reynaldo Hahn asking for his advice: 'The Stalactites of the Past', 'Reflections in the Patina', 'The Mirrors of the Dream', and so on.

carry no implication of loss. Nor will his 'remembrance' do, especially since, in the lines he is quoting, it occurs as the direct object of the verb form 'I summon up'. This compounds the misrepresentation of Proust's title. The thing that Proust claims specifically *not* to be doing in his novel is summoning up the past. *A la recherche* is a novel of memory that depends crucially on the Bergsonian distinction between voluntary and involuntary remembering, a distinction that Proust could confirm as existing from his own peculiarly rich experience of it. To summon up memories is a voluntary act, a getting of the past to do our bidding, as if we knew beforehand what we were going to find there. *A la recherche*, on the contrary, is a monument to the emotive power, the overwhelming completeness and the vivacity of the *un*summoned or involuntary memory. Proust had come to believe that the *real* past, the past as it actually was, is not recuperable by the intellect; it can return only if the intellect be somehow circumvented. Thus the narrator of the novel does not will himself to recall his childhood experience of Combray, it is given back to him in all its high significance by the accident of his tasting a piece of madeleine soaked in tea.

There is much to be read, then, into the deceptively plain French title, *A la recherche du temps perdu*; there is sadly little of the same kind to be read into the 'poetical' English one, *Remembrance of Things Past*: we have been carried out of philosophy and into literature. The change is symptomatic of the unhappy way in which Scott-Moncrieff contrived to play down the stringent intelligence of his author by conveying it in an English prose that is constantly looking to prettify. It's as if the translator had been taken aback by how acrid and how ruthless Proust can be in his exposure of the deep falsities of the inhabitants of the Parisian *beau monde*, and were determined to muffle its cruelty by the gentility of his English. Scott-Moncrieff's Proust is Proust made at least partly tame, a rather nicer, more clubabble fellow than the one known to his French readers.

In the 1980s, Proust's original English publishers at last decided that something remedial should be done with Scott-Moncrieff. They commissioned a revision of the entire text, from the late Terence Kilmartin. Kilmartin revised it in two ways. First, he took account of the new French text of the novel, which had appeared in 1954 when Pierre Clarac and André Ferré produced a fine new edition for the Bibliothèque de la Pléiade. The differences between this text and the one from which Scott-Moncrieff had worked were not enormous but they were significant, growing more frequent and more radical in the later sections. The variations introduced by Clarac and Ferré were based on the existing manuscript evidence as to what the novelist's own wishes had been. If the earlier text was sometimes faulty, that was largely Proust's own fault: his notorious method of rewriting his novel at the proof stage, and driving publisher and printers to distraction with his interpolations, transpositions and other second, third and fourth thoughts, meant that his directives were not always followed. And since he was still, when he died, deep in the correction of the later volumes, these suffered more than the rest in the printing.

Terence Kilmartin made many hundreds of changes, most of them very small, of a word or two at a time, to what Scott-Moncrieff wrote. He worked carefully and sensitively, but he still missed many chances of improving on the original, whether through diffidence, inadvertence or, which is most likely, fatigue. Editing a translation made by someone else is tedious, fiddly work and when the translation in question is as long as Scott-Moncrieff's, the task becomes altogether too much.

What he did, Kilmartin did well; the effect of his editing was certainly to sober Scott-Moncrieff down and make it more acceptably Proustian. Some small examples will show in what way. Where Proust's flatly descriptive phrase '*où l'eau bleuit*' had swelled in the excitable hands of Scott-Moncrieff into 'where the water glows with a blue lurking fire', Kilmartin reduced the swelling and translated it as 'glows blue' – though even 'glows' is overdoing things, when *bleuit* means no more than 'shows (or else turns) blue'. In Scott-Moncrieff, Proust's straightforward phrase '*comme le jour quand le soir tombe*' comes out as 'like the day when night gathers', where 'gathers' is a typical Scott-Moncrieff-ism, a poetaster's word, Kilmartin has 'like the daylight when night falls'. Again, Proust's *dévote*, used as a (mildly pejorative) epithet to describe a pious woman, becomes with Scott-Moncrieff 'instinct with piety' and with Kilmartin 'devout'. And finally, Proust's more or less oxymoronic combination of adjectives '*orageux et doux*' becomes Scott-Moncrieff's 'dear tempestuous', and Kilmartin's 'delightful, stormy', where the difference between 'tempestuous' and 'stormy' says it all: 'tempestuous' is not in Proust, 'stormy' is.

When translations date, they do not do so evenly: in a novel, translated dialogue dates more quickly than does translated narration or description. It is easy to see why, when the language that novelists put into the mouths of their speakers is so often intended by its colloquialism to display those same novelists' alertness and discrimination in reflecting the speech-changes of the day and the idiosyncrasies by which one speaker may be contrasted with another. Colloquialisms come a good deal into *A la recherche*, as enclitic marks on the diction of certain characters, serving at once to identify and to place them socially. Indeed, Proust makes greater use of speech in his novel than meets the eye – than literally meets the eye – because the spoken exchanges are introduced with only the skimpiest typographical indications and are not set apart from the surrounding narration as is the convention. This near-homogenisation of the printed page makes the contrast between the novelist's words and the words projected into the mouths of his characters the more striking.

Scott-Moncrieff does not give this contrast its due; the English that he puts into people's mouths is all of a piece with the rest and can on occasions quite miss the point. He is especially lax with the barbed vulgarisms that members of the Verdurin 'clan' go in for, for instance: their linguistic habits are intended by Proust to exhibit their ineradicable philistinism or mediocrity. I give two examples. When the dreadful Mme Verdurin claims that the young pianist whom she has taken under her wing is so brilliant as to have *enfoncé* (a transitive verb) two great virtuosos of the day, he has, according to Scott-Moncrieff, 'left both Planté and Rubinstein "sitting"'. As an English equivalent, this is weak, when the words Mme Verdurin has been given to speak should show her to be both ridiculous and possessive: Kilmartin's 'licked both Planté and Rubinstein hollow' is about right. Scott-Moncrieff also remains culpably deaf to the effects of indirect free speech, that favourite device of a novelist like Proust whereby phrases of a colloquial kind may be introduced into the narration without benefit of quotation marks but in such a way that we know at once that these words, whether spoken or merely thought, are ones appropriate to the character in question. Thus the words '*si ça lui chantait*' are slipped at one point by Proust into the narration, again *chez* Verdurin; they yield in Scott-Moncrieff the insipid 'if he felt inclined', which fails to declare itself as reported speech at all. Kilmartin again catches the tone ideally with 'if the spirit moved him' – a clichéd phrase that is purest Verdurin.

Finally, there are the indelicacies. There is no lack of bawdiness in Proust, who delights in putting the smuttiest thoughts into the smartest mouths and who gives free rein to such increasingly aggressive monsters of incivility as the baron de Charlus. Either because he didn't want to, or because his London publisher wouldn't let him, Scott-Moncrieff refused to be as scatologically explicit in English as Proust is in French: thus, a woman who in the French '*se soulage*' is said by Scott-Moncrieff to be 'doing something', but by Kilmartin to be 'relieving herself'; while another uninhibited character who exults in the thought that he can '*un peu les emmerder*' has to make do in Scott-Moncrieff with 'I can s-t on them' and wait sixty years for Kilmartin's 'shit on them'.

I have said that Kilmartin's revision of Scott-Moncrieff was on the right lines but insufficient. Only a few years after it was published, as if in recognition of this, the revision was itself revised, on the same right lines. This re-revision was likewise insufficient. The process is one that might go on indefinitely, the fact of the matter being that no translation flawed, as this one is, not by inaccuracies (there are impressively few of those) but by its style, can ever be made satisfactory in this piecemeal, schoolmasterly fashion. It would always have been simpler, and better, to have started to put Proust into English again from scratch.

In 1996, an entirely new English version of *A la recherche* was at last commissioned, by Penguin. It will be made not by a translator going it alone à la Scott-Moncrieff, but by six translators each doing one sixth of the whole. The arrangement is unusual, a division of translating labour inevitable no doubt for works of the size and diversity of the Bible, but audacious when asked to deal with the continuous work of a single author. Will it mean anglophone readers being given six rather different Prousts to read, once this *In Search of Lost Time* appears? Not if it has been edited with the patient and intelligent care that Proust's incomparable novel demands, to make sure that these six translators know their place and keep all of them consistently close to the substance and style of the original. I am one of the six translators myself, and extremely happy to be so. Proust is not an especially difficult writer to translate, but he is for sure the most rewarding, so infinitely well-stocked, so lucid and so frequently amusing is the mind whose thoughts you are hoping to reproduce. And, as if that weren't enough, one can persuade oneself daily, as a good competitor should, that one is on the way to doing better for Proust than did C.K. Scott-Moncrieff.

11

HENRI BARBUSSE

A fragile young poet in the 1890s, writing tearful *fin-de-siècle* verses, and by the 1920s an ultra on the Communist Left, proclaiming the achievements of Joseph Stalin: such was the curious course that Henri Barbusse's public life took, from his birth in northern France in 1873 to his death while on a visit to Moscow in 1935.

It is the early poetry, not the later politics, that must count as an aberration. Barbusse was born into the dissident classes, to a father from a Protestant family who took 1789 seriously and was an ardent secularist and Republican. But it was the sequence of formative events he lived through that drove him away from literature and into ideology: the Dreyfus affair, when he was in his twenties, which created the public space from where the new class of moralising 'intellectuals' could aspire to lecture the French nation; then, post-Dreyfus, the rallying to the army and to the militant nationalism of the *revanchards*, who looked forward to another war with Germany as the opportunity for France to take its revenge for the defeat of 1870; then, *post hoc* and perhaps *propter hoc*, the horrendous blood-letting of the war when it came, experienced by Barbusse at first-hand in Flanders; in 1917, first the February and subsequently the October Bolshevik Revolution in Russia, with its promise that a just, egalitarian society might at last be realised on earth; and finally, the threat to European peace newly posed in the late 1920s and early 1930s by the rise of German and Italian Fascism.

History had supplied reasons enough for the dandified young poet to enlist among the revolutionary hopefuls, though, true to his literary beginnings, Barbusse's ambitions for the future of his country and of the human race were always set self-defeatingly high. The redemptive ideas in which he dealt in the years following 1918, as he moved with growing stridency from an outraged humanism and internationalism to an eventual acceptance that violence was legitimate in a revolutionary cause, were absolute and uncompromising. They were so because they were surely required to suppress an ineradicable pessimism, to which, if it had been something of an affectation for the 1890s poet, Barbusse had good reason to hold after what he experienced in the trenches from 1914 to 1915. He took up generous causes, notably that of peace, yet so rigidly that it was the fight on their behalf, more than the causes as such, that seems to have been the attraction for him.

Barbusse's first reactions to the bleakness of the human condition were on the faint side. In the poems of *Les Pleureuses*, published in 1895, he retreats into the quiet of a bedroom or the shade of a fountain to make a subdued poetry from his unhappiness. Some of it is purest Verlaine, as when he writes, of inanimate objects, that 'Elles sont douces avec nous,/Caressant nos âmes craintives./Là-bas, les branches sont plaintives,/Tant nous avons pleuré dessous.' (They are gentle with us,/Caressing our fearful souls./There, the branches are plaintive,/So many are the tears we have shed beneath them.) There was poetic promise here, of a small kind, and Mallarmé, a teacher at the Paris lycée that Barbusse had attended, loyally subscribed to his former pupil's gift: 'You are, my dear friend, a poet . . . one of the best among us.' At the same time, Barbusse's future father-in-law, the *chef de file* of the Parnassian poets, Catulle Mendès, described him as 'the most remote and most exquisite of dreamers'. Which for a beginning poet was praise worth having; but 'remote' and a 'dreamer' was what Barbusse remained, even after he had abandoned poetry for good and begun to put himself forward as the apostle of an impossible 'simplicity' in politics.

A hundred years on, it's not hard to find signs, even in the lyrics of *Les Pleureuses*, premonitory of the ambition that was ultimately to turn Barbusse into an embattled director of consciences. He was aware from the start of the priestly possibilities for the writer in a secularising society – not for nothing had the aged Victor Hugo bent down to embrace him at a wedding when he was a small boy. The writer is empowered to play the role of intellectual – to contest authority and offer political guidance – because he possesses what Barbusse the poet calls 'the great benefit of language'. There are moments, even in *Les Pleureuses*, when he looks forward to one day expressing an 'implacable' truth on behalf of those who are insufficiently articulate to express it for themselves. (That 'implacable' is ominous, coming as it does from a future Stalinist.)

This was very precisely the role Barbusse took for himself twenty years later in his best-known book, *Le Feu* (Under fire). This novel, written in 1915 and published in 1916, was the most effective thing by far that he ever wrote, an account of life and death on the western front so unrelentingly grim as to strip the war once and for all of any notion that it might be either glorious or rational: *Le Feu* was an anti-war book that had sold more than three hundred thousand copies by the time of the Armistice in 1918 (and been read in England, too, where the profoundly disillusioned soldier-poets, Siegfried Sassoon and Wilfred Owen, both admired it).

It is written in two very distinct linguistic registers, the correct French of the narration being set against the unfamiliar argot of the soldiers in the dialogue. The use Barbusse makes of a rough, sometimes incomprehensible, trench demotic goes beyond any demands of realism; it is a political gesture. His private soldiers (no officers appear in the novel), with their unschooled syntax and obscure vocabulary, require an interpreter, someone of education who is fitted to mediate between them and the bourgeois reader; and this is Barbusse's own function as the more or less invisible narrator of the book. There is a moment in it when, recognising his intellectual superiority to themselves, the soldiers – who have earlier commented on the predictable absence of writers and intellectuals from the front line – ask that he should one day testify in public to the terrible truth of their ordeal, such being the new and urgent responsibility of whoever enjoys the 'great benefit of language'.

Barbusse had earned the position of privilege that he allots himself in *Le Feu*. He had joined the army in 1914 even though he was already forty-one years old and in uncertain health; and he proved himself a brave soldier, being decorated twice before he was invalided out. But *Le Feu* is far from being the documentary account of warfare that many who read it at the time may have mistaken it for. Its literary model was perhaps *La Débâcle*, Emile Zola's corpse-strewn, Naturalist novel about the humiliation of the French army in 1870. But Barbusse outdoes Zola in the dreamlike intensity with which he details the mutilations and destruction inflicted on men's bodies by bullets, shells, barbed wire and Flanders mud. The novel, he later said, was more important for its 'tendencies' than its documentation, and the most compelling tendency of all is that of healthy young men towards a gruesome and accelerated death. The novel is overpoweringly marked by what an Italian critic called its '*terribilismo*'.

To help ensure that it would not be read simply as a work of naive, and topical, realism, Barbusse began and ended it with scenes that are openly visionary, the one set among TB patients in an Alpine sanatorium situated literally *au-dessus de la mêlée*, the other on the battlefield itself. Both are designed to transcend the immediate horror and stupidity of the war in the direction of a future in which, as he says near the end of the book, 'entente between the democracies, entente between the immensities, the rising up of the peoples of the world, the brutally simple faith' must prevail. In the light of the blind slaughter that has continued all the way through, these final grandiloquent phrases may seem permissible, as looking forward to 'a universal republic' in which there will be no place for nationalisms, hence for war. Once the war was over, however, and Barbusse was looking to persuade the 'peoples of the world' that now was the time to rise up against the capitalist order which had sent millions of its 'slaves' to their deaths and had now resumed without a qualm its economic exploitation of the survivors, the extremism of his prescriptions became all too apparent.

The hallucinatory, didactic element in *Le Feu* assimilates it to the more obviously 'literary' novels Barbusse had published before the war. In the first of these, *Les Suppliants* (The supplicants), which appeared in 1903, the young hero, Maximilien Desanzac, envisions the destruction of the bourgeois world into which he resents having been born, but his one attempt to change it is a fiasco: in a hopeful moment of anarchism he builds a bomb with which to wreck his school, but manages only to blow out a window, after which he retires from the struggle, preferring the consolations of privacy to the hazards of activism.

Barbusse's second novel, *L'Enfer* (Hell), which came out five years after *Les Suppliants*, is more clearly indicative of the way in which his thought was evolving in these pre-war years. In itself, it's a dated book, dusty with the cobwebs of his earlier mannerism; seen, however, as a book transitional between the tormented inwardness of such as Desanzac and the will radically to purify a rotten society, the novel gains in substance. It contains all of Barbusse's youthful disgust with the ways of both God and man, but the assault on them is delivered with a new ferocity and a new precision of aim. The social topography of the novel is vague and the dialogue stylised, yet *L'Enfer* relates to an actual, not an imaginary, state of society. Looking back on it, Barbusse felt he had never been more extreme in his opinions than he was here, by which he meant particularly the attacks he makes on Christian belief and on the anti-German jingoism so widespread in France before 1914.

At this time, Barbusse was still an advocate of Tolstoyan non-violence, an absolute pacifist for whom war, or anything other than a peaceful revolution, was unacceptable on any terms at all. He was also, however, his father's son in being a fideist of Reason; and it was this arrogant, coercive rationalism that came eventually to outweigh any gentler philosophy in Barbusse, until the one-time man of peace proved able to accommodate himself to the barbaric logic of Stalin's terrorism, on the grounds that not to do so would be weakly sentimental. Barbusse after 1919, like Sartre after 1945, wanted to be seen as the fearless partisan of intellectual rigour, wherever it might lead, not as someone whose politics were founded on a vacuous humanism.

The truth was that the 'brutally simple faith' adumbrated on the last page of *Le Feu* might well require brutality if it were ever to be realised, because the peculiarly disturbing lesson of the war for a humanist such as Barbusse was that fellow members of the human race were quite ready, or even keen, to kill one another simply because they happened to have been born on different sides of a national frontier. It was all very well one of Barbusse's consumptive 'seers' lamenting, as he looks down on the battle, 'Two armies pitted against one another, is one great army committing suicide'; the sense of solidarity among the combatants that might have overriden nationalism is lacking. Barbusse himself could not forget that French soldiers had been prepared, when ordered, to form firing squads and execute those of their comrades who had been condemned for desertion. Given which, the momentary dream of 1916–7, shared by Barbusse, that the Socialist parties of France and Germany might together persuade their respective armies to withdraw from the war that their governments were set on continuing, seems peculiarly utopian.

There was after *L'Enfer* a new asceticism about Barbusse. That novel is full of what a critic at the time called 'exasperated sensuality' – which was no doubt one reason why it appeared in a new English translation in the mid sixties, even if by then Barbusse's perversities had come to seem pallid. During the 1914–18 war, however, sensuality, 'exasperated' or not, could be seen as a potentially demoralising distraction from the nation's cause. In 1917, passages from *L'Enfer* were read out in the Chambre des Députés, its apparently fortuitous conjunction of internationalist and secularist propaganda with scenes of sexual deviation being a handy card for the more bellicose deputies to play in their wish to discredit the best-selling pacifist author of *Le Feu*.

The novel's perversions take place in a single hotel room, where they are observed by a sensitive young man through a hole in the wall. His situation is that of the voyeur; but rather than a voyeur he is a seer: it's evidence of human ignominy he is after, not second-hand sexual kicks. To take a room in a fictional hotel is inevitably to book oneself into a microcosm, and what Barbusse's young man sees is offered to him as the dark truth about the corruption of personal and especially of sexual relations in a decaying society. He is, it is stressed, in no way extraordinary, but he has been elevated into a position of privilege, independent of the normal relationships that might otherwise lead him to identify with the human agents he is observing. He has no job and no friends, and through his peephole he can see other people without them seeing him: that is, record their behaviour without affecting it. The hotel room has become a laboratory, and the observer-hero is living out the hopeful claim Barbusse was to make later, in a novel – or rather, tract – of 1919 called *Clarté* (Clarity, or else Light), that 'Social science is a form of geometry.' At the time when he wrote *L'Enfer*, he was also editing a popular science magazine called *Je sais tout* (I know everything), and he uses science to help him make his morbid case, launching in the course of the book into two biological threnodies, dedicated one to the consumptive tubercle and the other to the different sorts of grub that feed off corpses.

Barbusse believed, as so many moralists unavailingly have over the centuries, that were everyone brought to share his own troubled awareness of mortality, human beings would come to their senses and stop killing one another. This awareness was fundamental to his postwar activism and *Clarté* is the novel in which, more explicitly than in *Le Feu*, he traces the process by which he was himself finally converted into a full-time propagandist. The book's hero, Simon Paulin, has a name patently echoing that of Christianity's great convert, St Paul. As a result of what he goes through during the war as an infantryman, Paulin is radically transformed, from a docile office-worker into a Barbussian sloganeer who believes that an intellectual commitment to the truth – Barbusse's truth – must lead on to a commitment to world revolution. This transformation involves Paulin sexually as well as intellectually. Before the war he had been a womaniser and an unfaithful husband. During the war, however, he learns his lesson, more than a little crudely, when he finds himself lusting in the old manner after a local farmer's wife. He can't stop himself from making advances to her, but the instant he does so, the woman is blown to bits by a German shell, fired in response to the novelist's punitive requirements. The newly austere, postwar Paulin substitutes 'tenderness' for the 'love' he had believed in when he was younger, which was simply another name by which to dissemble his aggressive sexual appetite. Only in a shared 'tenderness', all passion spent, suggests Barbusse, can there be equality between men and women and, by miraculous extension, between all the members of the human race. Sensuality has now to be sacrificed for a higher end.

Clarté is a mawkish novel that ends mawkishly, in the realisation of what Barbusse wants us to see as an ideal state of equality between Paulin and his wife. That equality is granted, however, on the man's terms and seems more like a final stage in his wife's grateful submission to his wishes. And read allegorically, that is to say, in political terms, her ready compliance is more sinister than uplifting, since if she is being asked to rehearse the part allotted in Barbusse's schemes to the previously mute or leaderless proletariat, Paulin, it seems, remains the one, the intellectual of the two, who determines the conditions on which their joint salvation will be won. The novelist has tried to disguise his hero's authoritarianism, but unsuccessfully.

Clarté was also the name given to the intellectual movement that Barbusse helped to found soon after the war ended. By now he had further grounds for both pessimism and optimism. The pessimism arose from the recognition, shared by many in France and elsewhere, that the Versailles peace terms were vindictive when they should have been generous and almost certainly meant that the pre-war *revanchisme* of the French militarists would now migrate to a defeated Germany (as it did). The countervailing ground for optimism was the success of the Bolsheviks in Russia, incomplete as yet in 1919, with the White armies still in the field, but on the way to a hopeful finality. Barbusse had a model to hand of a society founded, as he believed, on the extreme egalitarian – or 'simple' – principles he had been preaching.

The times were propitious for it, but the Clarté movement was not a success; it collapsed within two years. It did so partly because it failed to address those whom it sought in principle to mobilise, the working class. Thanks to the real and poignant camaraderie he had known in the army, Barbusse believed he was now in effect part of the proletariat himself. 'It was through them,' he wrote of his former comrades, 'that I, a bourgeois writer, was able to abandon that kind of abstract idealism that is the particular sin of intellectuals. It was through them that I was put in direct touch with the working class.' Yet his postwar activities display him as every bit as much an abstract idealist as he had been in his unregenerate days before 1914, the one great difference being that he was now more likely to be listened to, as the author of *Le Feu*.

Barbusse interpreted the war in that book in misleadingly narrow class terms. In his justification, let me add that these were the terms in which he had seen it from the start. Writing in *L'Humanité*, then still a Socialist newspaper, in August 1914, to explain how it was that he, a pacifist, had decided to enlist, he said: 'This war is a social war which will mark the decisive step – perhaps the definitive step – in the fulfilment of our [Socialist] cause.' And as a 'social war' is how it is portrayed in *Le Feu* and in *Clarté*, a war in which only the working class appears, whether on the French or, occasionally, on the German side. The officers are not shown; they are the class enemy, the guilty but invisible representatives of the callous, self-serving hierarchy that has sent all these men to their pointless deaths. The war for Barbusse the novelist is a conspiracy of the masters against the 'slaves'.

The *Clarté* movement had for its subtitle 'league of intellectual solidarity for the triumph of the international cause'. It attracted some support among intellectuals both inside and outside France, but never more than a few thousand of them. It began to break up when Barbusse went beyond its original, more moderate prospectus and came out in support of the Bolshevik concept of armed revolution. Many of his associates in Clarté refused to travel with him in that dangerous direction, the most prominent of them, Romain Rolland, seeing it as a sellout and an abandonment of those universal principles of justice and peace he believed the movement should stand for. Later, ironically, Barbusse himself was outflanked on the Left by a minority who wanted Clarté to become more active in a revolutionary sense, and who founded a journal, also called *Clarté*, to promote their aims.

Barbusse joined the French Communist Party in 1923, but as a member entitled by his literary celebrity and his well-known internationalism to be spared the full rigours of Party discipline. Both Lenin and, after his death, Stalin had soon grasped how useful to them prominent Western pacifists and internationalists like Barbusse could be, by pursuing their fundamentally Communist aims in apparent independence of Moscow. Stalin is reported to have told Barbusse face to face, early in the 1930s, that he could best serve the cause first, by not being a Communist; second, by always keeping within the law; and third, by writing about other things than the Soviet Union. The policy was that sometimes referred to as 'frontism', whereby the Comintern could manipulate and subsidise left-wing political activities in Western Europe without having to come out into the open.

Barbusse fell in with it readily enough. Throughout the 1920s and 1930s he was seldom silent, taking a prominent part in a confusing succession of 'front' organisations, the Ligue contre l'impérialisme et l'oppression coloniale, the Comité contre la guerre et le fascisme and the so-called Amsterdam-Pleyel congresses – the first held in Amsterdam, the second in the Salle Pleyel in Paris, which were called to rally support against war and against Fascism, even though by now it was quite widely appreciated that the inspiration for these groupings had come from Soviet Russia. In 1928, Barbusse founded *Monde*, a political and cultural weekly, which began as a Communist paper but quickly became rather surprisingly eclectic, publishing articles sufficiently far removed from Soviet orthodoxy to get it banned in Moscow.

But then Barbusse himself could be eclectic, choosing, for example, four years after he joined the Party, to write a book in praise of Jesus Christ. His is not, however, the Jesus of the Gospels but an atheistic class-warrior whose revolutionary teachings on behalf of the poor were all too soon incorporated and betrayed by an oppressive church. Barbusse imposes the present audaciously on the past in arguing that Christianity was originally 'a mass and a class movement', as if those emotive terms were sufficiently well-defined to be inserted into history at whatever point he fancied.

The Barbusse of these later years dwelt indeed in a starkly dialectical world, in which the victims of oppression are characterised by a heroic innocence, while their capitalist oppressors are wickedly clear-sighted in effecting their purposes. Thus black Africans suffering exploitation in the colonies are 'infinitely gentle by nature', until such time as the agents of their corruption arrive from metropolitan France; while the Russian 'peasants' sent to fight on the western front in 1916, who demand to be sent home when the news comes of the February Revolution, are instead deliberately sacrificed or else massacred by their 'monstrous' French commanders. This is sadly elementary stuff, and a sign of how blind or contemptuous of his audience Barbusse had by now become. But safe inside the carapace of his own 'simple' ideas, he had grown remarkably authoritarian. The Clarté movement had had as one of its declared purposes to educate the masses politically, to be an organ of enlightenment, an 'encyclopae-dia', like the great eighteenth-century *Encyclopédie*, whose publication had helped to bring down the ancien régime. But the postwar masses hadn't wanted to know and Barbusse as he aged gave up on them. They were not up to what he asked of them. And so, if the Bolsheviks had found that it took too long to 'educate' the Russian proletariat to think in the manner appropriate to a proletariat, he was prepared to see it violently purged.

Barbusse became a regular grace-and-favour visitor to the Soviet Union. But, like other visiting celebrities, he managed to see nothing he was not invited to see. There is a very bitter description of him in Moscow in 1927 to be found in the *Memoirs* of the revolutionary maverick Victor Serge. Barbusse had once been Serge's 'idol', but he now found him 'disgusting' with his complaints about his

— relatively speaking, very comfortable — living conditions in Moscow and, far worse, his evasiveness when the question of Stalin's terror tactics arose:

> When I mentioned the repression, he acted as though he had a headache, as though he didn't understand, as though he were rising to wondrous heights of thought; 'Tragic fate of the revolution, breadth, depths, yes, yes . . . oh my friend!' With a kind of cramp in my jaw I saw I was face to face with the human incarnation of hypocrisy.

Serge is a hostile witness, but this cruel description seems horribly apt, of a writer once eager to use the 'great benefit of language' for the general good but who ended by using it to benefit and protect mainly himself. Barbusse died in Moscow, of pneumonia, which he caught while discussing the making of a film about Stalin. He was taken back to Paris to be buried, and his funeral, in the Père Lachaise, was an event, a time for the French Left to turn out and be counted. The coffin was draped in the red flag and behind it walked girls carrying copies of his books on red cushions.

Barbusse would, I fear, have approved this *mise en scène* of revolutionary pomp, for the sin of which he was by the end of his life most conspicuously guilty was not the hypocrisy Serge accuses him of but vanity. Vanity is the intellectual's familiar recourse against the sense of his own ineffectiveness. The causes Barbusse had lent his name to — pacifism, internationalism, the proletarian revolution, anti-Fascism — had all of them, in practical terms, floundered or failed. As the subject of so ceremonious a valediction at the Père Lachaise, this tireless but frustrated beneficiary of language was simply having his final say.

12

LOUIS-FERDINAND CÉLINE

In November 1931, *La Gazette médicale* in Paris carried a curiously vehement piece on the treatment of bleeding gums. It was signed Dr Louis F. Destouches and it took issue, in a blizzard of exclamation marks, with the medicine of the schools, asking what help the professoriat and the textbooks were to a confused general practitioner who wanted to do something simply therapeutic for his patients. In the final few lines, this irascible, suspiciously literate broadside modulated into a puff for Sanogyl, a new remedial toothpaste. It was the last thing that Dr Destouches published before his prodigious debut in fiction one year later, as Louis-Ferdinand Céline, the author of *Voyage au bout de la nuit* (Journey to the end of the night).

There were foretastes of the writer Céline in the truculent medical journalism of Dr Destouches, but nothing to compare with the epochal vituperation with which the *Voyage*, like all of Céline's books, is filled; if he was to keep a practice the doctor required a cover. Céline was his cover, a name borrowed from this less than family-minded man's one tolerable relative, the grandmother who had been a fount of refreshing sarcasm for him when he was a small boy but who had died when he was ten. The *Voyage* raised the name Céline instantly to the heights, but he kept Destouches on, too, as an alias to practise medicine under, up to, during and even after the Second World War.

Céline earned money and leisure for himself from his books but he never let doctoring go altogether. His surgery hours in Clichy-la-Garenne, a working-class quarter of northern Paris, were the writer's field work, turning him into the licensed voyeur of the hurts and privations of his patients. Medicine had no cure for death, so his regard for its usefulness was limited, but he valued the company of the poor and unhealthy because they had two strong reasons to feel insecure and to know life for the harsh and precarious experience it was. So Dr Destouches stayed on, as a benefactor and as someone interestingly distinct from the impious Céline, the foul-mouthed anarchist who had written the *Voyage* and who in the late 1930s became the most crazily abusive of French anti-Semites.

Bleeding gums were just what the doctor ordered, to make Céline's case against the abstractions of academic medicine. As forms of bodily decay they are neither distinguished nor complicated enough to interest the Faculties. Céline cared only about treating disease, he resisted the idea that he should understand it as well; he put welfare ahead of technique. This, however, does not make him into a saintly altruist, toiling magnanimously in the back streets of Paris; his motive for practising as and where he did was as much revenge on the bourgeois medical establishment of which he had briefly been a part but with which he had broken, and that in its moneyed smugness knew nothing, he protested, of the abjections of proletarian life.

This was a role he had first prescribed for himself in the extraordinary thesis that he presented when he was qualifying as a mature student in the early 1920s (had the medical professors been as dim and narrow-minded as Céline claimed they were, they would have thrown it out). There was more of biography than of medical information in what Céline wrote, and years afterwards the thesis was published, on the back of his first novels, as *La Vie et l'oeuvre de Semmelweis* (The life and work of Semmelweis). Semmelweis was a gratifying discovery, a Hungarian doctor in the mid nineteenth century who was the first to realise that puerperal fever often proved fatal to mothers in labour wards because obstetric staff did not sterilise their hands or instruments and so passed it on. He was not listened to by the authorities in Vienna, where he worked, and young women continued to die. In the end, in Céline's telling of the story, Semmelweis is literally maddened by his failure to get others to see that he is right and infects himself deliberately and fatally. Céline had the facts of the case somewhat askew, but never mind; he tells a disheartening story with precocious verve and takes an unholy pleasure in its moral: that Semmelweis, genius, poet and, finally, outcast, was punished for having wished his fellow human beings too well.

Even in the functional columns of *La Gazette médicale*, Céline had to air his consuming grievance, that life is ghastly but that not everyone seems to know it. He did know it, he had had ghastly experiences, and if the world was to go on fiddling while he alone burned, then he would write his ghastly experiences up and share his hard-earned misanthropy with others. The *Voyage* is a formidable, monstrously accomplished start to this programme, the first instalment of an oeuvre all of which was to be devoted to the more or less apocalyptic portrayal of human society in moments of disintegration. Céline's finest books – the *Voyage*, *Mort à crédit* (Death on the instalment plan) and two that he wrote after 1945, *D'Un château l'autre* (Castle to castle) and *Nord* (North) – are a virulent commentary on what he wanted us to know he had been through in his life, from a stinted, inhumane childhood in Paris in the opening years of the century to a last decade of sour, fulminating reclusion on the outskirts of Paris after 1951.

Voyage au bout de la nuit is a novel narrated in the first person, and what a first person: Dr Bardamu, the most blackly humorous and disenchanted voice in all of French fiction. Like Dr Destouches, Bardamu practises in a poor quarter of Paris, but a quarter now renamed Garenne-Rancy (*ranci* = rancid), and in a house which can be reached along not Destouches's own rue d'Alsace, but the boulevard de la Révolte, past not one cemetery but two. Such are the distortions by which Céline set about re-organizing the topography of his own life into one so named as to display his morbid beliefs about life in general. When nervous challenges came, from local people who thought they might have recognised themselves or their surroundings, he replied: 'You have to blacken, and to blacken yourself.'

We are used to a literature that sets out to compensate the writer for his checks and fiascos, and we allow him his dab or two of glory to jolly up the picture, but Céline's novels offer a stranger form of compensation, as he savages himself for any idealism he may once have felt. He cannot seemingly forgive himself for having sometimes acted or believed in such a way as to deny the incurable viciousness of human life, and in everything he wrote an empty rhetoric of hopefulness is brought into conflict with the ignoble argot of experience. For intimate reasons, lying beyond the reach of hindsight, Céline had decided that argot must always win, and so he sets about him with his black brush.

If there is light amidst so much darkness, it is shed, faintly, by a wild, oceanic dream of freedom from all human attachments or obligations: a dream that there is no way of realising. At the end of the *Voyage*, the girl, Madelon, demands of her boyfriend Robinson that he return her love. Sex with him is not enough; she requires the surrender of his freedom. Robinson – the solitary Crusoe figure – refuses her, telling her brutally that 'the whole of life' stands between them. He quotes the grimness of that 'whole of life' at her in order to escape imprisonment by her passion. Madelon's answer is to shoot him dead as they drive home in a taxi. This is an oddly cinematic conclusion to the novel. The point, however, is that the louche, cynical Robinson has proved himself at the last to be a Célinian hero by his refusal to pretend to feelings he does not have and to compromise his autonomy.

Robinson's journey has ended, where such existential journeys must, in death; and death is awfully unmysterious in Céline, less mysterious, as he once remarked, than a game of cribbage. His writing is never more hectic and Rabelaisian than when he asks that we interpret a particular journey allegorically, as the trajectory of a whole life compressed perhaps into a few hours or days: the excursion to England, for example, in his second novel, *Mort à crédit*, which turns into a grotesque rout of vomiting passengers on a cross-Channel ferry that is made to serve as a Ship of seasick Fools. Or, for another example out of many, the train journey across Germany that Céline takes in his own person in *D'Un château l'autre* to attend the funeral of a Vichy Frenchman. The train, dug out from some weedy siding, is an absurd rococo relic of the last Kaiser, and on their way home to their Bavarian château of Sigmaringen, the party of Frenchmen are joined in it by a crowd of German children being evacuated to Switzerland. In no time, busy little fingers have made a shambles of the plush and velvet, and the smart military uniforms are reduced to shreds.

But it is the *Voyage* which contains the most revealing of all Céline's journeys, that of Bardamu to the heart of darkness in French colonial Africa. The name of the ship he travels on is a typical combination of pomp and the sort of physiological circumstance traditionally used to deflate pomp: the *Amiral Bragueton* (*braguette* = trouser flies). With the single exception of Bardamu, all the passengers – soldiers and colonial officials with their wives – are travelling at government expense. The sense of isolation and injustice which this fact provokes in Bardamu gets more and more acute, until he has developed a fine persecution complex. In order to defend himself he begins to meditate with an ugly delight on all the imperfections of the perishable and increasingly malodorous flesh that surrounds him, until finally, confronted with his aloofness by the ship's officers, he decides that survival is what counts and forces himself into grovelling contortions of jingoism to convince all those on board that he is really one of them. He dissembles his ferocious independence, that is, by the free and perfectly insincere play of language.

The elevation of bodily survival to the status of an absolute value has to be measured, however, against the courage under fire that Céline had long before displayed as a soldier. He in fact enlisted as a regular in the French army in

1912, and in the first months of the war, in 1914, he became a minor hero. He volunteered to carry a vital message near the front line and on the way back was wounded by shrapnel, an exploit that earned him acclaim in an illustrated paper and the Médaille militaire. Afterwards, however, Céline played down the gallantry and played up the wound: a smashed right arm only, according to the official records, but the source according to him of the headaches and tinnitus that he suffered from throughout the rest of his life – in extreme fits of self-commiseration he even hinted at a wartime trepanning.

Destouches the army volunteer had been a French patriot of the pre-1914 kind, and Céline will not forgive him for his naivety. His military experience is treated with unqualified derision in the *Voyage*. There, Bardamu enlists with all the rationality of a lemming making for the cliffs, when he gets carried away by the sound of a military band marching through the streets. He follows the music and, just as he is beginning to sense that this is unwise, the barrack gates are clanged shut behind him – by civilians, naturally. After which, the wartime passages of the novel contain no heroics, only the crassness and the physical horror of battle.

Once the wounded Bardamu is back among the civilians of Paris, with their braying patriotism, his exploits are versified by an effete young poet and recited at the Comédie-Française. The audience is easily stirred to paroxysms of patriotism and of sentimental attachment to the gallant *poilus* at the front, but Bardamu's own, less exalted idea of an appropriate reward for his bravery is to be able to sleep with the actress who has been eulogising him on the stage. Even in this he is disappointed, because another war hero gets in first.

The parade that Céline makes of his sensuality in his books may well derive from an incapacity to expose or to dramatise his deeper feelings. He has, on the other hand, an enduring aesthetic (or perhaps voyeuristic) regard for the human body, and for women's bodies especially. As a man he loved the ballet; he wrote for it, and he lived with one dancer – dedicating the *Voyage* to her – before he married another. The terrible mutilation or outright destruction of bodies that he had witnessed in 1914 is the main source of Céline's later pacifism, which was of an absolute kind. When, in the pamphlet of 1938 entitled *L'Ecole des cadavres* (School for corpses), he proposes that a peace pact should be signed between France and Hitler's Germany, he can claim that this is a truly patriotic solution to the deepening crisis because it will keep millions of young French bodies intact. Better fascism than another war: Céline was far from alone among First World War veterans in thinking that way.

It was thus hardly a political position, for he had no coherent politics. Doctors at least had something they could bring to a suffering human race in the shape of medicine; politicians and ideologues had less than nothing to offer. All abstract schemes of social betterment were, so far as Céline was concerned, futile. In the mid 1930s, he went to Russia, to try and collect the royalties that had accumulated there from the Russian translation of the *Voyage*. He found in Soviet society no sign of a dawn in the east. On the contrary: on his return to France he wrote a brief pamphlet, *Mea culpa*, in which he rejects Communism out of hand as being both glib and mechanistic, saying that it gilds the pill about human nature by professing an optimism which at least the medieval Christians had avoided.

Céline's own ideas as to how society might be regenerated were simple, insultingly so. It was no good humankind trying to think its way out of trouble; rationalist projects such as that put forward by Karl Marx could only fail, bloodily. If there is hope for us, it is to be found among those who act instinctively, among children or animals. The anarchic German children who lay the train waste in *D'Un château l'autre* are admirable in Céline's eyes for instinctively vandalising the outward signs – the uniforms and other trappings – by which we conceal our animal nakedness and vulnerability; this is Céline the atheist in his role of prepare-to-meet-thy-doom evangelist. (There is an equivalent moment in the *Voyage* when Robinson suggests that the ultimate in wisdom for a frightened soldier is to surrender to the enemy stark naked.) Also in *D'Un château l'autre*, it is Céline's pets, his cats and dogs, that recognise the footsteps of his returning wife, in a show of instinctive benevolence that he chooses to compare with the futilities of Einstein's science or Sartre's philosophy ('Hegelballs' is his name for that).

Heart, not brains, is what people need, and what, according to Céline, they now lack. 'Life isn't a question of heart' is the conclusion that Ferdinand, the narrator of *Mort à crédit*, comes to, after reflecting on the profound disappointments that have embittered the life of his father. In this novel, the defeat of the heart is symbolised on a grand scale by the career of Costal des Pereires, a balloonist and inventor who dominates the later pages of the book. Costal is an ambiguous mixture of charlatan and hero, whose fortunes are precisely figured in the balloon with which he has travelled France entertaining village crowds. With each bumpy landing it becomes a thing of more and more shreds and patches, until at last it is earthbound and due to be replaced by the aeroplanes of a new generation. Mechanical progress has won and we are prepared to regret it. Yet Céline still feels the need to persecute this giant vessel of his own disappointments, and after his death Costal is deflated like his own balloon when it turns out that his real name was nothing so majestic as Costal des Pereires, but Punais, which is only one letter short of the French word for a bug (*punaise*).

Hot air is what keeps Costal aloft; hot air is also what keeps Céline aloft, or that passionate upthrust of words by which he will work his passage in a world that does not deserve him. Passionate they may be, but those words did not come easily, and one of Céline's more justified grievances was against the assumption of critics that prose as scathing as his must be spontaneous, that he was therefore an artless writer. He was the opposite, he cared for what he wrote down to the smallest detail. (Report had it that he padlocked the manuscript of the *Voyage* to his wrist when setting out to deliver it to the publisher.) In a testamentary aside in his last book, *Rigodon*, which he finished revising on the day he died, he provides against any posthumous betrayal of his manuscript by underwriting it down to the last comma and refusing to have it edited with mere common sense, which is 'the death of rhythm'. Music – 'my little music': the phrase recurs over and over in his later books – was what he wanted his prose to have, and what very often it does have; because music persuades, it has the power to carry those who hear it away, as it had once carried Bardamu away.

Rigodon in the event was a somewhat croaky swan song, but along with *D'Un château l'autre* and *Nord* it makes a spectacular trilogy out of Céline's experiences in Germany in 1944 and 1945, after he had prudently decamped from Paris and the incipient nastiness of the *épuration*, fomented in his own case, or so he boasted, by murderous anathemata against him broadcast by the Free French in London. With his wife Lucette (Lili), an actor friend Le Vigan and the cat Bébert (named, revealingly, after a sick child in the *Voyage* that Bardamu is unable to save), Céline went first to Baden-Baden, then to Zornhof near Berlin, to Sigmaringen, the Bavarian asylum of the Vichy government and scene of *D'Un château l'autre* and finally to Denmark, where he spent two years in prison on charges of collaboration and from where he only returned to Paris after the amnesty of 1951.

There, behind his doctor's brass plate, his barbed wire and his mastiffs, Céline went on writing, eventually recapturing, in the trilogy, much of the misanthropic verve that had made his first books so compelling. The trilogy is stridently self-conscious as Céline's hardships are rolled into public view item by item and the narrative of his past halted for imprecations against his poverty, against the intrusions of journalists and others out to pillory him, and, above all, against the 'literary' life of Paris, in all its venal triviality. Anyone with power or popularity is the victim of torrential abuse: Jean Paulhan, who had treated Céline honourably, appears as Norbert Loukoum, the ringmaster no longer of the Gallimard publishing house but of a Revue Compacte d'Emmer-derie; Sartre is simply Tartre (tartar) or sometimes, more intestinally, Taenia; the Communist writer Aragon is l'Harengon (*hareng* = herring).

These elementary lampoons, however, are not the main business of the trilogy, which is offered as a 'chronicle' of the last months of Nazi Germany. To be present at the ruin of a regime, to say nothing of one advertised as a 'thousand-year Reich', was a favour due to Céline as a writer, not as a man: no addict of that monstrous but tasty sedative 'la nostalgie de l'apocalypse' was ever granted such a definitive dose. Much of what went on around him in 1944 and 1945 was momentous and disorderly enough to meet even Céline's requirements for a general insecurity of physical existence. As a chronicler of war he sees himself as having been released by history from any narrow obligations towards the truth; catastrophe surrounded him with a potential poetry of extremes that solicited his skills as a writer: life at Sigmaringen, for instance, he recognises as poised temptingly between the two orders whose trained intermediary he was, 'neither absolutely fictive, nor absolutely real'. The Vichy leaders, many of whom Céline attended in his capacity as a doctor, stumble uselessly about their Hohenzollern château, waiting on extinction amidst the derisory bric-a-brac of ten centuries of a rapacious devotion to inessentials. The rhetoric of their lives, whether it emerges in a political slogan or a military uniform, is eroded daily, and how gloatingly Céline's own anti-rhetoric reminds them of it: 'Blue Danube! . . . My arse!'

Particular scenes of degradation in Céline's last books are every bit as nightmarish as those in the early ones. In *Nord* the Célines and Le Vigan live amidst a grotesque community in Zornhof: a Junker Rittmeister of eighty and his family, including his legless, epileptic son; gangs of conscientious objectors hacking the wood for coffins out of the forest; Russian and French prisoners of war; a Nazi doctor with a fabulous cache of smuggled delicacies; prostitutes hauled off their beat in nearby Berlin to be treated for venereal disease.

The grisly life of this community is nothing compared to its deaths, however: the Rittmeister rides ridiculously off, sabre in hand, to turn back the Russian hordes single-handed and is eventually found pinioned in a ditch with the whores sitting down to dine off him; his son is dumped into a pond of fermenting beetroot juice during a concert by his giant Russian attendant. These warped and passionate inventions, registering an anarchist's glee at the fragility of any social order, as well as a nostalgia for the heroic and futile gesture of an aristocrat (the Rittmeister) too grandiose for the world he lives in, are an indispensable part of Céline's vision.

The ambiguity of Céline's position, as a healer in real life and a scourge of humanity in his books, is reflected in some of his characters, the Nazi epidemiologist Harras in *Nord*, for instance, who is constantly flying off to Lisbon to confer with specialists from the Allied side and lamenting the absence of pestilence in the modern world. Yet the name of Harras is an inescapable reminder of how sinister a fatalism Céline's concern with biology could become when exercised on a wider scale: *haras* is the French word for a stud farm and throughout the trilogy Céline hangs on to a demented vision of the coming mingling of the races, or what he calls 'the gametes' ball', a genetic Paul Jones that will put an end for ever to any idea of racial exclusivity.

This was the postwar version of his pre-war obsession with the Jews, seen as malignant aliens whose values threatened the wellbeing or even the survival of Céline's France. His objections to them were the familiar ones: Jews were too successful, too powerful, too cosmopolitan, too intellectual; and they were also warmongers, who wanted France to teach Hitler a lesson. Céline's was in essence an unusually lurid form of the anti-Semitism of the depressed urban class into which he was born, which had become accustomed to explaining its social and material insignificance by reference to some racial or categorical conspiracy. In *Mort à crédit*, the father launches himself on a career of paranoia by campaigning against the dogs that foul the pavement outside the family lace-shop (one animal instinct we could presumably do without), then moves up to an embracing condemnation of all Jews and Freemasons, as enemies worthier of both his time and his abuse. Céline's own abuse, in the three pamphlets that he wrote between 1937 and 1941, notably *Bagatelles pour un massacre*, achieves an awful virtuosity and is directed very much more widely than simply against Jews. But after the war, once the enormity of the Holocaust had begun to be revealed, it was naturally his anti-Semitism that caused him to be reviled.

In the trilogy, the Jews have been withdrawn as a threat, to be replaced by the Chinese, who will one day soon be arriving in the port of Brest and clapping degenerate whites into the shafts of their rickshaws. (Was it to put more weight behind this warning that *Rigodon* was written on yellow paper?) This crackpot updating of the source of France's doom, with Céline swapping *bêtes noires* in midstream, does something to undermine the gravity of his pre-war anti-Semitism, by showing it up as opportunism. What was important for him was to hold over his compatriots' heads whatever threats of destruction came the easiest to hand.

The style in which he uttered these threats is itself one of the most remarkable creations of twentieth-century French prose: mannered at its worst but wonderfully inventive and readable at its best. What Céline sought was a written French that was as emotionally charged as the spoken language is capable of being, the language as spoken, that is, by the resentful, disempowered members of society. Not that anyone ever has, or ever could, speak French with the energy and gift for neologism with which Céline – laboriously – wrote it. As time passed, his sentences became ever shorter and more emphatic. Conjunctions withered away, and his trademark became the *points de suspension* (. . .) that replaced them, often fortified by screamers (!), along with an extraordinary richness of argot, some of it standard, some of it of his own invention. His oeuvre had become what he wanted it to be: a sustained frontal assault on respectable usage.

Céline finished revising the manuscript of *Rigodon* in the morning of the day he died – a tamer but more moving abdication than that of another writer, Ernest Hemingway, who committed suicide that same day. Even in the French newspapers it was Hemingway who hogged the necrologies, or what Céline, always bucked to be informed of a noteworthy death, called the 'Parcae's column'. In his last years he had, if anything, stepped up the self-contempt that kept him young, and his final revenge on France for its neglect was to anticipate his own patriotic bones being tipped anonymously into a pauper's grave. He would have been gratified to have foreseen the coincidence of his own death with that of Hemingway, and the homage even of Paris being spent on the glamorous tourist of the 1920s rather than on a beleaguered native like himself.

13

A L'AINE ROBE GRILLÉE

Alain Robbe-Grillet is the incorruptible extremist of the *nouveau roman*, a writer who has always refused to depart from the rules he imposed on himself when he began writing fiction in the early 1950s or to move any closer to the supposedly more convivial methods of the 'conventional' novel. He is incapable of writing a novel that has a straight, contradiction-free plot or one containing 'characters' in the old, psychological sense of the word. His novels are true anti-novels, playful constructs written with the sardonic intention of demonstrating that the day of the linear, psychological novel is done, that in a world so impressively full of scientific facts as our own, fiction can no longer have any serious place.

Right from the start, Robbe-Grillet was taken more solemnly than someone so openly provocative and jokey should have been. His early novels were frequently misread, evidence no doubt that the literary world, whether in France or elsewhere, is slow to discern humour of the radical, undercover kind in which Robbe-Grillet has long specialised. *Le Voyeur* (The voyeur), *La Jalousie* (Jealousy) and *Dans le labyrinthe* (In the labyrinth) were novels, published in the 1950s, that were read, for all his teasing disclaimers, as genuine studies in psychological disturbance. They were seldom recognised as parodies of a genre that Robbe-Grillet believed was now defunct, practicable so far as he was concerned only in fun. It was only later, during the 1960s, that he was ready to come further into the open and be seen for what he had been from the outset: a humorist.

Robbe-Grillet published only two novels between 1960 and 1970. They are written to the same specification as the earlier, better-known novels. Nevertheless, there are particular aspects of *La Maison de rendez-vous* (1965) and *Projet pour une révolution à New York* (Project for a revolution in New York, 1970) which would make it wrong blindly to classify these fresh artefacts as mere clones developed from their canonical predecessors. They are, above all, noticeably less secretive about the logic of their own fabrication, as I shall hope to show by quotation from *Projet pour une révolution*. In this novel, Robbe-Grillet has not by any means decided to come clean and show us how he does it, but he has moved towards a greater explicitness. This relaxation could have been born of frustration, for he had been publishing novels since 1953 without any perceptible advance in the general understanding of his work.

If he had inaugurated instead of sustained his literary career with *La Maison de rendez-vous* and *Projet pour une révolution*, Robbe-Grillet's reputation could not have been quite what it is. For these two jocular and flamboyantly perverted narratives could never have been taken as earnestly as the earlier novels often were. The pawky commentators who debated tensely whether Matthias in *Le Voyeur* was or was not a sadistic killer, or who found melancholy echoes of Kafka in *Dans le labyrinthe*, would have needed less strait-laced exegetical equipment to tackle *La Maison de rendez-vous* or *Projet pour une révolution*.

In these novels, excess and a gross disrespect for the impedimenta of everyday life are inescapable. These are, unarguably, pop novels, simultaneously blowing up and sending up a certain kind of popular writing (or rather, thinking). It is possible that his experience of film-making manoeuvred Robbe-Grillet into this mode of comic amplification, since the novel offers him a release from at least two constraints inseparable from the cinema: the constraint of having to implicate living people, that's to say actors, of vulnerable flesh and blood, in his sadistic fantasies; and the constraint of having to introduce a 'real' background, in the sense of scenes and objects whose appearance on film we take as a guarantee of their authenticity. Thus the characters in *La Maison de rendez-vous* and *Projet pour une révolution* have become, if possible, less human than ever before, so grotesquely malleable are they and so liable to revert textually to the status of waxworks or dummies. The sort of perversions which the novelist enjoys practising on his female characters are, for obvious reasons, denied to the film-maker.

The matter of décor is more complicated. It was in the film of *L'Immortelle* that Robbe-Grillet first used exterior shots of an identifiable geographical location, the city of Istanbul (the château of *L'Année dernière à Marienbad* was recognisably a piece of existing architecture, not a plaster mock-up, but it was not situated in a real place called Marienbad). In *L'Immortelle*, Robbe-Grillet duly emphasised, as he needed to, that the Turkey in which his film was set was the Turkey of a picture postcard, an environment already pre-digested by the contemporary mind and so, it was to be hoped, void of possible documentary significance. In his later novels, Robbe-Grillet has dared to transfer this technique and has localised them in a way he had not attempted before. *La Maison de rendez-vous* is set in a scrupulously second-hand Hong Kong: 'everyone knows Hong Kong', as the text is forever recalling. There are rickshaws, coolies in conical hats, British policemen in shorts and long socks, Eurasian girls in slit skirts: in short, a décor fit for Sydney Greenstreet and Peter Lorre to be up to no good in.

The same goes for the New York of *Projet pour une révolution*, where there is a subway system, the streets are numbered, the buildings have prominent outside fire escapes, a handful of authentic toponyms are admitted. It would be exceedingly hard to claim that any of this constituted a source of information about the city. Yet even this modest integration of the real world into a blatantly fictitious narrative has its perils, for the innocent novel-reader has an urge to interpret all such detail, however shop-soiled, as representative or metonymic of a world outside the novel. If this temptation among his readers (and among his characters too!) could not be scotched, then Robbe-Grillet would be failing in his purpose, and there is one passage in the novel where he exposes the danger very tellingly. During one of various cross-examinations, the narrator faces a critic:

> 'Another thing: you talk about the Greenwich district, or the Madison subway station; any American would say "the Village" and "Madison Avenue".
>
> 'This time, I think it's you who are exaggerating! All the more so because no one has ever claimed that the story was being told by an American. Don't forget that it's always foreigners who make revolutions.'

There is, in fact, a necessary unfamiliarity between the storyteller and the setting of his story; but we are all, potentially, storytellers and share a common setting, which is the natural world. None of us is at home, or so the neo-existentialist Robbe-Grillet would argue. What he is invoking here is that hoary, very Sartrian topic, the alienation of God-less modern man, who persistently imagines myths or fictions in order to conceal the incompatibility between his own desires and a universe perceived as perfectly indifferent to them. This is the pathetic fallacy against which Robbe-Grillet has campaigned witheringly in his theoretical essays and very deviously in his novels; and the revolution somewhat erratically hatched in this particular novel is a further instalment: yet another ultimately frustrated effort at the subversion of the true, objective order of things by a cheerier, subjective one.

Hence the nice logic of reminding us that it is the 'foreigners' or 'étrangers' who are the culprits in this ontological plot, because the *étranger* has been, ever since Camus's Meursault first added new sememes to that word, the archetypal hero of our existential struggle to become reconciled to the unfriendly ways of the universe. It is not far-fetched, and it enriches the words at issue, to read the final sentence of the quotation above as a reinforcement, slyly made, of Robbe-Grillet's brusque dismissal of Camus, whose *étranger* enjoys the sort of collusion with nature which Robbe-Grillet finds both spurious and sentimental.

His wilful misrepresentation of New York usage in respect of these two place names is, additionally, a reminder that such attributable topography as the novel possesses is itself a structural element, to be justified by reference to its textual function and not by some vacuous test of assumed correspondence to the world outside it. The fragments of New York incorporated into *Projet pour une révolution* are only incidentally pertinent to the place of that name: it could perhaps be shown that Robbe-Grillet's New York is a by-product of these fragments, not the other way round.

This is a major inversion in the practice of fiction, but there is space here to look at only one example of it: the 'escaliers de fer', or iron fire escapes, running down the fronts of the buildings. These are at once a noticeable feature of the novel and a feature of the actual New York townscape publicised widely over the years in movies. They form part of our 'imaginary' New York. In the novel they are given a double but symmetrical function: they provide both an emergency exit from the building in case of danger and an illicit way into it for any would-be malefactors.

The malefactors in question are, we now know, bent on the ontological crime of wrenching the natural world into line with their emotional requirements; they are, that is, would-be novelists, so that the *escalier de fer* is the support for a culpable ascent from the real, as it were down-to-earth order of things to a heightened, fictive one. Correspondingly, the intended victim of a crime who is able to make an escape down the ladder is foiling the aspirations of the criminal. The *escaliers* thus have a double responsibility, for both the production and the erasure of a fiction; they are the locus of that contradictory motion out of which Robbe-Grillet has habitually constructed his novels.

But we have not finished with them yet, because the metal they are made from is every bit as significant as their role as transporters. Iron is a decisive element in the genesis of *Projet pour une révolution*, in its uses and, more important, its abuses. The major clue to its function comes, properly, right at the start of the novel, where the first object described is a door (which, just like the *escalier de fer*, is both a legitimate way out and a highly suspect way in to the building). The door is in the act of being closed by the narrator, with him outside on the doorstep; but we are never assured in so many words that this action is completed. If it were to be completed there would presumably be no novel, because the whole of the ensuing fiction depends on the dialectic between 'inside' and 'outside' and the various stratagems that can be employed to gain illicit entry (to people as well as buildings). The key to the door, which would be the answer to the narrator's prayer and a definitive assuagement of his anxiety, is envisaged inside the house, lying on a piece of furniture with the suggestive and (in the context of a Robbe-Grillet novel) reprehensible name of *console* – reprehensible because consolation is what he sees fiction as falsely offering us as its consumers.

But it is the description of the door that matters here:

> I am in the act of closing the door behind me, a heavy door of solid wood with a small, narrow, rectangular window let into it right at the top, the glass of which is protected by a cast-iron grille of a complicated design (a crude imitation of wrought iron) which masks it almost entirely. The interlaced spirals, made thicker still by successive layers of black paint, are so close together, and there is so little light the other side of the door, that one can make out nothing of what may, or may not, be found inside.

In French this original piece of ironwork is a *grille de fonte* and constitutes a serious obstacle to the transparency of the pane of glass in the door: functionally speaking, the same sort of obstacle as the *jalousie* or Venetian blind in Robbe-Grillet's earlier novel of that title. What lies on the other side of the glass will be the product not of observation but of imagination. But it would not be quite right to conclude that the *grille de fonte* is somehow the genetrix of the fiction; rather, it is the metallic equivalent of the novel itself, as can be demonstrated by the ambiguity of the word *fonte*. This means 'cast iron' but may also refer to the fount of type with which a compositor works. This second meaning enlarges the sense of the *grille de fonte* in just the way that the practised reader of Robbe-Grillet would expect. What is now designated is both a typographical disposition (the novel as actually printed) and an item of metalwork with a function to play in that novel; and the strange complexity of the grille's design is applicable to either of these meanings. Robbe-Grillet further validates this equation between novel and grille by stressing the artificial nature of the metalwork, which is an imitation of something that has itself been 'wrought' (*forgé* in French). The grille thus functions as the imitation of a work of art and displays what is, for Robbe-Grillet, the art of fiction's dominant characteristic, exaggeration, given that the imitation is a 'crude' one. After which subtly indicative opening, *Projet pour une révolution* becomes a novel in which the release, or *project*, of the imagination is constantly chargeable to the account of the one metal, iron.

The analysis of the *grille de fonte* could be prolonged, but the point is, I hope, made that the *escaliers de fer* are highly meaningful both because they are *escaliers* and because they are made of *fer*, and are not a random if plausible borrowing from the known townscape of New York. They are a feature of that city selected for Robbe-Grillet's peculiar structural needs, and so well adapted to them that he may easily have thought of the *escaliers* first and New York only second.

But underpin though they do the double movement of the novel, they cannot account for its impulsion: they are the scene, not the cause, of the movement from fact to fiction. To locate and determine this cause, one needs to look, logically enough, at the foot of the staircases, where the pernicious movement of ascent has to begin. The *escaliers* do not reach right to the ground but end three metres above it; the connection with the pavement can be made by a retractable ladder, though the criminals envisaged in the novel as going up the *escalier* spurn the ladder and pull themselves up on the bottom-most iron bar.

The retractable ladder is not, however, the only object in the novel of the correct length to overcome such a hiatus: two other substitutes, both three metres long and both in a manner of speaking retractable, are offered. The first of these is an ironing board of impressive versatility. Instead of remaining the innocuous domestic appliance that it ought to be, this ironing board becomes, first, a source of sexual stimulation for the girl who is using it to iron her dress after she has been aroused by a television film; while later on, the ravisher who breaks in on her re-allocates it as a custom-built torturer's aide, on which his victim can conveniently be strapped while he violates her.

The second member of this set of three is the graffito of a giant phallus, which has been added in black ink to an advertising poster in the street. This somewhat larger than life-size male organ has as its target – it is drawn vertically – the parted lips of a blindfolded girl, as if it were engaged in an imaginary act of fellatio. Like the ironing board it is participating in the series of acts of violation which recur throughout the novel.

Thus one can safely say that what gets this fiction off the ground is the sado-erotic impulse, that impulse which Robbe-Grillet sees as central to the fantasy life of contemporary West Europeans. *Projet pour une révolution* depends on a bawdy and sardonic magnification of this stimulus, whose emanations have here been inflated far beyond the point where we could take them seriously. Cagier books like *Le Voyeur* or *Dans le labyrinth*e may once have looked like some kind of psychopathological case studies, but not so this novel, which actually contains a number of allusions to the pleasure that is to be had from inflicting the sort of sufferings in question. What that means, naturally, is that there is pleasure for the imaginer in inflicting sexual tortures on his compliant because imaginary victims.

The violations, which form so prolonged and varied a series of events in *Projet pour une révolution*, might be brought together under the heading of 'acts of illegal entry'. They are, needless to say, the acts of conspirators or revolutionaries, whose objects in this novel are far from being political. One or two perverse or confused reviewers complained about this when the novel first appeared, and suggested that Robbe-Grillet was a fraud to give a title to the book which implied his espousal of an existing movement of subversion in the United States. His answer was that the sort of subversion open to the novelist is of a less direct kind, which lies in the promotion of the play instinct; and, he might have added, the sapping of the credibility of that auspicious art form, the 'bourgeois' novel.

The 'revolution' in this instance, it bears repeating, is one dedicated to the overthrow of the reality principle. The one scene of the novel where a clandestine political meeting seems to take place offers in actual fact some startlingly candid guidance to the true aims of the 'plotters' (and what a happily ambiguous term that is). When their deliberations are introduced we are given to expect an 'ideological exposé', and this indeed is what we subsequently get, except that the ideology is aesthetic and not political, even though the language used has, quite literally, a political coloration:

> The topic of today's lesson appears to be 'the colour red', envisaged as a radical solution to the irreducible antagonism between black and white. The three voices are each of them attributed, at present, to one of the major acts of liberation relating to red: rape, arson, murder.

Reds, blacks and whites, formally arranged into a Hegelian triangle where red, the colour of revolution, is the synthesis: the terminology is apt for a scenario of the racial division of the United States and its exploitation by partisans of the far Left. Yet *Projet pour une révolution* has no political content at all, in any useful sense of the word political, and the antagonism between black and white is certainly not ethnic. It is, instead, both typographical and philosophical. The word 'irreducible' needs to be taken literally, as embodying Robbe-Grillet's own belief that the antagonism in question cannot be legitimately overcome. What, then, is it?

In the first place, it is the dichotomy between white paper and black characters. Since the novel is, for Robbe-Grillet, something which should not, by rights, come into existence, white paper, unsullied by black marks, is an ideal, like the blank wall on which the incriminating marks of the millipede persistently appear in *La Jalousie*. In the second place, therefore, there is involved the general, epistemological antagonism between that which is and that which is not, between objective fact (white) and subjective projection (black). The resolution of this antinomy is the novel that we read, in which not only is the colour red made freely available but also two other, alternative syntheses: the colour grey, as a cross between black and white, and the mixed ethnic status of half-caste (the product of an attempt at artificial insemination which forms yet another of the novel's acts of serial violation).

Hence the considerable by-play throughout the book of white disguising itself as black and black as white, because this miscegenation is the unlawful possibility which only a fiction can realise. The chance of a radical change of pigmentation is what Manhattan window-gazers are actually offered: 'If you don't like your skin, change it!' urges a placard set amidst a display of masks and wigs, and ten pages further on this same placard is described as permitting 'every project, every dream', which relates it directly to the title of the novel (the shop window is qualified, equally revealingly, as a 'refuge').

'Irreducible', 'refuge', 'project' are not words one would once have anticipated finding in the text of a Robbe-Grillet novel. In *Projet pour une révolution* he has been unprecedentedly generous, however, in employing terms which, relating closely as they do to his programmatic writings, ought to alert his readers to his true purpose. From this novel could be extracted a substantial lexicon of such terms: 'subjective', 'anecdote', 'psychodrama', 'essential', 'fictive', 'humanist' and others besides, which he may have employed in his novels before but never so consistently. All of these words are two-faced: they have their textual role, but they also point outside the text, to the subjacent theory of fiction which Robbe-Grillet sticks to so rigorously. They constitute a skeletal metalanguage within the text, inviting us to perform small acts of criticism as we read and to enjoy the subtlety and good humour with which Robbe-Grillet makes his case.

The most striking of all these intrusive terms is that of 'metaphorical act', which is first used at the underground meeting of 'conspirators' referred to above. Everybody, by this time, must be supposed to have a good idea of what Robbe-Grillet's views of the metaphor are, and it is hard to see how any reader could pass over the words 'metaphorical act' without enquiring into them further. The metaphor, of course, is the evil influence in Robbe-Grillet's world, the figure of speech that leads the mind astray into forming a delusive relationship with the external world. It precedes the elaboration of the novel: 'The preliminary exposition, which was coming to an end as I arrived, must have been devoted to the theoretical justifications of crime in general and the notion of a metaphorical act.'

This last 'criminal' notion is thus an a priori of the text, which is the attempted realisation, or series of attempted realisations, of that act. (The 'preliminary' is a reminder that the novel opens on a *limen* or threshold). The metaphorical acts are not, at this point, explicitly identified with the criminal acts already adumbrated: rape, murder and arson. Later on they are:

> Crime is indispensable to the revolution, recites the doctor. Rape, murder, arson are the three metaphorical acts that will liberate the blacks, the ragged proletarians and the intellectul workers from their servitude, at the same time as the bourgeoisie from its sexual complexes.

The equation between the metaphorical acts and the actions of the novel is strengthened by the stipulation that there should be three of them; this is the language of the theatre, to which Robbe-Grillet has frequently resorted in order to underline the essentially theatrical, in the pejorative sense of the word, nature of the spectacles he is offering us. Near the end of *Projet pour une révolution*, after the three acts might be assumed to be complete, we are told that the dawn is near at hand and that, consequently, no time remains for the commission of a 'fourth act'.

Granted that it is the id, in its search for gratification by the projection of exorbitant private scenarios, which is held by Robbe-Grillet to be to blame for the human greed for fictions, it is understandable that the principal objective of the metaphorical acts in this novel should be the female sex organ. But while it is reasonable that rape and even murder should be practised on or via the pudenda, it is less so that arson should share the same target. Nevertheless, the series of cognate violations, of which these crimes are part, achieves a weird climax in an attempt at vaginal incendiarism near the end of the novel. This, the subsumption of the three acts taken independently, is the crime to end all crimes, the last fling of a thwarted imagination. And if anyone were still in doubt as to its ontological overtones, Robbe-Grillet has hit on another play on words to make these clearer, by having his assailant use *essence* (the French for petrol) to guarantee the desired conflagration ('The sex organ is soaked in petrol, which catches fire all of a sudden'). It is the unknowable 'essence' of things which Robbe-Grillet, the contented naturalist, has always banished from his philosophy, while recognising it as the lure that cozens the human mind into a false communion with nature, hence its location here at the entrance to the uterus. Hence also an extra ambiguity about the crimes perpetrated on the vagina in *Projet pour une révolution*, since they are the punishment meted out by the anti-novelist on the matrix of fiction itself.

This anatomical localisation of the creative urge is hardly being offered by Robbe-Grillet as a lasting contribution to the theory of fiction. It is acceptable only to the extent that it is trivially true, depending as it does on a pan-eroticism which reduces the term 'eroticism' to a synonym for 'energy' or even 'inspiration'. By Robbe-Grillet's lights, it would look as though the survival of the urge to make fiction is guaranteed by the physiology of the human race, which may come as a message of comfort to those who have deplored him as a terrorist set on the extermination of the novel altogether. But he is a man practised in irony and apparently indifferent about how intelligently the dialectic he has long conducted with the traditional novel is received. On the strength of *Projet pour une révolution*, there can be no enrolling him as a supporter of the view that, as a safe outlet for our murky imaginings, fiction is a genuine agent of therapy in our lives, since in this novel there are several caustic allusions to the supposedly cathartic properties of the novel form.

The denial of any psychological justification for fiction does not, however, turn Robbe-Grillet into a nihilist. The values of a book like this are ludic: the text is an invitation to take the author on in an ingenious, mind-testing game whose rules can be progressively discovered by close reading. The prize is a partial, never a complete, understanding of why the novel takes the form and follows the sequence it does, and what the exact principles of its construction are. Whether the co-operative reader will find that the intellectual agility demanded of him or her is sufficiently rewarded by the insights so acquired is another matter.

The novel as practised by Robbe-Grillet is no sort of threat to the survival of other kinds of fiction, whether 'Balzacian' or not. It simply offers a different experience of reading, and one, moreover, whose very real pleasures are in large part dependent on bearing in mind as you read the substance of Robbe-Grillet's quarrel with the methods of the conventional novel.

One difficulty of coming to terms with a Robbe-Grillet novel is that this can only be done satisfactorily with the French-language version. His ludic extravaganzas contain a great many plays on words, a good proportion of which will die out in translation, taking with them the sly evidence of what he is up to. Thus a wholly necessary sequence of words and events in the French will become an intermittently arbitrary one once it is conveyed in a different language, where some of the wordplay may still function, but never all of it.

I will end with an example of this wastage. There is an episode in *Projet pour une révolution* where Robbe-Grillet's two categorical villains, the linguistic and the libidinous, have been fused together with rare guile. It concerns what is referred to in the French text as a 'projet de repassage'. Now, in French *repassage* means 'ironing', as in the ironing of an item of clothing, and the girl in the novel, JR, is indeed in the process of ironing a dress. There is more, however, to *repassage* here than merely ironing; the word may also be taken to read *re-passage* and to allude to the inaugural act of the novel that I have quoted, of a passing back through the door into the house. In English, this wordplay is inevitably lost, since our 'ironing', unlike *repassage*, carries with it no suggestion of re-passing.

There is worse to come. Instead of ironing smoother her dress as she had 'projected', JR succeeds only in burning, with her iron, a triangular hole in, as it were, its private parts. It would be in keeping with Robbe-Grillet's clever but not impenetrable verbal schemes to have determined this episode – this textual 'accident' – by a veiled phonetic reference to his own name. For, granted that *l'aine* in French is a noun meaning the 'groin', that *la robe* means a 'dress' and that *griller* is a verb meaning to 'toast' or 'grill', we can say that, at this point of the novel, we are confronted with the project of 'à l'aine robe grillée'.

14

NATHALIE SARRAUTE

Nathalie Sarraute had her own, esoteric way of doing well at school. When, at her Paris *lycée*, her class was asked whether anyone had read *War and Peace*, thirteen-year-old Nathalie (née Natalya Tcherniak, in Russia), did not want to say that she had. She was fearful not of advertising how grown-up her reading had already become, but of what she might have to listen to should her teacher 'dare to touch' the book and the ineffable Tolstoy be invested by the crass discourse of a pedagogue. There was a severity about Sarraute even in her tender years: she knew by the fourth form it seems that language can mortify as easily as it can bring to life, and that the hardest of all the things we can do with words is to put the exactly right ones to our feelings.

This small, subcutaneous drama is fact; it is reported in the chronology of Sarraute's life that starts the Pléiade *Oeuvres complètes*. It could as well have been part of one of her novels, which are formed of a succession of private dramas no larger but just as searching. The situation in which a superior schoolgirl forgoes the admiration she might have earned for her precocity involves what, when she turned writer, Sarraute was to call a 'tropism'. The term is one that she took from the natural sciences, and when she adopted it she may have been thinking of Proust, who had recently made such apt and witty use of Maeterlinck's *L'Intelligence des fleurs* in describing the first, charmingly camp pas de deux between the baron de Charlus and his newest heart-throb, Jupien. In biology, a tropism is the instinctive movement that occurs when an organism responds to an outside stimulus: the often microscopic reorientation by which a plant or an animal reacts to what impinges on it. Tropisms are thus dramatic encounters of a sort, enacted without benefit of consciousness among the vegetable and animal orders.

With Sarraute they became the metaphor that gave her access to what she regarded as the one sound subject-matter for a modern novelist. Transferred to the human order, these protozoan manoeuvrings could serve as a type for the secret fencing matches fought out between any two people coming psyche to psyche, when one psyche will be out to take advantage of the other. Sarraute's long career in fiction was to be a search for new, ever more pared-down forms in which to turn these barely detectable fluctuations into words, so as to make them apparent for once in all their comic, damaging or simply lamentable ephemerality. She has carried that search on with rare single-mindedness and to wonderfully entertaining effect for almost sixty years, her last book (*Ouvrez*) having been published in 1997, when she, like the century, was ninety-seven years old.

Sarraute began writing in the early thirties, after several years of practising, half-heartedly and only because her father wanted her to, at the Paris bar. (This forensic experience helped later in the shaping of her fiction and it's one she shares, oddly, with the only other living French novelist I would compare with her as a source of intelligent pleasure, Robert Pinget.) She went about literature slowly once she had taken to it. *Tropismes*, her first book, was not published until 1939, seven years after she began writing it. It is a sparse but mordant collection of short scenes of social exchange whose ordinariness dissolves in Sarraute's acid-bath into something quite ominous. With a grim smile and a daunting accuracy, she flashes her torch down into those unlit places of the self where we re-arm for our intimate wars with one another. She had chosen to occupy once and for all the territory most favourable to her ambitions both as a novelist and as a moralist. In *Tropismes* she invented her own form of social Darwinism, by using zoological metaphors to indicate the – in truth, indescribable – predatory or else self-protective urges of our species.

Tropismes was not a success; its methods were unfamiliar, and 1939 was not a good year in which to publish your first book. Sarraute had to wait, and be a postwar writer. Although, as a Jew, she was under threat all through the Occupation, even divorcing her non-Jewish husband at one point in order to protect him, she survived and managed to keep writing. After 1945, she was taken up by Sartre, who had read *Tropismes* when it first appeared and had liked it. He thought he recognised a fellow spirit, someone like himself who was contemptuous of essentialist notions of human character, who saw the bourgeois world in which she moved as ruled everywhere by bad faith, and who knew what a tax our fear of judgement by others is on our 'authenticity' as social agents. Sarraute was indeed a Sartrian, but of a domestic not a philosophical kind, and she showed no liking for Sartre's wild-man politics. He encouraged her, publishing in *Les Temps modernes* an essay in which she laid brilliantly waste – and why not? – the claims to poetic greatness of the recently dead Paul Valéry, and then writing the introduction for her second piece of fiction, *Portrait d'un inconnu* (Portrait of a man unknown), of 1947.

This was *Tropismes* made continuous and drawn out to the length of a novel: a profound and engaging demonstration of the troubling things that are felt but do not get spoken whenever intimates, acquaintances or even strangers meet. Sarraute's victims – and it's families she has the wickedest fun with – come on stage as innocents awaiting their turn to be rumbled; they don't have to wait long: she is the arch-rumbler. No one, however coherent and assured a figure they may cut when they first appear in her books, will survive her attentions without serious damage, because their integrity is soon shown to be inauthentic, a false impression they give which, alas, the timid souls all around them are only too glad to go along with. For these timid ones are the individuals who can't bear to be individuals, they long for the security of 'fusion', of merging indistinguishably with some group or other. They feel nothing but veneration for the magisterial figures whom they mistake for enviable paragons of firmness and self-assurance. For their pains they are condemned by Sarraute to a condition of incurable anxiety, because anxiety, though unwanted, is a sign of life, indeed of humanity. She is on the side of the anxious, of that class of person singled out in *Portrait d'un inconnu*, the Hypersensitive: 'She who trembles at the faintest breath, whom the least contact causes to shudder and contract, she endures her blows without flinching. Barely other than a wavering in her, a vacillation – almost nothing.'

These 'almost nothings' are the exclusive stuff of Sarraute's oeuvre, the waverings that may escape the notice even of the waverer yet represent a crucial moment in the history of their emotions. In the instance above, the Hypersensitive one is a daughter on the point of coming desperately out against a bullying father and telling him triumphantly that she has at last met a man who is willing to marry her. 'Who would recognise her?' asks the text (or the novelist). That question is Sarraute's severe reproach to the inhabitants of the world she writes about, or to every one of us. By elaborating on this unhappy woman's passage from cowed symbiosis with her father to nascent rebellion, Sarraute shows her own humane hand. It's the put-upon who come out best in her fiction, and the seemingly invulnerable who have the furthest to fall. Like all the best moral pessimists, Sarraute is a great leveller.

Portrait d'un inconnu was not a success any more than *Tropismes* had been.

What struck people about it at the time – what still strikes some about Sarraute, depressingly – was that it was so 'abstract': nothing much ever seemed to happen, nowhere got properly described, none of the people had been given a name, the dialogue and the narration ran confusingly into each other. For the novelist the complaints were encouraging; they were after all withdrawal symptoms: by frustrating readers of their habitual fix – major happenings, well-marked characters, lots of scenery – she was alerting them to how deceitful she believed the conventions of the realist novel had become. By her abstractions she would be denying them the same illusory 'solidity' that is an object of such shameful desire in *Portrait d'un inconnu*, as in the novels that followed it.

Sarraute's methods were unfamiliar but they were not so new as to defy comprehension; her novels can be called 'abstract' only if your measure of 'reality' is one that has stood unchanged since Balzac was writing. Sarraute was a historicist. She had read widely (including in English: she did a year's history at Oxford in 1920–21); and when she started to write for herself she saw no point in attempting to do the same things by the same means as had novelists in the past. The thing was to keep the art of fiction moving on, in the direction laid down for it by the great names of the generation preceding her own – Proust, Joyce, Virginia Woolf. (There was also Dostoevsky, of whom more in a minute.) They had turned the novel definitively inwards and taken possession of areas of consciousness that might seem near to the limits of the sayable. Sarraute's tropisms were to be a way not of penetrating further even than Proust or Joyce or Woolf had been able to into the obscurities of the sub- or, in her case, better to say the pre-conscious, but of representing what was lurking there by other means. Her way is to display, never in so many words to analyse, our most fugitive sensations as and when they arise, not in the real time of the mind but in a fictive slow motion. Sarraute differs from her chosen predecessors by daring to be less explicit than they were. There are no explanatory captions as it were underneath her tiny scenes of intimate triumph or distress. Where Proust, for example, stands back and revels in the lucidity with which he can account for the behaviour of his (named) characters, Sarraute allows no such *cordon sanitaire* between ourselves and the nameless individuals overheard socialising in her novels. Having long ago made her escape from school, she isn't now going to play teacher and foreclose on the sensations she puts on display by declaring what their significance is. We're only too likely to do that for ourselves, and rather spoil things by 'fixing' the sensations so artfully presented to us in their true, labile state. But if Sarraute knows she is playing a losing game with our craving for definition, it's one she loses with great good humour.

As a novelist of adamantly progressive views where form was concerned, Sarraute inevitably got drawn into the fuss that surrounded the *nouveau roman* when literature's militant tendency in France took up its cause in the late fifties. This may have done her some immediate good, in giving a by nature discreet person greater visibility, but in the long run it was a pity, because it associated her too strongly with the brutalism of the *nouveau roman*'s front man, Alain Robbe-Grillet. Robbe-Grillet himself was never the literary vandal he found it useful in those days to let it seem that he was, but he was far less studied in polemic than Sarraute, who knew that the individual talent, however avant-garde, owes almost everything to literary tradition.

There was the great debt in her own case to her compatriot Dostoevsky, the nineteenth-century novelist from whom Sarraute clearly learnt most. In Dostoevsky, as we know, people act in the strangest, most contradictory ways, and we don't expect to be told what has led them to do so. As characters they remain in one piece only because they have names and an *état civil*; they can hardly be thought of as psychological entities, as they give way to what Sarraute calls their 'bizarre contortions'. Bizarre of course only because opaque: could we look inside these oddballs we would learn that their contortions are 'like the needle of the galvanometer which retraces, even as it amplifies them, the most infinitesimal variations in a current, those subtle, barely perceptible, fugitive, contradictory, evanescent movements . . . whose incessant play constitutes the invisible thread of all human relationships and the very substance of our lives.'

Had Dostoevsky had the techniques to hand that a twentieth-century writer has, he would surely, Sarraute suggests, have set about explicating the inner lives of his characters. In her terms, that would have been a disaster, because it would have had the effect of restoring 'order', the thing in life people seem to want most and which it would be braver of them not to want at all. She writes as a dialectician, pitting the forces of order, in the widest possible sense of the word, against the blind will to disruption. Order is bad, it is synonymous with the inert, the dead, the safe, the already known and labelled. The disorderly 'contortions' that constantly threaten it are, on the contrary, a gratifying evidence of life and of authenticity. They may not amount to much outwardly compared with the sensational volte-faces that are possible for a Karamazov or a Stavrogin, but in their modest way they are Sarraute's 'Notes from Underground'.

The overground to that underground is Sarraute's own bit of French society: bourgeois Paris. But it didn't have to be Paris or bourgeois or even French society, because what she has in her sights is the universal social condition, not a state of being peculiar to the domestic manipulators, professional dissemblers and culture snobs that she takes for her local examples. This universality is one good reason why the décor is always kept so bare in Sarraute, and why the dramatis personae remain anonymous. They are most of them personal pronouns only, a singular *il* or *elle* or, when there is need for the coercive voice of a collective to be heard, a plural *ils* or *elles*. They remain as pronouns because the pronominal is also the pre-nominal: there is no applying proper names at the tropismic level. Names in fiction keep their bearers at a certain formal distance from us and lend their contortions an objectivity which it is Sarraute's whole purpose to avoid.

And no names means no characters as such, except for purposes of parody, as in the novel that has a proper name for its title, *Martereau*, her third book. Martereau the man is a novelist's in-joke: he is someone who has been granted a good solid name (*marteau* is French for a hammer) but denied the consoling solidity of which it should have been the guarantee. He is a characterless character allotted a function in the plot that beautifully contradicts his solid name; for Martereau is an *homme de paille*, or straw man, who allows a house paid for by someone else to be registered in his name, as a tax dodge. But then comes the comedy of uncertainty: Is the foursquare Martereau what he seems, or is he perhaps a con man, who means to hang on to the house for himself? He could equally well be either. He is merely a source of ingenious speculation on the part of others whose status qua 'character' has no ultimate foundation. Sarraute's point is that to affix a name to a living and therefore indeterminate human being is to freeze them into a premature essence. ('Call no man happy till he be dead,' said the Greeks; 'Call no man anything till he be dead' is Sarraute's more comprehensive, post-existentialist version.)

This isn't just a matter of the novelist making an amusing case against superannuated notions of character in fiction. Sarraute is advising us on how we might best react to real life and real living people. Fictional characters don't remain safely trapped within fiction; they are the models we like to go to when pleasurably bent on our amateur readings of the 'contortionists' around us –

who, by a worrying reversal, may seem disappointingly pallid or unreal by comparison with their fictional originals. This on the face of it is outrageous, but one more Sarrautian proof needless to say of our craving for an intelligible solidity. She is having none of it; she would rather we went with the flux, instead of feebly abdicating from it under the illusion that we have now made safe sense of the people we know.

After 1960, Sarraute's books became more inward still, their settings more tenuous, their prose more measured. She became the supreme contriver of a new antiphony, by playing an overt, actually spoken, suspiciously trite dialogue off against another, covert dialogue that was the reverse of trite and seldom benign. This was her supporting *sous-conversation*, an undercurrent which is oral in its form but made unspeakable by its content, indecorous as it is and often inaccessible even to those imagined as engaged on it. Almost nothing now needed to be happening in the books to set this seditious music playing. *Les Fruits d'or* (The fruits of gold), a novel of 1963, has for its excuse a newly published novel of the same title as itself, and it plumbs delectable depths of inauthenticity in lightly dramatising the fatuities and concealed malevolence of smart book-talk. In *Vous les entendez?* (Do you hear them?), written a decade later, the nearest thing to an event is the sound of offstage youthful laughter as two pompous art-collectors sit admiring a pre-Columbian stone dog and their own good taste for admiring it. The laughter though is a worry for them: is it 'fresh and innocent' as one interpretation would have it, or is it, perish the thought, 'sly'? Who is to say? Not Nathalie Sarraute, though this was the first book she published after the epochal disturbances of May 1968, and since the precious stoneware ends up in the cellar with an oyster-shell ashtray fixed to its back, why doubt that this civilised but subversive writer had enjoyed the momentary eruption of youthful anarchy (and deplored the consequent restoration of 'order').

Youthfulness, and the harm that is done with and to it in society, is a theme all but pervasive in Sarraute. She is no Freudian, but more than willing to take the experience of childhood as a template for the future. Her grown-ups suspect, even if they never quite recognise, that in their most agitated moments they are responding in childlike ways, that they are still children while everyone else has apparently gained the security that comes with being adult. Yet by their regressions, and by kicking against the temptations to a dim dependency, the insecure ones are becoming painfully alive again.

In 1983, Sarraute published a book about her own early childhood, under the plainest of titles, *Enfance* (Childhood). She had always said before that she had no wish to write autobiographically, though she had come close to it I fancy in parts of the novel she describes as her own favourite, *Entre la vie et la mort* (Between life and death, 1968), a sometimes sardonic, at other times serious exploration of the conditions under which a word-obsessed child might be seen as predestined to write.

Enfance is far more direct than that, and Sarraute's one concession in all these years to an easy popularity. It's not on the other hand quite conventional in form. It is discontinuous, the writer's memories being kept independent of each other as she recovers them, not smoothed over into a single narrative; and when she senses a need to, she pauses from remembering and enters, by way of a *sous-conversation*, into a dialogue with herself, in which she wonders how truthful she is being in appearing to recall these particular moments of her past.

There could be no cleverer or more elegant a compromise between the formal and the confessional than that found by Sarraute in *Enfance*, and no more seductive entrée to her oeuvre. Her childhood was not perhaps a good one. Her parents divorced two years after she was born, and she lived first with her mother and her stepfather in Russia, and then, permanently though under the threat of being returned to her mother, with her father and young stepmother in France. A *What Maisie Knew* start to her life, and one retraced with pedantic composure by the writer, who is willing to guess how things actually stood between the various couples in the story, but unwilling to impose her guesswork on us as the final truth.

Sarraute is all scruples when it comes to distinguishing the factual from the hypothetical right from the start of *Enfance*, as with the first memory that she chooses to include there. This, typically, is a form of words, and foreign words at that, spoken to the five or six-year-old Nathalie by her German nanny: 'Nein, das tust du nicht' (No, you mustn't do that). The that which she mustn't do is stick a pair of scissors into the upholstery of a Swiss hotel room. The prohibition is futile; into the silk chair-back go the scissors, and at once 'something flabby, greyish is escaping through the split.' From such homely acts of insubordination are novelists formed; little Nathalie's scissors have been going in ever since.

'I'm going to slash it' is the bold answer that she remembers making to her nanny, an answer she is now prepared to develop à la Sarraute: 'I'm warning you, I'm going to take the plunge, leap out of this decent, inhabited, warm, gentle world, I'm going to wrench myself out of it, fall, sink into the uninhabited, into the void. . . .' This is what she reads into the event nearly eighty years later, drawing out its implications as they were to be determined by the future. The episode may be no more in memory than an exchange of German words, which are repeated several times over by Sarraute as she tries to get to the bottom of them, but how promising that little exchange turns out to have been. This is where her forensic side comes out, as the scraps of evidence are held up one by one and then interrogated, in this case quite briefly, to see what they might yield by way of a motive.

The *Oeuvres complètes* published in 1996 contains Nathalie Sarraute's twelve novels, six plays – all but one of them written for radio – the critical essays that she published in 1964 as *L'Ere du soupçon* (The age of suspicion) and the texts of the lectures she has given, in France and abroad. Complete, however, it isn't, for since it was published Sarraute has added the slim but by no means negligible *Ouvrez* to her oeuvre, and word is that she is writing still, every day, her one concession to her great age being to do so at home rather than at the café tables where she once preferred to work.

Sarraute has not done as well in English as she should have done. The first translations of her work, by Maria Jolas, were admittedly poor, a travesty of the prose that in French edges all the time towards poetry, so careful, compacted and rhythmical is it; the English of the later translations, done by Barbara Wright, is faithful in every respect, however, having had to pass the intimidating test of being read aloud to the author. That Nathalie Sarraute should have become a Pléiade author in her own lifetime is exceptional; it's high time the admiration for her outside France grew accordingly.

15

RAYMOND ROUSSEL

He was a writer, of sorts, and a man at once glamorously rich and mentally odd. His money he spent to the hilt in the furtherance of his oddness, for Roussel laboured to write the most uncommercial works and then paid to have them published. He set new standards indeed in vanity publishing, because he paid not only to get his poetry and his fiction into book form, but also to have his plays put on in Paris. The theatre does not come cheap for those who must be their own angels, but to see his uniquely inauspicious plays performed in public was a deep need, and Roussel did not stint on the satisfaction of it. By the end of his life his huge inheritance was exhausted.

Roussel was born, to the financial purple, in 1877. His father was a stockbroker, a wealthy man who had married into money. Young Raymond was more mothered than fathered, however, for in 1894 the father died suddenly – it was reported from drinking iced champagne on a hot day. The rich widow Roussel did not falter; she received the cultural *gratin* and she collected works of art, even if her taste was immaculately bourgeois, as her son's was to prove later on, to the extent of paying people to come in and read the *Three Musketeers* to her. The Veuve Roussel bought a yacht and cruised, so one story had it, all the way to India, where she would only look at the fabled shore through a telescope before ordering the captain to make an about-turn, for Cannes. (Her clothes for the voyage she stored in a coffin.) Either she really was eccentric or those who later reminisced about her wanted to make her sound so, as a fit progenitrix of the peculiar Raymond.

As an adolescent, Roussel was a musician, a successful student at the Paris Conservatoire, a future virtuoso even. But he was already writing and in his third year as a music student, in 1896, his 'crisis' happened. He was working night and day at a narrative poem, to be called *La*

*Doublure**, and doing so in a state of rare exaltation. In his own words, written long afterwards, 'For a few months I experienced a sensation of universal glory of an extraordinary intensity.' Or, as he was reported as saying by the specialist who later treated him, 'What I was writing was surrounded by radiance, I closed the curtains, for I was afraid of the least crack which would have allowed the rays of light coming from my pen to escape outside, I wanted to withdraw the screen suddenly and illuminate the world.'

For these few months, Roussel felt sure he was a literary genius, the peer of any writer who ever wrote. But then the exaltation passed and he entered on an adult lifetime of psychic distress. His childhood, when, he declared, he had known years of 'a perfect happiness', had gone from him. He became at some uncertain point the patient – the Roussel money talking, no doubt – of the top man in Paris for mind disorders, the great Pierre Janet, and appears under a pseudonym as a case study in Janet's book, *From Anguish to Ecstasy*. 'A shy, scrupulous, neuropathic young man, easily depressed,' Janet sums up his patient, whom he couldn't cure.

La Doublure, the poem Roussel was writing when the crisis came on him, trails no clouds of glory. It is in rhyming Alexandrines, but the language and the matter of the work are purest prose. Roussel invariably reads like a McGonagall of the Côte d'Azur:

> A Nice, cet après-midi, dans l'Avenue
> de la Gare, une foule énorme et biscornue
> Fête le dernier jour qu'on ait de Carnaval
>
> (In Nice, this afternoon, in the Avenue
> de la Gare, a vast, irregular crowd
> Is celebrating the last day they have of Carnival)

He asked that his poem be read as a novel, from the beginning through to the end: a first sign of how very highly he valued the act of narration. *La Doublure* in fact has a story running through it, flat and ordinary like its descriptions, of an incompetent actor who has a brief love-affair and ends up as a strolling player, with only his good memories of Nice in carnival-time to console him.

This melancholy work was published in 1897, at the author's expense. So unadmiring was its publisher that he never even announced the book's existence

* This, typically with Roussel, is a double-duty word in French. It can mean either the lining of a garment or a theatrical understudy.

in the *Bibliographie de la France*. Roussel had hopes, however, and tried complimentary copies on his relations and acquaintances, not forgetting young Marcel Proust, whose path he had very likely crossed socially – in the chic boulevard Malesherbes, the Prousts were living at no. 9 when the Roussels were at no. 25. Proust's short thank-you note later formed part of the dossier Roussel built up of the kinder things written about his work by others; the at that time unproductive Proust said naughtily how much he admired Roussel's staying power, in being able to write a hundred lines of poetry as easily as others might write ten lines of prose.

La Doublure met with an absolute silence; Roussel's fantasies of fame were exploded. 'I had the impression of having been dashed to the ground from on top of a prodigious summit of glory.' He developed rashes on his skin and then the nervous illness that he never shook off. But neurasthenia or no, he did not give up writing. Instead, he perfected a new method of composition, one both secretive and fertile, on which most of his later writing was to depend. This was Roussel's 'procedure', a form of wordplay which enabled him to write more or less mechanically. There is no telling from the strange texts so produced the strange manner of their making, but Roussel did not want to die without having revealed it. His literary testament, published only after his death, was an essay called 'How I Wrote Certain of My Books', in which he describes his creative method and gives a frighteningly detached account of his life in literature. He was revealing his method, he said, so that other writers might now make use of it; as indeed they might, though I question whether any ever seriously have.

In the procedure mark one, Roussel would find two French sentences very alike in sound but potentially quite divergent in their sense. The two phrases, for example: *Les lettres du blanc sur les bandes du vieux billard* and *Les lettres du blanc sur les bandes du vieux pillard*. These differ by only the one phoneme, the change from an initial *b* to an initial *p* which is enough in French to distinguish a billiard table (*billard*) from a plunderer (*pillard*). That is already quite a difference, but Roussel is only just starting. The semantic gap between the phrases can be further widened by taking their other nouns in different senses. In the first sentence, *lettres* may be read to mean typographical signs or characters, *blanc* as a cube of white marking-chalk and *bandes* as the cushions of the billiard table: leading, in English, to 'the characters in white chalk on the cushions of the old billiard table'. Which is not at all like the second sentence, where *lettres* are now missives, the *blanc* is a white man and *bandes* are the plunderer's hordes.

Thus, 'the white man's letters about the old plunderer's hordes.' Roussel now has two phrases with which he can start and finish a mini-narrative; all he needs to do is to construct a story which will join them up logically. This was to do what Mallarmé had once recommended that the writer must do: to 'cede the initiative to words'. Roussel himself adopted this procedure because he found it ideally inexpressive. It meant that he could work away at his writing without having to endure the, to him, painful risks of self-revelation.

From this one *texte-genèse* he claims that he was able to derive the whole of his *Impressions d'Afrique* (Impressions of Africa), the large prose work that he published in 1910, though neither of the key sentences occurs verbatim in that 300-page book. What such sentences gave him was first a plot and then a literary asylum. The plot involves the temporary captivity in equatorial Africa of a party of impossibly dextrous European tourists: acrobats, musicians, inventors, scientists, star performers all of them and the very stuff of Roussel's fiction. They are waiting to be ransomed and will pass the time in giving exhibitions of their supernal skills. Once he gets his ransom money, the local emperor, the 'old plunderer', will send them on their way. This remarkable novel is, in the words of Michel Butor, a 'festival of deliverance'.

Roussel's Africa is not, needless to say, the Africa of any known ethnology, but an Africa of the cheapest imaginings, as one might find it in contemporary children's stories. But the *Impressions* mark a passage in its author's mind, from the familiar to the alien, conditioned by his two near, not-so-random, homophonic sentences. For Roussel, the game of billiards was real, it was a pastime appropriate to the wealthy milieu in which he had been raised, hence one that he needed to escape from. Black African plunderers were something else, something made-up and unreal, an artistic milieu worthy of being escaped into.

His two big books, the *Impressions d'Afrique* and *Locus solus*, are a disjointed series of scenes, tableaux and stories in which human dexterity and obsession are taken to monstrous lengths. They are epics of prestidigitation, set in a world where technique is absolute. Roussel's own technique is first to amaze us with some enigmatic or marvellous spectacle and then to explain why it takes the form that it does. But the spectacle and its dubious rationale may be far apart in the text, because the writer wants to enthral us doubly, with first the presentation and only later the resolution of his puzzles. In the *Impressions*, for example, the enigmas displayed in the first half of the book are none of them explained until we get to the second half, when we find out how these European visitors came to be in Africa in the first place. Into the first edition, a perhaps nervous Roussel inserted a notice to the effect that readers not 'initiated' into his art should read the second half of the book first, even though, as a more or less complete unknown, it was a little too soon for him to have had anyone sufficiently prescient to be able to call themselves an 'initiate'.

The format of these two books is that of the circus or the music hall. Turn follows fast on turn, in a frantic accumulation of wonders. For a specimen performance, I take that of Skarioffszky, a very Hungarian Hungarian, who comes on stage in the *Impressions* having trained a giant but docile worm to produce music from a zither by using the contortions of its body to release drops of some unknown liquid onto the strings. Roussel goes into much obscure detail over the mechanics of this animal act, but since the means are as fantastic as the product, the technology, too, is fictive and fails to restore us to the everyday world. Then, two hundred pages further on, we get the story of how Skarioffszky first found and trained his worm. This redistributes the credit for his act somewhat, for it turns out that the worm was already a natural melomaniac when found by Skarioffszky, living in some magic medium that resembles water but is not water. As a worm-tamer, Skarioffszky has had things relatively easy. He had come to Africa as himself the star zither-player, but he abdicates cheerfully in favour of the gifted native (the French for a worm being *ver*, there may be a play here on *ver-tuose* or 'virtuoso'). Like so many of Roussel's fictional surrogates, Skarioffszky is adept at profiting from life's contingencies; his act is one of an inspired collaboration with alien forces and as such neatly analogous with Roussel's own collaboration with the French language.

But there is something else about the worm. Once trained in the use of its zither, it plays music every bit as *expressive* as that which Skarioffszky has been used to making. Roussel, the Conservatoire dropout, describes how the reptile attacks in turn a czardas, a medley of operetta tunes and a 'captivating' Hungarian rhapsody. The performance is scrupulously mechanical, yet its effects are held to be identical with those achieved by a human player. Worms being famously contemptible creatures, it might seem that Roussel is being sardonic in choosing one for his supreme artiste, but I think not. Rather, the worm is evidence of his passion to prove that expressiveness in art, whether in writing or in music, is a function of the medium, not of some supposed inner capacity of the soul.

In 1911, the zither-playing worm enjoyed a première, along with others of

Roussel's African prodigies, when his own stage version of the *Impressions* was mounted. The explicit theatricality of the book, with its sequences of turns and supporting narratives, lent itself to public performance, even if the consistent impossibility of all that happens must also have made its representation both arduous and disappointing – the natural laws are not so easily bent on stage as they are on the page. Roussel himself paid for everything, it seems: the hire of the theatre, the cast, the effects, the sets. This first time round, the *Impressions* lasted only two nights, because Roussel's mother then died and he called it off; six months later, it was put on again and was a noisy failure, the first of a series of similar costly fiascos which marked Roussel's efforts to get himself known as a playwright. Coins were thrown at the actors and the playwright was mocked. But there were a few enthusiasts in the audience: a knot of future Surrealists and Dadaists – Apollinaire, Marcel Duchamp, Picabia all attended – who were the first to take Roussel up. In the twenties, he was to become quite a favourite with the avant-garde, who loved the fact that someone of such deplorable and solemn good taste could produce works so bizarrely way-out.

At the end of 1913, Roussel published his other masterpiece, *Locus solus*, which is as richly and freakishly imaginary as *Impressions d'Afrique*. There was no need this time for him to travel anywhere as fictive as 'Africa'; the setting of *Locus solus* is a private estate only a quarter of an hour out of central Paris. The owner of this 'solitary place' is Martial Canterel, who shows off its astonishing tableaux and contrivances to select parties of guests. Canterel is a scientific magus, a figment comparable with those dreamed up by the writer whom Roussel most revered, Jules Verne. He enjoys an inordinate power both over things and, through his words, over people. For not only is Canterel the creator of an awesome science-park, he is also a guide with a positively Orphic ability to charm: he is 'one of the champions of the word'.

Canterel's feats of invention are extravagant, even measured against those of the *Impressions*. What, for instance, of his paviour's beetle, suspended from a small balloon, which is slowly creating a mosaic picture out of a vast store of human teeth (painlessly removed by some patented new method). Some of the teeth are a healthy white, others have been helpfully yellowed by nicotine, others still are blue or black, or reddened at the roots from their extraction. The mosaic is polychrome, therefore, and also figurative: it shows a Germanic knight or *Reiter* asleep in a crypt beside a subterranean lake, with other figures wreathed in smoke representing emanations from the knight's dormant brain. The mechanism by which the beetle operates is recounted in unintelligible detail, as though this were some authentic if whimsical form of new technology. But in order to make it set the teeth down where they are needed for the picture, Canterel has first to become a master of meteorology, since the aerostat controlling the beetle is itself at the mercy of the winds. Canterel, happily, is able to predict wind conditions with total accuracy up to ten days ahead, so the rightful completion of his mosaic is assured. As with Skarioffszky and his musical worm, Canterel's prowess combines the aleatory with the deliberate, or accident with hard work. Such, for Roussel, was the specification of artistic creation.

His own hard work in the making of *Locus solus* was of a slightly different kind from that which he had put into the *Impressions*. His procedure had by now evolved into a mark two version, though there was still a touch of mark one in the fabrication of the beetle. For this, Roussel had started from the words *demoiselle à prétendant* or 'young girl with a suitor' and converted them into *demoiselle à reître en dents* or 'paviour's beetle (another meaning of the word *demoiselle*) with a *Reiter* out of teeth': he came to lean very heavily on the versatility of the prepositional form *à* in his semantic games.

The procedure mark two involves twisting existing French words or phrases phonetically into new ones: for instance, the phrase *Napoléon premier empéreur* (Napoleon the First, emperor) he turned for his creative purposes into the near-nonsense string of substantives, *Nappe ollé ombre miettes hampe air heure*. Hence, in the text we get Spanish dancers (*olé*) dancing on a tablecloth (*nappe*) on which there is a shadow (*ombre*) of some crumbs (*miettes*), followed by a wind (*air*)-driven clock (*heure*) mounted on a pole (*hampe*). Or another choice example: the brand name *Phonotypia* gave him in the first instance *fausse note tibia*, and then, once the narrative element is in place, a Breton fisherman who plays flute tunes on his own amputated tibia. This more evolved procedure enabled Roussel to work from series of dislocated nouns, to which his own contribution would be the narrative syntax linking them. But the Phonotypia example shows, too, how freely he distorted the sounds he began with; this was a looser procedure than the earlier one and gave him a wider choice of possibilities.

To many, Roussel will seem a petty or a futile writer: a punster who even hid the evidence of his punning. But the wordplay on which he counted was a most serious business for him; it kept him working, and in work alone lay the promise that the lost 'glory' might be won back, as ultimate literary fame if not as an immediate radiance. Roussel's is a literature of therapy and its hallmark is a concern with flawless repetition. The elaborate performances in which his two large books abound cannot go wrong, the command that is invested in the performer is total. And with command there comes release, deliverance. Among the geniuses of the *Impressions* is a young female impersonator, Carmichael, who sings perfect soprano. But trying to repeat the lines of a crushingly repetitive epic poem written by the emperor in celebration of his own exploits, Carmichael actually gets a word wrong. The emperor punishes him with a three-hour detention. The next time he recites the poem, Carmichael is word-perfect, and both he and the other Europeans are then allowed to leave 'Africa'. Life returns, you might say, only once the text has been got absolutely right.

Roussel served through the 1914–18 war in the French army, by his own account as a driver, though no one believed that a man reputedly incapable of unscrewing the cap on a bottle could have learnt to drive a lorry. After the war he returned to his writing. *Locus solus* was expensively adapted for the stage and performed in 1922, to more derision. The Surrealists defended it, but elsewhere there was much humourless grumbling about rich men being able to hire public theatres and put on rubbish. Concluding next that adaptations would never succeed, he wrote two plays directly for the stage, but these failed too. The second of them, *La Poussière des soleils* (The dust of the suns), passed off almost quietly, and his jovial claque felt cheated, worried that their man might be declining fatally into good sense.

For seven years Roussel worked also on his *Nouvelles Impressions d'Afrique*, a poem written in Alexandrines (even the footnotes are in the same classical metre) which he calculated had cost him more than nineteen thousand hours of work. The *Nouvelles Impressions* are scarcely more African than the *Impressions*, even if each section of the poem does set out to describe a particular scene in Egypt. But it is very quickly led astray, as Roussel pursues the promptings of language rather than those of the landscape. From the banks of the Nile to a Paris salon is for him the shortest of steps:

> Rasant le Nil, je vois fuir deux rives couvertes
> De fleurs, d'ailes, d'éclairs, de riches plantes vertes
> Dont une suffirait à vingt de nos salons

> (Skimming the Nile, I see two banks receding covered
> With flowers, with wings, with lightning flashes, with rich green plants
> One of which would suffice for twenty of our drawing rooms)

And once we are in the salons there is no going back to the Nile, as Roussel's verses devolve into a sequence of parentheses, the next of which invariably opens before the previous one has closed, so that you may come upon embedded parentheses up to the power of five or six, which does nothing for the poem's continuity. For all its occasional charm, the *Nouvelles Impressions* was another commercial flop. The text was too short to make a book on its own, so Roussel thought to get it illustrated. The artist he hired through a detective agency, but he refused to meet him or let him actually read the poem before providing the pictures. Instructions were sent, however, and the pictures were done. But they appeared in the book as a block, all fifty-nine of them, rather than placed where appropriate throughout the text, and the book itself was printed in such a way that until the pages were cut only Roussel's contribution to it, the verses, was visible.

Roussel continued in these years to be treated by doctors. In 1928, he was in the same *maison de santé* as Jean Cocteau, then being treated for opium addiction. Cocteau noticed, as others had, how like Proust Roussel was – in voice, in physique and in nervousness. Roussel, on the other hand, spoilt the comparison by asking Cocteau one day why he, Roussel, could not be famous like a very much less highbrow writer than Proust, the 'exotic' novelist Pierre Loti. By the end of the twenties, it seems certain that Roussel had spent his way through his family money. He took new and this time more practical steps towards securing a name for himself once he was dead. He sold the villa in Neuilly which he had inherited from his mother, on the understanding that if a projected road was one day made through part of the gardens, it would be called the avenue Raymond Roussel (it never was); and he bought for himself a concession in the Père-Lachaise cemetery, ordering for it a large monument in best Carrara marble which would show him standing authorially before a bookcase (this was never made either). The sculptor was to work from a photograph, but one taken when Roussel was still a hopeful nineteen year old.

In 1933, Roussel went to stay in Palermo, in the same hotel in which Wagner had written *Parsifal*. With him was Charlotte Dufrène, who had been his 'mistress' for many years, taken, it was generally assumed, to serve as a cover for his homosexuality. He was now on a regime of barbiturates. In Palermo he took an overdose but was quickly found and revived. The death wish in him was strong, but not yet strong enough for him to be able to end his life by his own hand. He turned one last time to his money to ease the way: first he tried to bribe Charlotte to shoot him with his own revolver and then, when she refused, asked his valet to cut his wrists. The valet wouldn't. So Roussel cut his own wrists, in the bath, but at once called for help – and was saved once again. Finally, still a guest in the same – remarkably tolerant – hotel, he took a second, this time definitive overdose of Soneryl. He was buried where he had wanted: in the Père-Lachaise, without his statue but in a vault divided into thirty-two compartments, in apparent homage to another of his ludic obsessions, the game of chess. (Who, I wonder, did he envision as his posthumous opponent, occupying the other half of the board?)

Roussel is a writer who comes and goes. He came first in the 1920s, condescendingly lionised as he then was by the Surrealists; only to fall back into obscurity once the vogue for him had dwindled. He came again in the 1960s and 1970s, when François Caradec's life of him appeared and his methods of composition were taken as a model by the ludically inclined members of the OuLiPo, a body actually brought into existence in order to encourage Roussel-like experiments in the generative powers of language. And in the 1990s, just when this quiet revival in Roussel's literary fortunes was starting to lose way, a cache of his unpublished manuscripts came to light, whose eventual publication will ensure that his next relapse into obscurity is some years off. Some of what Roussel so laboriously wrote is no fun to read, but there was a method in his literary madness which we do well to attend to, because it makes explicit the degree to which, when we write, we ask language to call the tune.

16

BORIS VIAN

Around two a.m. Boris suggested a cup of coffee; we sat down in the kitchen and we talked till dawn: about his novel, about jazz, about literature, about his job as an engineer. I could no longer find anything affected in that long smooth white face but an extreme kindness and a sort of obstinate candour; Vian was as fiery in his detestation of the *affreux* [the frightful ones] as in loving what he loved. . . . We talked and the dawn came too quickly.

The description is Simone de Beauvoir's, in one of her volumes of autobiography, *La Force des choses*, and the occasion of this all-night conversation was a party given by Boris and Michelle Vian in March 1946. Boris Vian was then twenty-six and the ideal embodiment of the convivial, anarchic spirit of postwar Saint-Germain-des-Prés: the young *cave*-dweller who was to become the annalist of that renowned Left Bank neighbourhood when, some years after his early death, his *Manuel de Saint-Germain-des-Prés* was published.

At the time, Vian was a close friend of Sartre and Simone de Beauvoir, and an existentialist by instinct rather than by any formal affiliation to that philosophy. As it had been so very lengthily expounded by Sartre during the war in *L'Etre et le néant*, existentialism was for Vian matter more for satire than for the solemn acceptance it had met with from others. What suited him about it was the romantic, not to say fantastic, idea that, for as long as we are alive, we are each of us free to be what we will: this was an idea that Vian did his best to live out. Be a specialist in everything was what he once advised, and he had himself the zest and variety of mind to be a specialist in unusually many things. His education had been mathematical and technical: his degree was in engineering. Having graduated, he worked in an office for three and a half years, at something called the Association française de normalisation, a body whose name and function could but strike someone like Vian as ludicrous, he being already certain that the ab- or anti-normal was to be preferred to the normal. In 1946, he gave the job up, and thereafter engineering turned from a profession into an amusement: he kept it up as a lover of old cars, as an inspired DIY man and as the inventor in his books of such technological luxuries as a 'pianocktail', a cross between a musical instrument and a bartender, which mixes apéritifs in obedience to the jazz tunes that are played on the keyboard.

Born in 1920, Vian was twenty-four when the German occupiers were expelled from Paris, a liberation that served as an encouraging prelude to his own liberation a year or two later, from the constraints of regular work in an office and what he saw as the prevailing cultural staidness. The time was one of Americanisation in Paris, of a new passion among the young for what Raymond Queneau's fearsome *gamine*, the phonetically challenged Zazie, refers to as 'cacocalo' and 'bloudjinnzes'. The United States had first sent soldiers to help liberate France and then, under the Marshall Plan, they had sent money to restore the economy. Gratitude was in order, and the form it took was often one of an unprecedented openness towards American culture. This might be deplored for its barbarism by the older cultural mandarins of Paris, but it was an inspiration for free spirits such as Boris Vian.

He had strong American tastes already, in movies, in crime writing, in science fiction and especially in jazz. This last took off in France on the postwar wave of philo-Americanism. Vian was a trumpet player, a good one, in a style said to have been modelled on that of the Chicagoan Bix Beiderbecke, and the groups he played with, amateur though they remained, were the best known in France. Vian played jazz and he also promoted it, as a publicist and as a discographer. When its American giants of those years came across to Paris – Miles Davis, Duke Ellington, Charlie Parker – Boris Vian was their host and advocate on the Left Bank.

It was there, indeed, in the liberated environment of its *caves*, or 'basement clubs' – of the celebrated Tabou (taboo) above all – that Vian found a setting that could sustain him both socially and financially. He enjoyed the caustic, self-indulgent company of the boisterous Sartre and co., who took to this erratically talented young man. Sartre it was who launched him into literature. The first piece of writing that Vian published under his own name, a short story called *Les Fourmis* (The ants) appeared, remarkably, in the June 1946 issue of Sartre's very serious journal, *Les Temps modernes*. In the same issue, there appeared also the first of five items contributed by Vian under the teasing title of 'Chroniques du menteur', or 'The liar's column', a by-line that gave him the freedom to write more or less anything he chose, since a liar can't so easily be held responsible for what he prints in case he turns out not to believe it himself. In the event, Vian's parasitical column soon turned on its host, criticising first the journal's format and then the narrowness of its political and literary focus. The liar was dropped; but it is to the credit of the Sartre of those relaxed years that he should have invited this untameable drinking companion to contribute to his journal, knowing as he did that Vian was the exact reverse of an *homme engagé*.

In the years that followed that first appearance in print, Vian wrote and published a great deal: poems, stories, songs, scenarios for films and for operas, translations from English, six novels and three and a half plays (the half was barely longer than a squib). He did not, however, become widely known. He lacked the authorial vanity that is so useful to a writer in France, and seems to have been happy to publish anywhere, on the most casual terms. With one exception, the novels that were to be taken up with huge enthusiasm after his death were published for the first time by small, financially pinched houses, and they flopped, selling mere hundreds of copies, if that. (The one exception was *L'Ecume des jours* [Froth on the daydream, or, in the US, Mood indigo], which was published by Gallimard, thanks to the support it received there from Raymond Queneau; but it still sold poorly.) If Vian was known at all in his lifetime outside Left Bank circles it was first as a *chansonnier* (a writer and performer of vaudeville songs) and then as the pseudonymous author of four 'American' *romans noirs*, or crime novels.

By the reckoning of his bibliographers, Vian wrote approaching four hundred songs, many of them to order and in a few minutes only, with a wit and facility that were the wonder of the trade. He himself had no sort of singing voice or technique, but he went onto the stage and sang nonetheless, to good effect, liked perhaps for his amateurishness. The songs themselves were in the best tradition of their cabaret genre: a mixture of the polemical, the sentimental and the seditious. One of them in particular struck a topical chord and gave Vian a wider fame: 'Le Déserteur' (The deserter), a song that he wrote in 1955, in the early days of the war in Algeria, when young French conscripts found themselves being sent to try and suppress by force of arms the increasingly successful movement for independence in the colony. Unlike Sartre, with whom by this time he had broken, Vian was no extremist on the issue; he declared that his song was 'pro-civilian' rather than anti-military, a distinction that does him credit.

Monsieur le Président
Je vous fais une lettre
Que vous lirez peut-être
Si vous avez le temps
Je viens de recevoir
Mes papiers militaires
Pour partir à la guerre
Avant mercredi soir
Monsieur le Président
Je ne veux pas le faire
Je ne suis pas sur terre
Pour tuer des pauvres gens
C'est pas pour vous fâcher
Il faut que je vous dise
Ma décision est prise
Je m'en vais déserter.

(Monsieur President
I'm writing you a letter
That you'll read perhaps
If you have time
I've just received
My call-up papers
To go off to war
By Wednesday evening
Monsieur President
I won't do it
I'm not here on earth
To kill poor people
It's not so as to annoy you
I have to tell you
My mind's made up
I'm going to desert.)

Sublime simplicity was ever the satirist's best weapon, and the faux-naïf manner here is essential to the *chansonnier* tradition: it should make the words of the song seem more, not less, angry. 'Le Déserteur' was in fact less savagely anti-authority than others of Vian's songs but, written and sung when it was, at the most divisive moment in French postwar history, it might easily have led to his being beaten or even killed by colonialist fanatics in metropolitan France.

Vian was also known as the 'translator' of the scabrous crime novels of an American author called 'Vernon Sullivan'. He wrote four of these and the first of them, *J'irai cracher sur vos tombes* (I'll go spit on your graves), landed him very profitably in trouble with the censors. The book was a clever pastiche, written in the space of ten days after he had made a typically friendly promise to produce something for a publisher in need of a best seller along the lines of *No Orchids for Miss Blandish*, the James Hadley Chase novel that had recently had an enormous success in French translation. As it turned out, *J'irai cracher* was a best seller, selling, so it was said, more copies than any other book published in France in the whole of 1947.

It was also prosecuted for indecency, in a case that lasted for three years, before its author was in the end fined the modest sum of 100,000 (old) francs for an 'affront to public decency'. Having had to admit to authorship of the incriminated volume, Vian was from then on known to a far larger public than before, as a practising libertarian. The most prominent of those who had claimed that *J'irai cracher* was an incitement to the young to commit acts of debauchery was an architect named Daniel Parker, whose reward was to be given the role of hero in the next Vernon Sullivan novel, *Les Morts ont tous la même peau* (The dead all have the same skin), in which Dan Parker is a bouncer in a New York nightclub who believes, wrongly, that, though his skin is white, he was born into a black family. He is blackmailed, murders his blackmailer in desperation and ends by committing suicide, having become the unfortunate bearer of Vian's simple, anti-racist moral, that skin colour counts for nothing in the face of the mortality that we all, black and white alike, have in common.

Everyone with whom Boris Vian came into contact at this time of his life was liable to be made use of à la Dan Parker, though, given how fantastic much of this usage was, it would be going too far to say that what he wrote were *romans à clef*. Some of his friends step straight into literature in their everyday clothes. One Jacques Loustalot, for instance, was given a hilarious role as a one-eyed army major, while Claude Léon, a fellow jazzman, was turned into a most unlikely hermit. In 1947, Vian was disappointed when the best, and ultimately far and away the most successful of his novels, *L'Ecume des jours*, did not win a literary prize for which it was a candidate, and in the novel that he produced shortly afterwards, *L'Automne à Pékin* (Autumn in Peking), he inserted references both friendly and unfriendly to some of those involved, according to whether they had been for or against him in the debate over who should win the prize in question. One of his supporters, Jacques Lemarchand, is rewarded by having an avenue named after him – a mark of respect he shares with two of Vian's jazz heroes, Sidney Bechet and Louis Armstrong – and by being described as 'the heroic defender, all on his own, of a barricade against the Prussians in 1870'. While among those thought to have scuppered Vian's chances of the prize, the influential critic Jean Paulhan appears as an unlovely tycoon, the baron Ursus de Janpolent, and the author whose book had actually taken the prize, Jean Grosjean, at that time a Catholic priest, is renamed the abbé Petitjean and asked to recite forms of catechism far removed from any authorised by the Church.

Vian was writing in the first instance for the amusement of those around him, who knew him well enough to pick up his allusions and identify the objects of his satire. This is nowhere clearer than in the first of his novels to be published, the endearingly titled *Vercoquin et le plancton* (*Vercoquin* = *ver* + *coquin*, or 'worm' + 'rascal'). In this skit he takes his revenge on the Association française de normalisation where he had spent three and a half bored and futile years, and preaches for a first time the gospel of anti-work that meant so much to him. This was Vian's simplified version of another Sartrian, or Marxian, theme: that of alienation. Work, of the mindless, nugatory kind described here and elsewhere in Vian's oeuvre, is against nature, and to submit to its disciplines is to die inwardly. Against work, in *Vercoquin*, are to be set the surprise-parties that represent an autonomous, natural, unscripted way of life. ('Surprise-parties' were called by their English name and seem to have become something of an adolescent fashion among the bourgeois young even before 1939; Vian himself loved going to them and giving them, and he wrote *Vercoquin* in part to remind those who might have forgotten what a precious element of youthful experience they had been.)

Vercoquin is nothing if not a high-spirited book, an early demonstration of Vian's gift for *loufoquerie* or 'fantastic humour'. The knockabout has a cartoon or silent-movie quality, involving as it does a regular modification of the laws of nature so as to make the lived environment more congenial to human wishes. And it fits happily with the easy hedonism that so appealed to Vian, whose surprise-parties, convened in order to breathe life back into the moribund souls of the stupefied office workers, are liable to lead on to a more advanced sort of gathering, to the *partouze*, or 'orgy'.

The unclouded sexuality of *Vercoquin* was soon, however, to prove exceptional in Vian's writing. In the books that followed, the relations between young men and young women grow more troubled, and the comedy starts to acquire a dark edge. Things were not well in Vian's private life: he had trouble both maritally and medically. He had married very young, at twenty-one, during the war, and already by the mid 1940s that marriage was deteriorating (it ended in a divorce in 1952, by which time Michelle Vian had had a notorious affair with

Sartre). That was one cause for depression.* Vian's medical state made things even worse. He had had serious heart trouble ever since an attack of rheumatic fever in childhood; characteristically, he made no allowances for it, and went on playing the trumpet even after doctors had told him he was risking his life by doing so. He was under threat physically as well as psychologically, and this downward turn in his life became reflected in the trajectory that he imposed on the plot of his best-known novel.

The physical erosion of a desirable young body is the poignant theme of *L'Ecume des jours*. That erosion is brought about by means that are fantastic, though its effects are not so, since they end in the cruel death of the childlike girl who has to endure them. The novel begins in the neat, hopeful setting of a young man's apartment into which there shines not just one sun but two; it ends with the same living space shrinking day by day into the grimiest of dying spaces. The young man, Colin, is an innocent, lustful but a little timid, who meets a girl, Chloë (named for a Duke Ellington number), who is as innocent as himself: this is the cheerful surprise-party world over again. Once the two of them are married, however, the atmosphere becomes punitive. On their honeymoon they drive ominously through a copper-mining district and past groups of the degraded men who are obliged to work there, before Chloë happens to breathe in some snowflakes and contracts the strange disease that will kill her, as a water lily grows inside her lung. The fatal affliction is ambiguously poised between the charmingly floral and the macabre.

The water lily is not the only agent of destruction in the novel; there is also the obsession that leads to the penury, solitude and eventual death of another of the characters, Colin's friend Chick. The obsession is at first sight a comical one: Chick is obsessed with collecting the manuscripts and other memorabilia of a famous philosopher called Jean-Sol Partre – Colin envisages at one point doing the same for Partre's companion, the duchesse de Bovouard. Partriana, however – his discarded pipes, a pair of his trousers, a thumbprint – cost money, thousands in the local Vianesque currency of 'doublezoons', and Chick, who is an ill-paid engineer, can satisfy his obsession only with hand-outs from the well-heeled Colin. What with lending doublezoons to Chick, however, and paying for rapacious and ineffectual doctors to treat Chloë, Colin's money runs

---

* A comment in Raymond Queneau's published journals, for the year 1952, casts a rather bleak light on Vian's state. This was the year when the divorce was finalised, and Queneau quotes his friend as saying 'A case of acute blue-stockingitis. . . . Now she says I harmed her, that it was "traumatic" for her. . . . The best thing would be if she had a fatal car accident.'

out, which is terrible news in a Vian novel, because those without money must go out and earn some. Colin's attempts to do so are predictably grim and unavailing.

Vian's by-play with the revered thinker Jean-Sol Partre, now the author of a twenty-volume encyclopaedia on 'vomit' and of *La Lettre et le néon*, a treatise on illuminated advertising signs, is benign enough, and includes an extravagantly slapstick account of a meeting addressed by Partre, to be read as a satire on a famous lecture on existentialism that Sartre had given before an unnaturally excited Paris audience in 1945. At the same time, Chick's absurd and disastrous hagiolatry is surely meant as the iconoclastic Vian's warning against what had since become a local cult of Sartre as the revered genius of the Left Bank. Chick is the first, but not the last, of Vian's characters who is made to embody the threat to health and happiness that may spring from obsession; in the last, and least comic, of his novels, *L'Arrache-Coeur* (Heartsnatcher), a young mother of triplets is so obsessively maternal that she encloses them in cages behind a 'wall of nothing' so as to ensure her own secure possession of them.

The hatred of work also takes on a blacker hue in *L'Ecume des jours* than it had in the simpler days of *Vercoquin*. The leering copper miners whom Colin and Chloë see from the safety of their car are ugly, sinister figures, dehumanised by what they are asked to do. Colin himself, who as yet has plenty of money and an apartment ingeniously fitted out so as to relieve anyone who lives in it of degrading chores, embodies the greatest truth of Vianism: that work is plain bad unless it is work aimed at the reduction in the amount of work that needs to be done. Vian would not have hung back from welcoming with open arms the advances in mechanisation and robotics that we have seen since his death.

He was enraged by the docility with which people surrender their autonomy by becoming employees: to belong to a category of any kind is to abandon one's identity. In *L'Ecume des jours*, when those ultimate bogeys the *flics* turn out under the command of their 'seneschal', they all answer to the same name, the name of Douglas, for some no doubt excellent personal reason. In *L'Equarrissage pour tous* (Knackering made easy), a frantic squib of a play supposedly set in a Norman horse-knacker's yard on D-Day, the members of the opposing armies end up dressed in one another's uniforms after a game of strip poker. In *L'Automne à Pékin*, the same scorn is shown towards bus conductors and homosexuals, categories ridiculed by Vian for acting 'inauthentically', in a manner imposed on them from outside by the expectations of the society in which they find themselves.

There is the category also of priests, the cassocked ones. Vian clearly saw no use in them, but his attitude is nuanced. They may have entertainment value, like the monk who, in one of Vian's more harmless songs, picks up the new 1950s rhythms from America on his home-made radio and emerges from his austere cell gambolling to a familiar French round:

> Frère Jacques
> Jupon vole
> Chantons tous ensemble
> L'frock and roll.

> (Frère Jacques
> Skirts a-whorl
> Sing it all together
> Frock 'n roll.)

The collusion between the Church and show business is brought out more pointedly in one of the plays, where an abbé has a dressing room in his church and gives interviews to reporters after delivering an especially brilliant sermon. In *L'Ecume des jours*, Colin and Chloë are married in a church, to the bizarrest of rites, involving various jazz instruments, dancing children and two high-camp 'fairies of honour'. This is religion as spectacle, if nothing else, and prepares the way for the (egg-shaped) church in *L'Arrache-Coeur*, whose incumbent preaches that God is a luxury. When, after Chloë's funeral, Colin asks Jesus on his crucifix why he had done nothing to save her, the same Jesus who had looked on benevolently at the time of the couple's wedding merely shifts to a more comfortable position and purrs contentedly like a cat. At which point, Vian's ambivalent stance in respect of religion gives way to resentment at the futility of its proferred consolations.

In the face of death, Vian can offer nothing more comforting than defiance, and a refusal to live one's life by society's meekly utilitarian rules. Going into Vian's apartment in Paris, so someone said, was like going on holiday, and the holiday spirit is the one he was adept at creating in his books. It was made more, not less, desirable of course for being exposed, in *L'Ecume des jours*, as a desperately fragile state of mind. Exopotamia, the desert country – not obviously anywhere near China nor in any sense autumnal – that he invented in

L'Automne à Pékin, defeats all attempts to build a railway line across it, and at the end of that book we are told that the future of the country is perfectly unpredictable, that anything at all might happen there: such was Vianland.

Boris Vian died suddenly, of a heart attack, in 1959, aged only thirty-nine – 'I shan't live to be forty,' he had been used to saying. It happened suitably in a place of pleasure, a cinema, where he was watching the preview of a movie made from *J'irai cracher sur vos tombes*. This shockingly early death meant that posterity could take him permanently for what he had been when young: he had been spared the sclerosis of mind that might have come even to Boris Vian in middle age. And that now irrevocable youthfulness ensured success in the future for his writings such as he could not have conceived of in his lifetime. In the early 1960s, Raymond Queneau was suddenly able to say: 'Boris Vian is about to become Boris Vian.' And so he did. The novels were re-issued, by more enterprising publishers this time, in more visible editions, and they sold, especially *L'Ecume des jours*, whose eventual sales over the next few years approached a million copies.

When the events of May 1968 came, with the benign if doomed wish of their student fomenters and activists that Imagination now take precedence over the reality principle in the conduct of public life, who better for them to take as their prophet than Boris Vian, the young man who had as a pastime created an alternative reality where the spirit of play had been installed in power? Boris Vian's moment had arrived.

17

RAYMOND QUENEAU

In 1948, Jean-Paul Sartre asked the question 'What is Literature?' and answered it in a substantial, profoundly *engagé* book in which he declared that Literature was 'in a word . . . in its essence, the subjectivity of a society in a state of permanent revolution'. At much the same time, a contemporary of Sartre's, Raymond Queneau, answered the same question in three *désengagé* lines of *faux-naif* verse. Writing, he said, was

> Un jeu simple
> que j'invimple
> dans la nuimple

or in English, ignoring the twist Queneau has given to the tails of two French words for the sake of a rhyme, 'A simple game/ that I made up / in the dark.'

The style of these lines is hardly Sartrian, yet the philosophy, once it has been teased out, is. For Queneau took a gloomy view of the human condition, and his philosophy might fairly be described as existentialism with a human face. Like Sartre, he knew that we must all of us live, metaphysically speaking, in the 'dark', as transients of scant significance in a cosmos seeming to possess a degree of rhyme but absolutely no reason. But where the ebullient Sartre contrives to raise our dereliction into a perverse source of grandeur, on the Romantic assumption that we deserve better of the Universe in which we find ourselves adrift, Queneau remains wryly down-to-earth, unwilling to see either his humble self or any of those around him in the exalted guise of an existentialist hero.

Nor did he begin to share the optimistic beliefs that the Sartre of *What is Literature?* held as to the pragmatic possibilities of writing. Sartre thought that writers could change the world, politically and morally, by 'unveiling' society to itself; Queneau thought no such utopian thing. For him, the literary and the topical were two quite distinct spheres, a point he made robustly enough in his first novel, *Le Chiendent* (The couch-grass, 1933), where the local newspaper is good only for being torn into small sheets and hung up for active service beside the lavatory-pan. Writing for Queneau was not politics but play, a game, though by no means as simple a one as he may sometimes have pretended. It was also his life, or the activity at which he spent his time, and a serious matter too, therefore; if he chose to write playfully it was because he thought writers had a duty to remain modest and to keep a sense of proportion about their importance in the scheme of things.

Sartre and Queneau had more than a certain philosophy in common: they also had the town of Le Havre. Queneau was born there (in 1903), and for five years in the early 1930s Sartre taught in a *lycée* there. In *La Nausée*, the novel which Sartre began writing at that time, Le Havre, a place he loathed, has been renamed Bouville (*boue* = 'mud'), and a lawyer's clerk whom he had come across turned into the character of the Auto-Didact, a mournful figure who sits daily improving himself in the public library. Raymond Queneau to the life, one might almost say: for Queneau once described himself as a boy sitting in the public library in Le Havre, reading systematically through the *Encylopédie Larousse*, volume 1, A to Bello (Andrès). Not that, as he saw it, there was anything at all contemptible in having, or in feeding, a strong desire to know things; it was to stay with him throughout his life.

Queneau's appetite for books was remarkable, and precocious. By the age of sixteen, he was reading Nietzsche and finding Proust on first acquaintance 'soporific'. When his journals were published in full in 1996, nearly two hundred pages were taken up by the lists of books that he had read at different stages of his life. He was a great reader and a great maker of lists, given from childhood on to the pleasures of tabulation. In January 1945, a month like any other, he records having read thirty-three books in thirty-one days, on literature, history, art, mathematics, physics, travel, plants and other subjects besides. There was more to this gluttonous programme, however, than the replenishment of an unusually encyclopaedic mind, for in the objectivity that reading demanded he looked to find relief from the anxious self-concern that otherwise afflicted him. There was, as he recognised, a strong, and uncomfortable, element of willed mental distraction in this piling-up of impersonal knowledge.

In the mid 1950s, Queneau found what many would have supposed was the job for which his many years of miscellaneous browsing had been preparing him: he was invited by his own publisher, Gallimard, to take charge of the new Encyclopédie de la Pléiade that was being planned. He became its presiding editor; yet his gross appetite for information notwithstanding, he was never at ease in the part of encyclopaedist, let alone in that of an editor. He saw himself rather as a failed metaphysician. Queneau had won all manner of prizes at school, and might when he left have gone in several intellectual directions. In the event, he enrolled to read sciences at the Sorbonne, a course that could be expected to satisfy the rigorous, empirical side of his intelligence. There was another side to Queneau when young, however, a speculative one that led him beyond the secular metaphysics of the philosophers into a concern with religion, with the various conceptions of God and with the purposes, if any, of the Whole. The 'way' that he foresaw himself following most happily in his life was that of an unspecific 'transcendence' – a vertical transcendence outside of Time, that is, not the horizontal transcendence within History of a revolutionary politics. But he found in the end that he wasn't the transcendent sort: 'But there,' this is a journal entry from 1927, 'I'm incapable of it. I mean not of meditation, but of tackling the universal – or better still: I can't detach myself from the individual, the particular. . . . That's . . . the tragic aspect of my intellectual life.'

At this stage, Queneau can have had no real idea of how he might turn this 'tragic aspect' of his intellectual life to advantage. Once he became a writer of poetry and fiction he did so turn it, however, to our great advantage as well as to his own. What had once seemed tragic came to seem a source of comedy, as he resolved the tension between the divergent tendencies of his mind by playing the philosopher-clown and smuggling his old transcendental perplexities into novels that might appear to their amused readers to contain nothing beyond the particularities of local and preferably low life.

That low life is invariably urban: Queneau was the complete townsman. If there is lyricism in his poetry, the town alone is able to bring it out, never the countryside, which is a place without the least claim on him: 'abuser du temps qui passe / voilà tout ce qu'à la campagne / fait le monsieur de Paris'(misuse the time that passes / that's all the gentleman from Paris / does in the country). As an adolescent in Le Havre, in intervals of reading, Queneau enjoyed such public amusements as were going, the cinemas first of all and eventually the bars, duly recording in his journals the numbers of hours that he spent playing billiards there. In his novels, bars serve as a true locus amoenus, they are the idealised settings in which his raucously urban characters can spar with one another in a conviviality made richer by the inspired French demotic Queneau puts into their mouths.

After 1921, when the family moved to the Paris outskirts, he became expert on the layout of the Métro and on the numbers and routes of Paris buses, more knowledge that he puts to work in his books. He was himself the most knowing of Parisians, unlike the character in his famous metropolitan novel, *Zazie dans le métro* (Zazie on the Metro), who is constantly getting the city's landmarks muddled up even though he has lived there all his life. Queneau had a chronic need to know, whether about the city he lived in or about the dauntingly numerous other topics that he pursued. His encyclopaedia was never far away, and even by 1950 he was still telling himself off for failing to resist 'the temptation to read Larousse pen in hand'. He especially couldn't resist items of what he called 'stray erudition', wayward knowledge of the sort he employs to fine effect in his novel *Les Enfants du limon* (The children of the clay), which contains surprising quantities of information about the deluded but determined eccentrics who have struggled vainly in the past to square the circle, trisect an angle and solve other insoluble puzzles.

Mathematics was in fact the subject about which Queneau knew and cared the most. He was an anti-realist, believing that the structures of mathematics reflect the structure of the human mind. They are not provably real, in the philosophical sense of existing objectively in nature, independent of the mind that contains them; their truth is consensual and pragmatic, because they are agreed on by the community of the mathematically informed and they can be succesfully applied by working scientists. They are therefore, in Queneau's terms, both 'fictif', 'factif' and 'effectif'. He thought it deplorable that mathematics should have the quite low cultural standing that it does have and be looked on by many as obscure. He would have liked to popularise mathematical knowledge, and condemned above all the self-satisfaction with which literary people boast that they don't understand the first thing about them, as if the literary and mathematical worlds were mutually exclusive. It was a question not of intelligence but of character, declared Queneau: 'Anyone is capable of understanding mathematics, or, if you prefer, "the mathematical method". All it takes is a good teacher and not too many complexes.'

Mathematics interlocks most simply with literature in the determination of literary forms. This is readily apparent in poetry, whose forms must involve some intrusion of the numerical: the sonnet, for example, is a poetic form the number of whose lines, their division into groups and even their syllabification is fixed by numerical convention. Queneau had an extensive knowledge of poetic forms and a mathematician's desire to exploit and, whenever possible, to develop them – a desire that led him, late in his life, to help found the OuLiPo, whose function was, and is, to experiment along these lines. His own most celebrated OuLiPian exercise was an opuscule entitled *Cent mille milliards de poèmes* (A hundred thousand billion poems), which consists of a sonnet whose fourteen lines are all interchangeable with one another and able therefore to be re-arranged in a vast number of permutations, computable if need be as factorial 14 (14 × 13 × 12 × . . .). The exercise was typical of Queneau: ludic yet highly instructive, in drawing attention to the element of the combinatorial that exists in all writing, even if we prefer not to acknowledge it. Writing can but consist in the combining of words and, living as we do in the age of Chomsky, we have come to understand better the nature and extent of the constraints that affect verbal combination.

There is mathematics in Queneau's novels too, where he uses it, surreptitiously, as a determinant of their structure, thus bringing fiction and poetry closer together. In a novel called *Les Fleurs bleues* (*Between Blue and Blue* in its English translation), for example, particular integers have been given particular functions. The book has twenty-one chapters in all, and the barge or ark on which one of the two principal characters lives is no. 21. Of the twenty-one chapters, the seventh and thirteenth are structurally different from the others, because the numbers seven and thirteen were propitious for Queneau, seven because his surname had seven letters in it, thirteen because it 'denied good fortune'!

In a similar spirit, and in the same novel, he also resorts to what could well be called rhyme in order to give a coherent structure to the plot. *Les Fleurs bleues* is effectively one long rhyme since it derives from the mental activities of two dreamers, each of whom dreams the life of the other. They start the book 700 years apart, but the senior of the two, historically speaking, is soon striding towards the present 175 years at a time. This as it happens is the time-gap dividing two very significant meetings of the States General in France, in 1614 and the revolutionary year of 1789, and also the time-gap dividing the latter year from that when the novel was begun, 1964. This is what Queneau, following the Surrealists, would have called a *hasard objectif* or 'objective chance', a suggestive coincidence offered to him by the historical calendar. And any such *hasard objectif* was an excuse for the writer to take wing, as in *Les Fleurs bleues* he very engagingly does.

The second of Queneau's great intellectual passions was for language, a passion that is everywhere apparent in his writing. It had begun when he was still at school. Aged eighteen, and in a 'period of intellectual euphoria', the 'Major Projects' that he listed for future fulfilment included: 'Re-learning English, Latin, Greek, learning Italian, German'; and, on the theoretical side: 'Linguistics, Saussure (in depth) – Meillet – Bréal – Grammont.' These were the leading French-language linguists of the day, and that he should have been reading Saussure as early as 1921 is impressive; the epochal *Cours de linguistique générale* was little known and less understood at that time, having first been published only five years before.

But then the very orderly Queneau was someone well able to think structurally about language even before he had read Saussure. One opposition of which much is made in Saussurian linguistics came to influence him more than any other: that between *langue* and *parole*, or a language understood theoretically, as a system, and language as it is actually practised, as a daily event. Queneau's interest became centred on *parole*, or language in action, and above all on the striking differences that exist within any particular language between its formal and informal usages. His most attractive books are founded on a logomachy in which fine words are pitted against the not so fine, or an exaggeratedly correct French against an equally exaggerated demotic that is mainly of Queneau's devising and is both funnier and more subtly allusive than anything one can imagine overhearing in the streets, bars or Métro of Paris.

Queneau offered this inventive compromise between the two extremes as 'a third French', in the wish that under its influence the formal written language might be revitalised by being brought closer to the spoken. The narrative passages of his novels are often conspicuously elegant and conspicuously learned in their vocabulary: they are close to being stylish parodies of the high style. In between them come what are beyond question the most entertaining tirades and barrages of dialogue in all of modern French literature. What we hear then is the vox populi as it ought to be, were the actual populus as verbally resourceful as Queneau's very flattering imitation of it.

Politically, Queneau has to go down as an instinctive anarchist, for whom a total disrespect towards the forms and wielders of power in society was second nature. Language has a vital part to play here, as in the seditious slogans with which Zazie cuts a swathe through Paris during her brief visit there: 'Napoléon mon cul' (Napoleon my arse), her 'murderous clausula', as Roland Barthes called it (employing an arcane term, 'clausula', that Queneau will surely have appreciated). By an extension of the same irreverence, Queneau enjoys now and again practising gross distortions on the standard orthography of French, to show how far spelling and pronunciation can drift apart (not that they were ever so very close togther). Hence the alarmingly agglutinative word-form 'doukipudonktan' that is likely to stop readers in their tracks at the start of *Zazie dans le métro*, or the even lengthier 'imélaminhocudlastar'*, whose decryption is more testing still.

This is excellent fun, and characteristic of the jokey ways in which Queneau chooses to advance arguments that he himself takes seriously. It is the same in the case of philosophy, a subject in which he was exceedingly well read but which he would never have contemplated introducing into his novels except in the same humorous disguise. The most openly philosophical of these is the first, *Le Chiendent*, in which there is a character, Etienne Marcel, who, shades of the Cartesian *cogito*, takes on substance only once he starts to think and who, shades of Husserl, also experiences a phenomenological *epoche*, or moment of pure perception of the phenomenal world. This being Queneau, however, what Marcel's eye falls on is first two plastic ducks swimming around in a waterproof hat in a shop window (Queneau's father sold hats in the shop he kept in Le Havre), and then a large sign saying 'Chips' on the front of a rundown café. (At times like these Queneau seems to be satirising the Sartre of *La Nausée* even before that novel had been written.) Queneau had begun as he would go on, making esoteric fun of the philosophy he had been reading and pleasing those readers who were clever enough to get the point. In his own eyes, he was a 'hermeneutic', never a 'hermetic', writer, meaning that one might have to work hard to understand what he was up to, but that the clues were there in the text and in sufficient numbers to supply an interpretation.

Queneau's journals are an intriguing mixture of the impersonal and the confessional: impersonal in recording the sayings, thoughts and actions of others; confessional when he turns, reluctantly so he says, to record the many *emmerdements* of his life, or the things and the people that bugged him, not least

---

* Both are complete sentences. The first would normally be printed in French as 'd'où qu'il pue donc tant', which is syntactically insufficient but would mean something like 'how come he smells so much then'; the second would read 'il met la main au cul de la star', meaning 'he put his hand on the star's bum'.

himself. He remarks at one point that the advantage of keeping a journal is that it should make it less of a temptation to write autobiographically elsewhere. In his own case, the journals appear to have done their job: Queneau is not to be caught being unequivocally himself in his novels (with his poetry it is different). Yet there is no question but that his intimate concerns surface in his fictions, in a sublimated form which he could only have hoped would at once ease and mask the distress that they clearly caused him in his life. He was a chronically uneasy man, and nowhere more so than in the matter of sexuality. In a long, explicitly autobiographical poem, he writes of how, quite early on in his life, he had taken fright at 'the mixture of filth and innocence present in the creation'. Rather than 'in the creation', he might have said, in himself. He found it hard to come to terms with the sexual and other 'filth' that he knew to be part of him.

Queneau was in analysis at two different periods of his life and he coined, typically, a portmanteau noun to sum up the benefit that he hoped to get from his treatment: *psychanasouillis*, the latter part of which derives from the verb *souiller*, meaning to 'soil' or 'pollute'. He later claimed that analysis had done him good, that he was better off for having faced up to the shameful contents of his unconscious. He appears to have been concerned as an analysand above all by doubts about his virility. 'No Don Juan, R.Q.,' as he ruefully observed of himself, following yet another failure with a woman. He wondered on occasion indeed whether he wasn't gay, or *hormosessuel* as the inventive Zazie likes to put it, giving one to wonder in turn whether his uncertainties may not have found slapstick expression in the sexual ambivalence of Zazie's uncle Gabriel, stage name Gabriella, who performs nightly as a *danseuse de charme* in a gay nightclub.

Filth in various forms plays a teasingly prominent part in the novels. The sludge, for example, in which the barge is trapped at the start of *Les Fleurs bleues* but from which, at the end, it is released, strongly suggesting that the novel has fulfilled some hidden therapeutic purpose. Or the cascade of household waste that is the inaugural event of a superficially benign fiction, *Loin de Rueil* (Far from Rueil): 'The garbage tumbled out from the metal tin and thundered down into the dustbin, eggshells, cabbage stalks, greasy paper, peelings.' The hint is at once there, that the story that follows contains more of a troublingly personal nature than might meet the innocent eye.

Of all the intimate preoccupations that Queneau has projected in this oblique fashion into his novels, the one most deserving of being singled out is the preoccupation with modesty, a quality that he hoped to find in other people and which he struggled to possess for himself. His are novels written in genial celebration of those unassuming members of society who neither exert power over others nor desire ever to do so: of individuals like the feckless, exploited but endlessly resilient Pierrot of *Pierrot mon ami* (Pierrot my friend), or the endearing simpleton Valentin Brû of *Le Dimanche de la vie* (The Sunday of life). Presumption on the other hand is a quality that Queneau punishes, as in the last of his novels, *Le Vol d'Icare* (the flight/theft of Icarus), whose hero is ultimately, like his mythological forebear, brought humiliatingly low for having presumed to fly too high. (Queneau's Icarus is in fact a refugee from a novel in progress, who thinks that he will have a better life once he has escaped from his author. He ends, however, trapped as he falls between the covers of that same author's book, having been taught a cruel lesson in authorial opportunism.)

For Queneau the writer, modesty was a problem. For how can one indulge the vanity that inheres in the act of publication while continuing to think of oneself as a modest person? The problem is made worse if you declare in public, deconstructively, that you aspire to being modest, which is to sacrifice the very quality to which you aspire to a contradictory desire for admiration. This moral aporia is one which Queneau has discreetly transferred to the character of Valentin Brû in *Le Dimanche de la vie* – a man, be it noted, with a suspiciously feminine name, since *la bru* is French for a daughter-in-law (can a circumflex be enough to guarantee masculinity?). After a spell as a shopkeeper, Brû finds himself recalled to the army when the Second World War breaks out; just as in 1939 Private Queneau was himself recalled. Private Brû is someone of impeccable modesty – until the day when he is overcome by a desire to become a saint. The road to sanctity lies, he believes, through first a close acquaintance with 'filth' – volunteering for all the dirty, literally shitty jobs – and then the potential sacrifice of his life – getting himself posted to the Maginot Line. Now in the wartime section of his journals, Queneau reveals that he himself made this same request more than once, to be posted, despite his age (he was thirty-six), to a place of danger where he might be killed. He asks himself why he should have done so and concludes that it could only have been out of vanity, that real heroism does not lie in gestures of that grandiloquent kind, but in quiet endurance. What had looked to him like a saintly self-abnegation turned out to have been culpable narcissism. This small detail from the journals lends complexity and true pathos to Valentin Brû's abrupt and apparently ludicrous decision to become a saint.

The title of *Le Dimanche de la vie* comes from some curious lines of Hegel's that Queneau must have found wholly sympathetic: 'it is the Sunday of life, which levels everything and banishes everything bad; men endowed with so good a humour cannot be fundamentally bad or vile.' Levelling was the unvarying purpose of Queneau's own humour; in their sabotaging of pretension, in life as in language, his books are arguments in favour of an uncomplicated egalitarianism. Queneau is never in his writing the misanthrope that he was accused of being away from it; he is generous in his belief that, when it comes to judging people, small is beautiful. He has a character who literally embodies this conviction, moreover: the dwarf Bébé Toutout, who, thanks to his own lowly perspective on the world, finds stiff-necked giraffes absurd and the guinea pigs who live so close to the ground perfectly sympathetic.

18

GEORGES PEREC

The Underwood machine at which Georges Perec did his typing was old but a survivor, and it can't often have been at rest during the twenty-odd years of his writing life. For Perec was productive: by the time of his early death in 1982, he was the author of one large book, half a dozen short, or very short, books and a whole catalogue of sundries – radio plays, film and television scripts, book and art reviews, essays, articles and two gatherings of crossword puzzles. The large book was his vastly entertaining novel, *La Vie mode d'emploi* (Life a user's manual), a multi-story masterpiece that launched Perec among anglophones with an auspicious éclat when it appeared in English translation in 1987. Since then, most of the short, or very short, books – *Les Choses* (Things), *Un homme qui dort* (A man asleep), *W ou le Souvenir d'enfance* (W or the memory of childhood), *La Disparition* (A Void), and the unfinished '*53 Days*' – have also been translated (as has a selection of his shorter pieces, translated by myself). All of these books are either fiction or contain elements of fiction, even if there has to be something of Perec himself in the anomic anti-hero of *Un homme qui dort* and rather more of him in *W ou le Souvenir d'enfance*.

No other recent (or not so recent) French writer has been translated into English on quite the comprehensive scale that Perec has now achieved; and that is heartening – all the more so for being unexpected. I remember well how I warmed to Perec the moment I first read him, as a likeable and an ingenious writer in a familiar French vein; but I would not then have supposed him likely to be taken up to this extent among English-language readers. He seemed the wrong sort of French writer for that.

He was the sort of French writer, that is, who has things too evidently under close control, who is cool to a fault and too much in love with the formalities of writing. *La Vie mode d'emploi* is not the kind of novel we're used to admiring, for example, transparently artificial as it is, starved of 'real' people by way of

189

characters and filled with pointers to the elaborate way in which it has been organised by the novelist. It's an entertaining yet tremendously thought-out book, whose high popularity was not to be expected. And the same goes for *W ou le Souvenir d'enfance*, inasmuch as it is an unnaturally poised and in some respects obscure attempt to come to terms with the tragic aspects of Perec's early life.

Georges Perec is not, then, the writer to turn to if it's the cordial, unobstructed airing of feelings that you admire. It is characteristic of him that when he writes, in an essay called 'The Scene of a Stratagem', about his time in psychoanalysis his subject is not the *what* of that analysis but the *where* and the *how*: he gives us the structure as it were without the event. He lets us know that analysis was in the end effective in relieving him of some intimate angst or misery, but without letting us know what form this angst or misery took. Reticence is the mark of everything that Perec wrote where the subject comes close to home. There is only the most fleeting indication, for example, when he describes, in note-form but in detail, what has been happening over time to the buildings in a particular Paris street, that this is the street where he had himself lived as a small child before he was brutally orphaned by the Second World War.

And to reticence Perec may add humour, which is the most convivial means of all for a writer to keep in with his readers without letting too much of himself show. Almost all of Perec's writing has the blessed, underrated quality of *lightness*, which was one of the qualities that his friend, the incomparably light Italian writer Italo Calvino, said belonged among the prime literary virtues. In Perec lightness and humour are all the more sociable for masking as they do a pessimistic view of his own and the human condition. The French writer he most reminds one of is Raymond Queneau, who influenced the young Perec a great deal when he was starting out. Queneau, too, was a depressive man who wrote broadly comical novels while letting us see that the comedy was a cover, that life wasn't so very amusing once you stopped to think about it.

Like Queneau, Perec took refuge in language, as an absorbing medium with rules of its own, by dalliance with which you can play consoling tricks on reality. And again like Queneau, he is a great believer in all that is most ordinary in human affairs: an unassuming laureate of the everyday, never in any danger of seeming remote or pretentious. Perec was a Parisian and an intellectual in many of his tastes, but too nervous and too sincerely democratic ever to have wanted to start pronouncing on this and that in the megaphone role of a Paris intellectual. Paris intellectuals were celebrated in their day for laying down the ideological law from their strategic headquarters in one or other Left Bank café; Perec, too, went to Left Bank cafés, not in his case to lay down any law but to play the pinball machines – to the point where he used to get blistered fingers from twiddling the controls. Which is a more human way than most of coping with ennui.

Behind the lightness and escapism of Perec's writing there lay trauma. He was born in 1936, in Paris, the child of Polish Jews who had moved to France towards the end of the 1920s. The father went to work in a foundry, the mother kept a hairdressing salon in Belleville, a rundown quarter in the north-east of the city. When the war broke out in September 1939, Perec's father joined up and, because he was still a Polish citizen, was posted to the Foreign Legion; in June of the following year he was fatally wounded by shrapnel, more or less simultaneously with the signing of an armistice with the victorious Germans. For the next eighteen months, the boy Perec lived in occupied Paris with his mother. At the end of 1941, by which time the threat to French Jews was becoming more immediate, he was sent south into the unoccupied zone, to a village near Grenoble, where he lived with an aunt and uncle. His mother remained behind. Early in 1943, she was rounded up along with other Jews and sent to Germany. She was never seen again, and is presumed to have died in Auschwitz. Georges Perec was subsequently brought up in Paris by the same aunt and uncle with whom he had lived, and survived, in the south.

These are terrible facts of his childhood that anyone reading Perec is the better off for knowing, since not knowing them will make some at least of his writings seem much less affecting than they actually are (for example, the supremely objective description of the street in Belleville I cited earlier). 'I was born in France, I am French, I bear a French first name, Georges, and a French surname, or almost, Perec'. In this 'almost' there lay a painful and incurable awareness of difference for Perec. His surname didn't have quite the written form it should have done; had it been truly French it would have been written Pérec, with an acute accent, or possibly Perrec, with a double r to ensure that the first e was given the right value. The faintly foreign form that it in fact took was for him the telltale mark of his difference. His was the uncertainty of the assimilated but still identifiable Jew. To the French he was different for being by birth Jewish; to other, unassimilated Jews, including members of his own family, he was different because he was French, steeped in a Gentile culture.

The fate suffered by his mother, and by others of his Polish relatives, and his own guilt perhaps at having survived, can be read into what I shall call the *willed* objectivity that characterises Perec's writing, a poignant objectivity provided one bears in mind how hard-won an attitude this was. Like other victims of the Holocaust, Perec was obsessed with memory and with the forces of oblivion that threaten it. This helps to explain his commitment to registering the 'infra-ordinary' and his belief that we none of us give enough attention to what is truly daily in our daily lives, to the banal habits, settings and events of which these lives almost entirely consist. The infra-ordinary is what goes, literally, without saying. Perec, however, the modest, watchful student of the everyday, will take on the job of saying it, as in the novel that first brought him to notice, *Les Choses*, in which a discouraging passage in the lives of a young French couple is told almost exclusively in terms of the household goods that they either own or would like to own.

At one stage of Perec's life, this unusually concrete mode of literary sociology had a political programme behind it, derived from Marxian teachings about the use- and labour-value attaching to even – or especially – the most nondescript products of human manufacture. But the left-wing allegiance of Perec's youth was shallow and didn't last. He was never the man to react against it, however, and what did survive in his case was an unregenerate if far from crusading materialism, a way of seeing the world in very physical terms that he extended to the act of writing and to language itself.

Materialists of language of Perec's kind take full advantage of the fact that language's constituents, words, are so many objects existing in the first place materially, in the form either of a graphic inscription or else acoustically as an ephemeral sound made in the mouth and received by the ear. Linguistic materialists like to exploit the possibilities that are inherent in words as manipulable things, that is to say as 'pure' signifiers (a suspect purity, but we can let that pass). Most of us, for most of the time, are 'immaterialists' of language: we take the materiality or thingness of words to be unimportant and pass directly on to their meaning, to the signified. Perec was a writer waiting, you might say, for structuralism to happen and to bring to wider public notice its suggestive division of language into material and semantic aspects. It is a division rich in possibilities for anyone who has decided, as he already had, that language is a raw material there to be enjoyed by the writer (or speaker) and worked on.

He wasn't alone in this; others in Paris felt the same way. A key moment in Perec's life came with his co-opting in 1967 by the OuLiPo, an association of the like-minded that has by this time acquired a certain celebrity both in France and abroad but which was then more or less unknown. There is a nice pedantry to the acronym it took to itself, with its upper- and lower-case letters, apt because it is the acronym of a body that is as fond of pedantry as it is of wordplay. The OUvroir de LIttérature POtentielle, or 'workshop for potential literature', was formed in 1960 by a subset of writers and mathematicians who were all of them interested in the possible connections between the practice of mathematics and the various formal constraints that have to be satisfied in the writing of poetry. Perec was no sort of mathematician and had no ambitions as a poet, but the interests and above all the advanced experiments in formal constraint that the members of the OuLiPo went in for were greatly to his liking. He became a key and resourceful member of the group, proving himself capable of OuLiPian feats of transcendent skill.

Perec has a claim indeed to have been the most formidable player of OuLiPian games in the long history of *Homo ludens*, and he gave as his reason for taking to them so wholeheartedly that had he not been bound to observe tough formal constraints when writing, he would have been unable to write anything creative at all (shades of Raymond Roussel). He needed to have the possibilities narrowed down in advance, to be made to feel less free in respect of language. He had, he said, not 'one carat of inspiration', didn't believe indeed that there was any such thing. And the virtue for a reticent man of compositional methods such as those practised by members of the OuLiPo was that they were anti-expressive, *un*revealing of the practitioner's feelings or his state of mind.

Of Perec's various OuLiPian exploits, two stand out. One is a palindrome to end all palindromes, the longest surely in the history of palindromics: it runs to some five thousand characters. It makes little or no consecutive sense but it is beautifully reversible and a dazzling monument to the persevering intelligence that worked to create it. The second of Perec's most notable exploits is his equally prodigious lipogrammatic novel, *La Disparition* (or, in the stunning English version of it made many years later by Gilbert Adair, *A Void*).

This OuLiPian masterpiece is of a quality such that it asks for the technical background to be filled in. We have heard a lot in recent times, chiefly thanks to the neo-Freudian teachings of Jacques Lacan, about 'floating signifiers' and the way in which they may bob anchorless around on the deep waters of meaning; we have heard very little about sinking signifiers, or language items that have stopped bobbing and been sent silently to the bottom, if not for the duration then at least provisionally, while we see how well we can do without them. To scuttle a signifier in this arbitrary way is to play at lipograms, an elementary language game that has been around for two and a half millennia.

This *lipo* has nothing to do with surplus fat, waiting to be drawn off from hips and thighs by the liposuctionist's vacuum cleaner: it comes from a Greek verb meaning 'to leave out'. The lipogram is a piece of writing from which one or more letters of the alphabet have been excluded, preferably common letters if the game is to be worth playing. There is in theory no reason why there shouldn't also be spoken lipograms, or lipophones; indeed, I can imagine that, the bit once between their teeth, composers of lipograms find themselves talking lipogrammatically, either because they can't stop or because they think it will help them to keep in training.

The earliest lipograms are thought to have been composed in the sixth century BC, but none have survived; maybe they were never actually written down, only imagined, to circulate among the clerisy as instant legends of verbal skill. One Greek lipogrammatist is said to have written poems in which he left out the letter sigma because he didn't like the hissing sound it made when spoken; a more ambitious fellow Greek rewrote the *Iliad* excluding a different character from each of its twenty-four books: no alphas in book one, no betas in book two and so on – odd that the number of books in the *Iliad* and of characters in the Greek alphabet should be the same, unless, perish the Perecquian thought, that is *why* the poem is divided into twenty-four books. The sigmaphobe, with his euphonic *arrière-pensée*, was in fact missing the point of the lipogram, which is not designed for the writer's convenience. The *Iliad* man was the purist of the two; he had grasped that the lipogram should be a purposeless ordeal undertaken voluntarily, a gratuitous taxing of the brain, and the severer the better. It should make the business of writing not pleasanter but harder.

The lipograms composed and published in the past – in those nicely decadent moments of cultural history when according the signifier precedence over the signified has been seen as the enlightened pastime that it is – were, with rare exceptions such as the lipogrammatised Homer, of modest, parlour-game size: a neat quatrain leaving out a particular vowel or consonant perhaps, or a page or two of similarly deprived prose. Perec, however, had gone into the bibliography of these things and found examples where the lipogrammatist had kept going and produced a text aspiring to gigantism. Notably, there was a lipogrammatic novel written earlier this century by 'an American sailor' called Ernest Vincent Wright. It was published in Los Angeles in 1939 and declared its achievement somewhat naively in its subtitle: *Gadsby: A story of over 50,000 words without using the letter E.*

With this nautical predecessor in his sights, Perec undertook to write the mother of all lipograms, an ultimate OuLiPogram. It came out in the late sixties, a king-sized *e*-less novel with a suggestive though by no means giveaway title, *La Disparition* (The disappearance, or more morbidly The death, given that *la disparition* is the commonest of all French euphemisms for death). This was several thousand words longer than *Gadsby*, whose title and author – minus the Ernest, for obvious reasons – are fraternally evoked a number of times by Perec in his own text, Wright being at one point awarded the degree of Auctor Honoris Causa at Oxford and later ennobled as Lord Gadsby.

Perec having kept mum about the nature of the constraint under which *La Disparition* had been written, there were those at the time by all accounts who read the book without noticing that it was *e*-less. This is just about credible. *La Disparition* is a delightfully amusing book to read, deliriously full of stories, objects, allusions, characters and bizarre incidents: a learned display of what in an afterword (still *e*-less) Perec called 'his passion for accumulation, for saturation, for imitation, for quotation, for translation, for automatisation' (I quote from Gilbert Adair). A plot so hyperactive, even by Perec's unusually robust standards of plotting – see *La Vie mode d'emploi* – might have aroused suspicion, as might his glaring and often hilarious refusal throughout the book to limit himself to one permissible word when the sentence allows of another ten such to be introduced in close conjunction with it. Yet even with the title there to help you, it wouldn't be so easy to tell that its paradoxical verbal opulence had originated in the absence of a certain letter of the alphabet. You can either *see* that a text has no *e*'s in it or you can't.

It wasn't long before the word went round: *La Disparition* hadn't a single *e* anywhere in its 300-odd pages. Knowing this, readers could begin to spot and so to enjoy the many clues that it contains as to its own ludic nature. The name of the main protagonist for a start, Anton Voyl, decryptible without too much difficulty as the suitably de-vocalised form of *voyelle*, the French word for 'vowel' – the more accurate but strange-looking Voyll would no doubt have made the whole thing too obvious. And then there are the many stories, and the many stories within the many stories, to which *La Disparition* is the ample host: they have all to do with sudden disappearances, with violent deaths, with pursuit, with the revealing, or not, of secrets. The book is a sort of parody of the Lacanian theme of the 'lack', or that painful, permanent but creative absence that Lacan has it is the source of our endlessly renewable human desires.

Perec presumably enjoyed knowing that not everyone who read *La Disparition* at the outset had rumbled him, that for all its eccentricities of wording and syntax it had seemed near enough to linguistic orthodoxy to be read as if it had been written by someone able to call on all the elements of his native alphabet. On the other hand, he could hardly have wanted those who didn't realise it was a lipogram to go on not realising it, since whatever admiration they had felt for the book would then rest on the wrong, insufficient premisses. This is the classic dilemma of the practical joker: whether to play your joke and creep quietly away without revealing yourself, or to wait immodestly on the spot for the acclaim to start.

To do without the letter *e* in French may be marginally easier than to do without it in English. Perec was denied the use of some invaluable word forms: *je, se, le, ce, elle, de, les, des, avec, après, quel, que, est* – the list is potentially long, and daunting. Written French, on the other hand, allows of elision, so that some of these banned substances can be welcomed back in by the lipogrammatist in the form of *j', s', d', qu'* and so on. Perec's English translator was not so lucky. For him there can be no *he, she, we, they, the, be, see, before, after, then* – an even more daunting list of tabooed items when you are setting out to 'translate' a book of three hundred pages. Nor is elision a legitimate way out in English: short of shifting Perec's action to Yorkshire and introducing a lot of apostrophes of the 'troubl' at t'mill' variety, Adair was faced with doing without the definite article; and short of cheating in a rather different direction, and going in for quasi-poetical apostrophe *d*'s, he was faced with doing without a great many English past participles.

Whether or not Adair's work should count as a 'translation' of Perec is an interesting question. *A Void* certainly sticks closer to *La Disparition* than one might have expected. All the many personal and place names in the original can of course be reproduced as is, though Adair has rightly altered the name of the hero to Anton Vowl. And the multiple plots and subplots follow much the same erratic course, except where a detour has been made necessary by the shortage of suitable vocally challenged English words. Since Perec's text might be said to be all detours anyway, this is no great hindrance. If anything, it is the reverse. On those many occasions when an exact correspondence of one lipogrammatic text to the other becomes impossible, the translator is out on his own, free to revel in the rare pleasures of periphrasis just as Perec was before him, and

showing himself in Adair's case to be a dab hand at visiting some of the remoter
attics and cellars of our local word-hoard:

> But whilst a goatishly rutting Albin was ravishing Anastasia just as (if you know your
> classical mythology) Apollo had had his way with Iris, Adonis with Calypso, and
> Antinous with Aurora, his gang, complying with his wish, was attacking that studio
> adjoining Anastasia's caravan, blowing it sky-high with a ton of TNT, illuminating a
> pitch-dark night with its conflagration and making an almighty Doomsday din. It was a
> sort of Walpurgisnacht. Its poor occupants . . . ran this way and that, shouting and
> howling in panic. Most got it instantly, struck by a burning plank, by a scorching
> whirlwind, by a boiling rock torn out of its soil, by a spray of stinging-hot, skin-
> riddling coals, or by a smoking brand whooshing up as if from out of a volcano.

In its tipsy verbosity, this paragraph from *A Void* gives just the right hectic
impression of the paragraph of *La Disparition* from which it has taken off. It's
arguable that translation is in fact made easier when certain words are forbidden
to you as a translator, on the same OuLiPian principle that writing in general is
made freer by being obliged to conform to rigorous constraints. The translator
engaged on translating a lipogram has the best of both worlds: a text to work
from that will keep him from getting lost; and the freedom to stray and indulge
himself whenever some chicane is placed in his way by the original wording.

At the time of his death, Georges Perec had a small but select reputation in
his own country and none at all to speak of outside it. That has certainly
changed. And what an excellent thing that a writer so unassuming, so
sympathetic and so playful should be read by the many, for no one represents
more winningly than does Perec a French tradition of literary humour that has
seldom been given its due.

Index

199